THE NEW QUEST FOR
PAUL
& HIS READING OF
THE OLD TESTAMENT:

THE CONTRAST BETWEEN

THE "LETTER" & THE "SPIRIT"

IN 2 CORINTHIANS 3:1-18.

Already the author of an important study of Pauline anthropology, Laato here turns to the differences brought to Paul's reading of Scripture and, particularly, to his understanding of the Mosaic law by his faith in Jesus Christ. Although the heart of his study is a detailed examination of 2 Corinthians 3, implications for Paul's relations with Judaism are drawn out and Laato's debate with the New Perspective on Paul is taken a step further. All in all, a timely contribution to current issues in Pauline scholarship.

Stephen Westerholm
Professor Emeritus, McMaster University

The "New Perspective on Paul" is not new any longer, but its pervasiveness necessitates a corrective reply that is both biblically-faithful and historically-nuanced. In this fine book, Timo Laato does just that.

Robert L. Plummer, Ph.D.
Collin and Evelyn Aikman Professor of Biblical Studies
The Southern Baptist Theological Seminary

Written with verve, close attention to the text, and rich theological reflection, Timo Laato's new reading of Paul's distinction between the work of "the letter" and "the Spirit" will benefit many—and stir up fresh debate. It is a welcome contribution.

Mark A. Seifrid
Senior Professor of Exegetical Theology
Concordia Seminary

Timo Laato tackles one of the most difficult texts in Paul and provides a fresh and most stimulating interpretation. Laato doesn't merely repristinate Luther's reading, even though his interpretation fits with Luther's understanding in many respects. Scholars and readers will profit from Laato's fascinating interpretation of letter-Spirit in Paul. The book abounds with insights and deserves a wide reading.

Thomas R. Schreiner
James Buchanan Harrison Professor of New Testament Interpretation
Associate Dean
The Southern Baptist Theological Seminary
Louisville, Kentucky

Timo Laato has done a rare thing in presenting a coherent interpretation which takes account of the radical newness of Paul's theology, while also doing justice to the apostle's deep rootedness in the Old Testament. This is a detailed and eloquent examination of 2 Corinthians 3 which will offer up a challenge both to some Lutheran interpretations, and to the New Perspective, as well as to the Paul within Judaism school. Laato's work has been a vital contribution to Pauline scholarship for over thirty years, and the same vitality and exegetical skill is just as evident in *The New Quest for Paul* as it always has been.

Simon Gathercole
Professor of New Testament and Early Christianity,
University of Cambridge
Editor, *New Testament Studies*
Fellow, Tutor and Director of Studies, Fitzwilliam College

THE NEW QUEST FOR
PAUL
& HIS READING OF
THE OLD TESTAMENT:

THE CONTRAST BETWEEN

THE "LETTER" & THE "SPIRIT"

IN 2 CORINTHIANS 3:1-18.

TIMO LAATO
FOREWORD BY
BROR ERICKSON

ACADEMIC

Published by:
1517 Publishing
PO Box 54032
Irvine, CA 92619-4032

Publisher's Cataloging-In-Publication Data
(Prepared by Cassidy Cataloguing Services)

Names: Laato, Timo, 1963- author. | Erickson, Bror, writer of foreword.
Title: The new quest for Paul and his reading of the Old Testament : the contrast between the "letter" and the "Spirit" in 2 Corinthians 3:1-18 / Timo Laato ; foreword by Bror Erickson.
Description: Irvine, CA : 1517 Publishing, [2023] | Includes bibliographical references and index.
Identifiers: ISBN: 978-1-956658-34-7 (hardcover) | 978-1-956658-35-4 (paperback) | 978-1-956658-36-1 (ebook)
Subjects: LCSH: Bible. Epistles of Paul—Theology. | Bible. Epistles of Paul—Criticism, interpretation, etc. | Bible. Corinthians, 2nd—Criticism, interpretation, etc. | Bible. Old Testament—Criticism, interpretation, etc. | Paul, the Apostle, Saint. | BISAC: RELIGION / Biblical Criticism & Interpretation / New Testament. | RELIGION / Biblical Criticism & Interpretation / General. | RELIGION / Biblical Studies / New Testament / Paul's Letters.
Classification: LCC: BS2651 .L33 2023 | DDC: 227.06—dc23

Printed in the United States of America.

Contents

Foreword

Working with Dr. Timo Laato on his insightful projects is always an honor. This time *The New Quest for Paul and His Reading of the Old Testament* proves exceptional.

Dr. Laato has long been known as an opponent of the so-called "new perspective" and a defender of a traditional Lutheran understanding of the Pauline corpus. In this book, he seeks to move beyond that debate and open new vistas in Pauline research. In the book's conclusion, he says the New Perspective has run its course because it has failed to show any essential change in Paul's understanding of Judaism post-Damascus, so a *new quest* for Paul is needed. To expose the failure of the New Perspective, Timo first dives into a detailed exegetical study of 2 Corinthians 3, examining the interpretational problems associated with Paul's distinction concerning the letter that kills and the Spirit that gives life. He shows that contrary to popular opinion, this does not mean a "literal-letteral" reading of the law is to be avoided because it kills.

On the contrary, it is to be read as literally as possible so that it can do its work of killing! In other words, it is not a call for a softer, more lenient reading of the law. The whole purpose of the law is to kill so that the Spirit can, in turn, give life to that which is dead—that which the law has killed. Against the "literal-letteral" sense of Scripture, Paul reads the Old Testament according to the "literal-spiritual" sense. He does not just pick up some minor faults in his former thinking. No, he now understands the need for a totally new mode of existence. Paul emphasizes that Christians fulfill the whole Mosaic law including every single commandment, even those instructions relating to circumcision, meals or foods, festivals, sacrifices, and temple service.

However, he argues that they do not fulfill the numerous orders of the Torah "in flesh" and according to their "literal-letteral" meaning but "in Spirit" and according to their "literal-spiritual meaning."

To prove this, Timo draws on similar wording in Romans written at approximately the same time as 2 Corinthians and several passages in the Old Testament from Exodus, Jeremiah, and Ezekiel. The result of this study shows that the more Jewish a person makes Luther, the more Lutheran Paul becomes. However, this also demands a break with Käsemann's "Lutheran" understanding of a Paul who disregards large chunks of the Old Testament as useless. That sort of Lutheran understanding is not Lutheran, but it also does a disservice to Paul, who saw works of the law as being any work being done in obedience to the Torah, whether or not that work would fall under a ceremonial or moral classification by modern standards, which Paul did not recognize. It is a disservice to Paul's theology to see him as a proto-Reformed Jew of the modern era.

In the end, Timo argues for a new quest for Paul that will abandon both the clichéd Lutheran view of Käsemann and the facile views of the New Perspective.

Your Brother in Christ,
Rev. Bror Erickson

Preface

There are many books. Maybe far too many. The Biblical writer reminds us: "Be warned, my son . . . Of making many books there is no end, and much study wearies the body." (Ecclesiastes 12:12). Especially, there are many books on Pauline theology. Some of them are good; some others are not so good. There are also a few really bad books. Hence, it seems necessary to write my plea for this book. What is it all about?

For many decades, the so-called New Perspective on Paul has dominated the academic research. Sometimes, you get the impression there are no longer any other alternatives. "They have spoken, the matter is settled." I doubt that. The New Perspective has run its course. It has failed to explain Paul's break with Judaism. For sure, saying something like that causes many readers to frown and look perplexed. They might decide not to read my book, or they read and sharpen their pencils and write a morbid criticism. They have a right to do so. But still, research has to move ahead. It cannot get stuck here. Therefore, I suppose you should read this book. *Tolle, lege!*

To reach my goal, there is a long way to run. Indeed, there are no shortcuts to victory. We know: no pain, no gain. Therefore, I first decided to study 2 Corinthians 3, a chapter that has a reputation of being a nightmare for Pauline scholars. The contrast between the letter and the Spirit (v. 6) has given many academics an especially hard time and caused them a gray hair. I myself grew older in doing this study. Now, the work is over. It seems that the gain was really worth the pain. Fresh insights into the complexity of Pauline thinking are reached. They help us to better understand the Pauline line of thought. In the new light, the New Perspective appears very old-fashioned. Instead, the New Quest is needed, and that is what this book is about.

In my conclusions, I sum up my book as follows:

Taken as a whole, Paul puts himself at odds with any kind of Judaism. On purpose, he drifts into a frontal collision with it in his reading of the Old Testament. He speaks for a new mode of existence. That's why there is no room for the old manner of living as Jews truthfully try to do what is written in the Torah. All the same, they still do it "in flesh" and only according to the "literal-letteral" sense of Scripture. In consequence, they are without exception bound to fail. It is indeed a total failure. To say this is not to say that old-fashioned and outdated distortions (or conscious falsifications) of the Jewish religion in exegetical research in the end prove right.

Against the "literal-letteral" sense of Scripture, Paul reads the Old Testament according to the "literal-spiritual" sense. He does not just pick up some minor faults in his former thinking. No, he now understands the need for a totally new mode of existence. "The old has gone, the new is here!" (2 Corinthians 5:17).

* * *

I dedicate this book to one of my grandchildren, Timoteus. He was the reason why I tried to finish my research as soon as possible after a long period of diligent work. I was afraid of a psychic break-down because of his serious illness. He has had to fight for his life. By God's grace (and after nine operations so far), he is still alive and progressing. I admire his power to survive. I am not sure if I will do it. The war in Ukraine made the situation even worse. People are dying. It hurts so much to read about their deaths, especially the deaths of little children. But life still goes on. According to our Christian faith, life will never die! Let me put it in this way: If Timoteus has survived, he encourages me to survive through the necessary academic debate about the validity of the argumentation in each research. Instead of psychic breakdown, maybe—God willing—the theological break-through will follow.

I thank Bror Erickson for correcting my English. If my text is worth reading, it shows that I finally have learned from him to write better. He has never spared his efforts in teaching me. For all those reasons, a big fat "thank you"!

In the final stage, Kathleen Crenshaw read my manuscript once again and polished my English as much as possible. Her corrections were precise and perfect. I thank her for her diligent work. Any remaining errors are my fault.

In addition, I thank Steve Byrnes for encouraging me to finish this book and publishing it in New Reformation Publications.

Timo Laato

1
Introduction

2 Corinthians 3 as a problem

It is hard to escape the impression that a veil lies over our minds whenever we analyze or interpret 2 Corinthians 3.[1] The chapter has a reputation of "a tortuous passage."[2] All the more, it might be called "the Mount Everest of Pauline texts as far as difficulty is concerned."[3] As a whole, it ends up "one of the most difficult passages to understand within the Pauline corpus."[4] There is a wide panorama of similar assessments featuring the inaccessible terrain of the present bewilderment.[5] It reminds the readers of the old discouraging saying: "Abandon all hope, ye who enter here."

---

[1]   Hays 1989, 123. See further Baker 2000, 1.

[2]   Martin 1986, 72. He also comments that 2 Corinthians in general, has come to be known as both "the paradise and the despair of the commentator" (x). Further, he adds that "no other New Testament book, it seems, is in need of such careful exposition" since "this letter is one of the most difficult writings in the New Testament." In conclusion, he resignedly points out: "Much, however, has to remain speculative in our inquiries, and we can only hope that we have guessed accurately at Paul's meaning in several parts of the letter [. . .]."

[3]   Hanson 1980, 19. He also speaks of 2 Corinthians 3 as "the sphinx among texts, since its difficulty lies in its enigmatic quality rather than in its complexity." In reference to him, Stockhausen 1989, 32.

[4]   Hafemann 2005, 1.

[5]   See, e.g., Philpot 2013b, 156: "Among all instances of quotations or allusions of the OT in the NT, 2 Corinthians 3:7-18 is perhaps the most challenging to interpret." Later on, he underlines that "Paul's argument in 3:7-18 has puzzled interpreters for centuries" (ibid., 166). Fitzmyer (1981, 630) regards

It adds up to the perplexity of New Testament scholars that they apparently do not know with certainty what to search for in 2 Corinthians 3 and, precisely, from which angle to read, study, and explicate the whole chapter. E. Käsemann puts emphasis on the herme-neutical application of the letter-spirit antithesis (2 Corinthians 3:6). The terms "letter" and "spirit" mark two possible ways of seeing and interpreting Scripture. The former denotes a perverted, prin-cipally Jewish approach to the Old Testament "under the veil of the Torah in its misunderstood character as a demand for good works," whereas the latter designates an undistorted, specifically Christian redirection to the Old Testament "in the light of the lifting of that veil through Christ" and with regard to "the message of justification" (2 Corinthians 3:15-16). The contrast between the two poles takes on "a hermeneutical function."[6] Hence, Käsemann speaks of a deliber-ate tension of "scripture against scripture" viz "the law as promise against the Torah as a demand for works."[7] He distinguishes "a canon within a canon." It summarizes the heart or generative principle of Paul's theology. Besides, it forms the basis for his hermeneutics as

---

2 Corinthians 3:4 as "a very complicated passage" and "one of the most sub-lime ways in which Paul sums up the effects of the Christ-event." Van Unnik (1963, 156) writes as follows: "It seems as though the obscurity of this passage [= 2 Cor 3] is impenetrable and that the commentaries lead us to the conclu-sion: 'so many men, so many minds.'" Cover (2015, 3) underscores: "Paul's sustained exegesis of Exodus 34 in 2 Cor 3:7–18, which leaps unexpectedly from the epistle like an interpretive bolt from the blue, has proved a perennial riddle and resource for its interpreters, modern and ancient." Savage (2004, 105) emphasizes: "Scholars have invested much time and energy trying to make sense of this chapter." Moreover, he avows that "its argument is nearly impossible to follow, hindered at many points by mixed metaphors" or "puzzling allusions" (ibid.). Childs (2004, 620) avows: "The difficulties of understanding II Cor. 3 are so many that one hesitates to enter the arena." He further utters: "Unfortunately, there has emerged nothing which even begins to resemble a consensus of opin-ion among New Testament scholars in spite of considerable attention to these problems within recent years." Stockhausen (1989, 2) affirms: "II Corinthians is unquestionably the most difficult of Paul's letters. Its argumentation is fre-quently obscure to the modern reader, its contents unfamiliar, its construction apparently haphazard, and its *Sitz im Leben* foggy." (See also p. 8.)

[6] Käsemann 1971, 155. See also Richardson 1973, 208.

[7] Käsemann 1971, 160 (cf. 165).

he decodes the Old Testament texts as an expression for the content of his gospel.[8]

On the other hand, S. Westerholm maintains that "the letter-spirit antithesis has nothing to do with Pauline hermeneutics." The terms do not "refer to an inadequate and an adequate way of reading the sacred scriptures." Rather, "they are used of man's obligation to God under the old and new dispensations." Consequently, the letter-spirit antithesis copes with "Pauline ethics, not Pauline hermeneutics."[9] In conclusion, Westerholm suggests that it would indeed "be difficult to find a better starting-point for a study of Pauline ethics than the letter-spirit antithesis." He repeats one more time that the two terms should be understood as they were originally intended.[10]

2 Corinthians 3 in context

Side by side with a variety of different perspectives on the letter-spirit antithesis, a note of caution is called for. We run the risk of losing sight of the context. In 2 Corinthians 3, Paul does not write an excursus on hermeneutical methods or ethical principles (even if he surely says something about those issues as well). Instead, he intends to present an efficient apologia for his apostolic ministry. He sets out to show that his grieving and suffering are to be integrated with his divine vocation and mission. Thus, 2 Corinthians 3:6 does not sum up a detached, dogmatic maxim to be read as part of Paul's larger idea of something supposedly "more important," whether for hermeneutical or ethical reasons. No external premise of his "isms" prove determinate for the exegetical analysis of his actual texts.[11]

Conversely, we just as easily run the risk of keeping the letter-spirit antithesis apart from the overall theological setting. The contrast between the two poles should not be maintained in forced

---

[8] Ibid., 164-166.

[9] Westerholm 1984, 241.

[10] Ibid., 246.

[11] See Hafemann 2005, 30, 33; Hays 1989, 124-125, 149-151. Cf. Seifrid 2014, 99: "It is the legitimation of *Paul's* apostolic ministry to the *Corinthians*. Neither he nor they can be abstracted from the argument." Similarly, Balla 2007, 758-759, 761, Newman 2017, 230, Richardson 1973, 209-210. Cf. also Friesen 1971.

isolation from other relevant texts. Paul deals with the same or similar issues elsewhere. Especially in his letter to the Romans, written not long after 2 Corinthians and, as known, in Corinth itself, he is caught up in related subjects. The specific letter-spirit antithesis occurs there as well (Romans 2:29, 7:6).[12] Thus, any outcome of an academic survey of Paul's hermeneutics and ethics, based on that contrast, should apply to all data and not only part of it. In another case, his line of thought has scarcely been followed correctly.

2 Corinthians 3—guidelines for the interpretation

Therefore, while entering the exegetical labyrinth of 2 Corinthians 3, we should strive for a wide-ranging discernment that reads as little into the text as possible. It is further no less necessary that the core concern of the passage for the defense of the apostolic ministry does not escape our sight.[13] Any analysis or examination of Paul's hermeneutics or ethics along those lines must then remain within the limits of his hermeneutical or ethical principles and practices as demonstrated in the whole chapter. Whatever conclusions, they must be derived from his reasoning in the context of, say, 2 Corinthians 2:14-4:6 and not taken apart from it. Otherwise, his own voice disappears into thin air.[14] It appears definitely reasonable to expect that in practice he really stands for the principle that he espouses. If not, his fatal inconsistency becomes apparent through critical inquiry.[15] Finally, the big picture of Paul's thinking should not fade into the background. The results of the study should be checked against his other writings, especially Romans.

Furthermore, the radical shift in Paul's thinking took place and shape as a result of his conversion. At that moment, he started to regard his previous pharisaic orientation and proclivity as "crap"

---

[12] Schneider 1953, 196.

[13] Martin 1986, 66.

[14] Hafemann 2005, 30, 33. See further Balla 2007, 753-755, 762, Lambrecht 1983, *passim* (especially 345-347), Philpot 2013b, 157, Savage 2004, 103-105. Cf. Stockhausen (1989, 6) who in addition avows: 2 Corinthians 3:1-4:6 "lies in the central section of the epistle which is regarded as its doctrinal heart." Moreover, the unity of 2 Corinthians 2:14-6:10 "is the least questioned in the letter."

[15] Hays 1989, 125.

(Philippians 3:4-11). To be sure, he does not directly deal with his altered or transformed reading of the Old Testament as a consequence of his turning to Jesus as the Messiah in any of his letters. Nonetheless, his fundamental reassessment of the meaning and use of Scripture strongly relates to that specific event since his former religious activity and the core of the traditional Judaism revolve around and rest on the conscientious interpretation and application of the biblical data.[16] Accordingly, the hermeneutical and ethical reorientation of Paul should be recognized and understood as an inference from his faith. His veil was taken away as he put his trust in the crucified and risen Messiah (cf. 2 Corinthians 3:16). Then, the bright divine light was shed on or in his dark heart and illuminated him (cf. 2 Corinthians 4:6). His theology is truly about *theologia regenitorum*! Notwithstanding, the original historical setting of the Old Testament serves as an absolutely necessary condition for his explanations and conclusions. In other words, they do not develop from his pure, pious imagination. On the contrary, they do arise from his careful reading of the texts themselves in the light of his Christology.[17]

The intertextuality between the Old and the New Testament in Paul's theological thought, the hermeneutical or ethical implications of his selective scriptural quotations and perceptive biblical interpretations, the logical deductions from his Christological axioms, and whatever—the terms and concepts of modern academic research look like anachronistic expressions. Definitely, they are. But the questions and problems, as defined above, are not. They are still relevant and awaiting any response or solution.[18] To that purpose, I hope, this book is worth reading.

My task and method

My task is to analyze and evaluate in-depth the line of thought in 2 Corinthians 3, especially from the perspective of the antithesis between the "letter" and the "Spirit" in v. 6. Not every feature and

---

[16] Hays 1989, 122-123.
[17] See Laato 2021, 29-86.
[18] Cf. Hays 1989, 122-123.

detail of the passage are taken into consideration. The following lines do not sum up an "ordinary" commentary on this or that. The point of commenting next to all kinds of stuff is well chosen in another context. But here, concentration on the main content of the chapter is warmly welcomed. The focus lies on the possible hermeneutical and ethical implications, entailed in the antithesis between the "letter" and the "Spirit" (2 Corinthians 3:6) as well as in the comparison between the ministry of Moses and Paul (2 Corinthians 3:7-18). If required, also other relevant Pauline texts are read and studied to shed more light on the central problems. Especially the Epistle to the Romans, written not long after the Epistles to the Corinthians and in Corinth itself, comes to grips with the same contrast between the "letter" and the "Spirit" (see 2:29 and 7:6). It obviously carries weight and makes the difference in the overall argumentation.[19]

Consistent with the definition of the task, the history of research (chapter 2) accounts for the main clarifications of the tricky antithesis between the "letter" and the "Spirit." They make plain the wide and long roads travelled ever since in separate directions. In the case of a dead-end street, the need for a groundbreaking step forward becomes all too evident. To that purpose, a profound analysis of the structure of 2 Corinthians 3:1-18 (chapter 3) is hoped-for. The loose parts of the text are put together to plot the route ahead. It proves how to proceed to get from A to B or from beginning to end. Next, a close inquiry into the linguistic and semantic multiplicity of the language in 2 Corinthians 3 (chapter 4) shows the complexity of the task. There is no easy way out. Many challenges lie ahead. A more in-depth study of the Old Testament framework (chapter 5), then picks up the under-lying traditions for the apostolic proclamation of the gospel to rest on. It prepares the ground for the fulfillment of the New Testament as delineated in 2 Corinthians 3. That is where the exegetical inter-pretation of the text to a great extent starts. A comparison of the

---

[19] For the concentration on 2 Corinthians 3 as such, cf. Hays 1989, 216 n 5: "It is conventional to treat the pericope as beginning in 2 Cor. 2:14 (despite the link-ing conjunction *de*) rather than in 3:1. Certainly, major themes of 3:1-4:6 (suf-ficiency for ministry, commissioning by God) are sounded already in 2:14-17. For the purpose of this book, however, I have chosen to begin with 3:1 because it introduces a new cluster of metaphors related to writing and reading."

ministries of Moses and Paul (chapter 6) as well as a reexamination of the contrast of the "letter" and the "Spirit" (chapter 7) bring to the fore the apostolic theology. Fresh insights are achieved. They, so to speak, pave a path through all but impassible terrain of academic scholarship. Thereafter, attention is still drawn to the importance of the results in the wide theological context of the so-called "Lutheran" Paul (chapter 8). What was wrong with him? Or was there anything wrong with him? Here, the line of reasoning from the perspectives of Church history and Christian dogmatics leads to the same direction as the previous exegetical analyses. "What goes around, comes around." Finally, the outcomes of this research are to be related to the state of research (chapter 9) in order to know which way to go. All blind alleys and back roads should be marked in red. After a rather short summary and wide-ranging conclusions (chapter 10), the map is ready to be used. The new quest for Paul is now on track![20]

---

[20] Since the secondary literature on 2 Corinthians 3 is vast or next to endless, the references below are selective and not all-inclusive. The list of literature solely contains the books and articles that are quoted or discussed. Other publications are omitted for compelling reasons. Occasionally, a more thorough academic analysis is found in my other publications.

2

The antithesis between
the "letter" and the "Spirit"—
the brief history of research

History of research—troubles and problems

It appears next to impossible to write a history of interpretation of
2 Corinthians 3. The attempts would require at least a wide-ranging
monograph and many in-depth analyses to address all of the exegetical and hermeneutical issues in the research so far.[1] At any rate, the
whole complex of diversities seems to revolve around the antithesis
between the "letter" and the "Spirit" (v. 6). A thorough study of this
precise contrast, then, permeates the further reading of the whole
chapter. Accordingly, one tiny detail of the text has a strong bearing
on the context before and after.[2]

Besides, the antithesis between the "letter" and the "Spirit" has
every so often been understood on the basis of the meaning of the
"letter." Then, from the definition of the first part of the contrast
follows a definition of the second part of the contrast: the meaning
of the "Spirit." Obviously, the latter is the opposite of the former. To
a large extent, the reading of the rest of 2 Corinthians 3 hinges on a
presupposition like that.

Here, the brief history of research is primarily outlined by the
different meanings of the concept of the "letter" and secondarily by

---

[1] Cf. Hays 1989, 136-137.
[2] Cf. Westerholm 1984, 229.

the different meanings of the concept of the "Spirit." As a whole, the opposite poles of the contrast stand out. Four main alternatives are presented together with a critical evaluation of each of them.

1. The "letter" as the literal sense of the Old Testament

By tradition, the "letter" has been understood as the literal sense of the Old Testament. It provides a literalist approach to the text. The reader is stuck or caught in an external and superficial "word by word"-meaning without seeing any internal and profound significance there. In contrast, the "Spirit" denotes the spiritual sense of the Old Testament or, much more narrowly, the "spirit" (in lower-case s) as the real intention of the law or, much more generally, the common Christian ability of spiritual discernment. At least in most cases, the spiritual perception amounts to the allegorical interpretation of Scripture.[3]

However, nowhere in Pauline letters—nor in the whole New Testament—does the "Spirit" denote the deeper meaning of the text. In the context and throughout chapter 3, πνεῦμα stands for the Spirit of God.[4] Without doubt, the πνεῦμα in v. 6 harkens back to the πνεῦμα Θεοῦ ζῶντος in v. 3, where the Spirit does not mean the true meaning of Scripture but more correctly a divine agency at work within human life.[5] It follows that the contrast between the "letter" and the "Spirit" does not call any attention to the allegorical interpretation.

Yet, the question arises if the emphasis on the literal and spiritual senses of the Old Testament has an element of truth in Pauline theology on the whole and in 2 Corinthians 3 as well. For instance, more than a few Church Fathers take no decisive stand on the issue. In actual fact, they hold to *two* interpretations (by mistake or, rather, on purpose). On the one hand, they firmly stick with the literal and spiritual senses of the Old Testament. On the other hand, they strongly persist in the alternative perception that the "letter" simply

---

[3] Historically, the main proponent of the first alternative is Origen. For his interpretation, see, e.g., Schneider 1953, 166-168. For the interpretations of Church Fathers in general, see ibid., 165-184.

[4] Gleason 1997, 71.

[5] Thrall 2004, 234.

denotes the written law (not a *sense* of it) and the "Spirit" broadly designates the third person of the Trinity and his divine power (see the alternative 4 below).[6] Frankly speaking, why do they ultimately think in that way? It seems to me worth considering.

2. The "letter" as the legalistic misunderstanding and misuse of the Mosaic law

According to another common interpretation, the "letter" represents the Mosaic law as understood and used in an entirely legalistic sense. It stands for the Jewish distortion of the Torah as a means of meriting salvation. Thus, it promotes human achievement. In consequence, it perverts the true intention of the whole Old Testament. In contrast, the "Spirit" embodies the right approach. The Torah is understood and used as Holy Scripture that validates and substantiates the apostolic proclamation of the gospel to an absolute exclusion of earning salvation by the works of the law.[7]

Rather than speaking of a perversion of the law, Paul simply refers to the initial law-giving in v. 7. He does not talk about any subsequent misuse of the Torah in vv. 7-11.[8] He would hardly have attributed a degree of glory (v. 9) to a distortion of the divine revelation.[9] Neither would he propose that Moses was a minister of a badly maltreated law.[10] It is the "letter" *per se* that kills, and it does that by any actual reading (v. 6). To read a misreading into the concept of the "letter" is a misreading not to be read!

Notwithstanding, the Jewish misunderstanding or hardening, as disallowed in vv. 14-15, is related to the reading of the "letter" (v. 6) or the "old covenant" document (v. 14) or the books of Moses (v. 15). Hence, Israel's failure *does* include an intellectual dimension that does not merely comprise rational perceiving or thinking but a spiritual rebellion in active disobedience. For sure, it ends up in a legalistic perversion of the law in one way or another. All the more,

---

[6] Schneider 1953, 163-187, especially 184-187.
[7] Particularly, see, e.g., Provence 1982, 65-68.
[8] Gleason 1997, 74; Thrall 2004, 235; Westerholm 1984, 240.
[9] Gleason 1997, 74, Westerholm 1984, 240-241.
[10] Gleason 1997, 74; Westerholm 1984, 240.

the question of the meaning and function of the "letter" in the context of 2 Corinthians 3 escalates. At the very least, it is hard to find any reasonable explanation that integrates the several traits of the chapter pointing in different directions and combine them into a coherent setting of theological unity.

3. The "letter" only as an outward conformity to the Mosaic law and devoid of any inward obedience

Every so often, the "letter" is taken for something merely external just like the Ten Commandments (or "words") of the old covenant that were written on stone tablets. However, the outward writing of them does not yet put them within the human heart. On the contrary, they exert an alien and tyrannical control over those under their authority. The religious coercion directly results in moral subjugation that is imposed from the outside. Since no inward consent to the Mosaic law ensues, no internal transformation of the mind follows. Accordingly, the antithesis between the "letter" and the "Spirit" is not understood dialectically, but rather and more precisely in continuum. Through the "Spirit" (or "spirit") of the new covenant, the "letter" of the old covenant is utterly internalized. They belong together, and they should be kept together. Deep down, there is no change in the Mosaic law but in the ability of the believers to obey the Mosaic law. They are now finally enabled and empowered to fulfill it. Their willing obedience does not in the least suggest the end of the Torah, which remains intact.[11] Hence, the contrast between the "letter" and the "Spirit" ultimately turns into a complementary relationship between the two.

Ostensibly, the former reading of a consonant development of the old covenant into the new covenant is gaining approval and popularity nowadays.[12] It indeed contains many valid points. They draw attention to main features in Pauline theology. So, the preaching

---

[11] Most clearly, Balla 2007, 761. He emphasizes that "the 'written code,' the OT 'letter,' does not kill if it is read through the Spirit who leads us to Christ and to a Christological reading of the OT." See also Hafemann 2005, *passim* (especially 265-287). Similarly, Philpot 2013b, 165-166.
[12] Grindheim 2001, 97.

of the gospel always upholds continuity with Torah in terms of the fulfillment of the whole Scripture. Even if the Mosaic law certainly does not save, it has not been renounced but still prevails as an expression for an ethical code in sincere love. Once all imaginable dissimilarities have been taken into account, an indisputable similarity stands as firm as ever. Hence, the interpretation of the contrast between the "letter" and the "Spirit" as a controversy between the external or internal conformity to the divine will has a lot going for it. The very complex of open questions and half-finished surveys must be resumed later. Here, there is nothing more to be said about them.

Nevertheless, the overall explanation of an outward and inward obedience to the Mosaic law as an all-inclusive reading of 2 Corinthians 3:6 fails to carry conviction. Rightly, M. Seifrid writes that the history of interpretation may be understood as a record of different attempts to tame the "letter" that kills in order to liberate the "Spirit" that gives life.[13] In the present context, Paul does not describe the Torah as a fiasco or a failure. He does not define it as ineffective or insufficient. In fact, the very opposite is the case! The "letter" delivers death. It executes those under its sway. Accordingly, the Mosaic law "cannot be regarded as a mere problem to be overcome." It serves a divine purpose to the exclusion of any earning of salvation and every boasting of one's own works.[14] In other words, it paves the way for the proclamation of the gospel and the new life in Christ through his resuscitating Spirit. Seifrid concludes: "Only that which has been put to death can be made alive."[15] This critical and crucial aspect should not be lost in the abyss of modern sophisticated theological analyses.

4. The "letter" as the Mosaic law that condemns and kills the sinner

The negative assessment of the "letter (γράμμα) that kills" for sure stands in close correlation with the law of Moses, in consideration of the

---

[13] Seifrid 2014, 130.

[14] Ibid., 132.

[15] Ibid., 128.

engraving "in letters" (ἐν γράμμασιν) on stone that marked the inau-guration of the old covenant (2 Corinthians 3:6-7).[16] Correspondingly, the positive assessment of the "Spirit that gives life" stands in clear opposition to the law of Moses, taking into account that it was "writ-ten" or more precisely "chiseled" (ἐγγεγραμμένη) on tablets of stone but not "with the Spirit of the living God" (v. 3).[17] Further, the "letter" that brings death ushers in a metonymy of "Moses being read" in asso-ciation with a veil covering the reader's heart (v. 15).[18] Accordingly, the "letter" and the "Spirit" should be understood in contrast and not in continuum (as in the third alternative). They denote two dif-ferent sides of the divine revelation, a dichotomy of either producing condemnation and death or providing justification and life. The fun-damental dualism of the traditional Reformation (or Lutheranism) between law and gospel simply holds true.[19] To put it another way: the very essence of that special distinction reaches out to the definite division between "Moses in action" and "Christ in action."[20]

Without doubt, the discourse in 2 Corinthians 3 turns up strongly antithetical but not in a monolithic fashion. What is inscribed and prescribed on the tablets of stone is described as the old covenant in strict contrast to the new covenant. Yet in both cases, there is an amount of glory, shedding (bright or surpassingly bright) light on people.[21] Besides, it should not escape notice that the exact dis-tinction prevails between the "letter" and the "Spirit," but, in actual fact, *not* between law and gospel. In chapter 3, Paul *never* uses the word "law" (νόμος). More strikingly, he uses it *nowhere* in the whole Epistle! Therefore, the question of the real target and intention in 2 Corinthians 3 partially remains unresolved.[22]

---

[16] Thrall 2004, 234. However, she herself does not represent the fourth but the third alternative above!

[17] Thrall 2004, 226.

[18] Gleason 1997, 76 n. 50, Seifrid 2014, 152.

[19] Grindheim 2001, 97, 102-114. Similarly, Gleason 1997, 75-77. See already Kamlah 1954, 282: "Meinem Urteil nach ist des Apostels Unterscheidung von γράμμα und πνεῦμα in dem lutherischen 'Gesetz und Evangelium' vorbildlich systematisch sktualisiert."

[20] Seifrid 2014, 128.

[21] More on this, see below.

[22] See Dunn 2013, 165.

Other suggestions

In addition to the former four main alternatives, there are many minor variations too. They are not to be dealt with here.[23] If required, they will get more attention later. However, it should be acknowledged that sometimes some of the four main alternatives might be mixed together to facilitate the notorious difficulty of deciphering 2 Corinthians 3. For instance, J. D. G. Dunn amalgamates the second and the third alternatives. He writes that numerous Jews were "content with the outward appearance of keeping the law, whose observance was superficial, perhaps only to impress others, or to keep up appearances of being a faithful Jew." Then, he severely reproaches "thinking of keeping the letter of the law as a punctiliousness in observing detail, including minute detail, while missing what the law was really about."[24] These and similar harsh reprimands from the pen of one of the prominent proponents of the New Perspective come as a provoking surprise (cf. the second alternative). What did he have in mind? It seems that in his eyes Judaism badly amounts to a hypocritical and casuistic religion of vilest art![25] Besides, Dunn maintains that the "letter" sums up all that is outward and visible whereas the "Spirit" pins down all that is inward and hidden.[26] He asserts that freedom from external bondage of pedantic literalism liberates to internal dependence on creative ingenuity. Consequently, submission to the law in an outside manner rules out commission of the lawgiver in an inside manner (cf. the third alternative).[27] Admittedly, Dunn has much more to say. Still, more of the same does not avert from him the arguments above that call into question his overall position. It is very telling that he does not properly discuss the killing effect of the law as such (cf. the fourth alternative) but rather the killing effect of the law "at a superficial level" or according to an adamantine, "verbal submission to the

---

[23] For a more extensive history of research, see, e.g., Gleason 1997, 70-77, Hafemann 2005, 1-35, Hughes 1962, 96-102, Provence 1982, 63-68, Seifrid 2014, 130-150.

[24] Dunn 2013, 167 (see also 169-174).

[25] For an overall assessment of Dunn's position, see my article 2019, 302-306.

[26] Dunn 2013, 167.

[27] Ibid., 169-174.

law."[28] Apparently, it takes a lot of effort to get some sense out of the complex academic discussion that gains momentum here and now.

What to do?

On the whole, the history of research has taken us down a blind alley that leads to a dead end. The problem is still there unresolved in a kind of self-imposed blockade. Thus, it remains unclear what 2 Corinthians 3 does mean in general and the antithesis between the "letter" and the "Spirit" in particular. We are trying to get it right and find a straight path out of the impasse. To start with, much more light is to be shed on the target text of our study.

---

[28] Ibid., 169. Later on, Dunn (ibid., 173) writes: "Here again, Paul does not identify the law as *gramma*; it is not the law itself that is *gramma*, but the law treated only at the *gramma* level, the letter of the law as determinative in the way it is understood and obeyed."

3

The structure of 2 Corinthians 3:1-18

General observations

The text to be analyzed is the whole chapter 2 Corinthians 3.
Recurrently, it is discussed together with the preceding passage
(2:14-17) and the subsequent passage (4:1-6), which are parts of the
near context. To be sure, they are taken into account below but not
dealt with *per se*.[1]

A very heavy-laden line of thought runs through chapter 3.
Sometimes it is difficult to follow how the argumentation actually
proceeds. Nonetheless, the main points clearly emerge. It is all about
the relationship between the old and the new covenant. The giving of the Mosaic law and the figure of Moses permeate the text
thoroughly. The notion of "tablets of stone" (v. 3) refers to the Ten
Commandments. The talk of competence that comes from God
(v. 5, cf. already 2:16) alludes to the dialogue between Moses and
God (LXX Exodus 4:10, see below). The "letter" (v. 6) stands for the
Sinaitic legislation. Then, vv. 7-11 cope with the glory of the Mosaic
ministry and vv. 12-18 deal with the veil of Moses. The former passage is based largely on Exodus 34:29-32, the latter passage mostly
on Exodus 34:33-35.[2]

Paul's argument falls naturally into three parts. He seems to
underline the transition in chapters 3 and 4 with a recurring expression as follows:

---

[1] See above, chapter 1.
[2] Guthrie 2015, 204, Harris 2005, 276. Cf. Provence 1982, 68.

3:4 "we have such confidence as this" (πεποίθησιν δὲ τοιαύτην ἔχομεν)
3:12 "having such hope as this" (ἔχοντες οὖν τοιαύτην ἐλπίδα)
4:1 "having such ministry as this" (ἔχοντες τὴν διακονίαν ταύτην)
4:7 "we have such treasure as this" (ἔχομεν δὲ τὸν θησαυρὸν τοῦτον)[3]

Thus, Paul's argument falls into 3:1-3, 3:4-11, 3:12-18. Further, 3:4-11 falls into two parts as indicated by the three "how much more" (*qal wa-homer* or *a minore ad maius*) juxtapositions in vv. 7-11. Besides, the rhetorical question of vv. 7-8 indicates a continuation of the argument of v. 6.[4] Finally, the last verse 18 functions at the same time as a summary of the whole chapter (see below). Taken as a whole, 2 Corinthians 3 consists of passages 3:1-3, 3:4-6, 3:7-11, 3:12-17, 3:18.

Verses 1-3

At large, vv. 1-3 turn around the question of letters of recommendation. Paul does not need them. The Corinthians themselves are his letter of recommendation. He explains the meaning of his view with the help of lining out the structural parallelism in v. 3:

a contrast of means (*materia qua*)
   "*written not with ink but*" (ἐνγεγραμμένη οὐ μέλανι ἀλλὰ)
      "with the Spirit of the living God" (πνεύματι θεοῦ ζῶντος),
a contrast of sphere (*materia in qua*)
   "*not on tablets of stone but*" (οὐκ ἐν πλαξὶν λιθίναις ἀλλ')
      "on tablets of fleshly hearts" (ἐν πλαξὶν καρδίαις σαρκίναις)[5]

As well-known, v. 3 primarily refers to Exodus 34:1-4. It stands in contrast to Jeremiah 31:31-34 (LXX 38:31-34) through the verb "write" (see below). It stands also in contrast to Ezekiel 11:19 and 36:26-27 through the notion of "stone tablets" (see below).[6]

---

[3] Belleville 1992, 192 n 1. See also Balla 2007, 754.
[4] Hafemann 2005 268.
[5] Guthrie 2015, 191.
[6] Johansson 1990, 76. Similarly, Legarth 2004, 51-53.

Verses 4-6

The task of writing with the Spirit of the living God is a divine commission, the real mission impossible. Who can accomplish it? According to vv. 4-6, the adequacy or competence comes from God. He has made Paul and his co-workers competent as ministers of a new covenant.[7] In this respect 3:6a harks back to 2:16b. The expressions in them are paired with each other as follows:

ἱκάνωσεν	ἱκανός
ἡμᾶς	τίς
διακόνους καινῆς διαθήκης	πρὸς ταῦτα[8]

Obviously, 2:16b alludes to Moses who in LXX Exodus 4:10 (cf. LXX Joel 2:11) declares that he is not competent (οὐχ ἱκανός εἰμι) as a minister of the old covenant. He is qualified only because God sustains and supplies him. In a similar way, Paul and his co-workers solely trust in God as ministers of the new covenant and get their power from him in the midst of oppressions and persecutions (cf. the self-description of Paul as "one of born" but "out of due time" in 1 Corinthians 15:9).[9]

In addition, 3:6b speaks of death and life ("for the letter kills, but the Spirit gives life") in resemblance to 2:16a ("the odor from death unto death" and "the odor from life unto life"). Thus, the ties between the two verses are close.[10]

What is more, 3:6 also forestalls 3:17-18, which speaks of the Spirit of liberty with an emphasis on the divine and eternal glory. The spiritual reality functions as a kind of *inclusio* in chapter 3 (see vv. 3,

---

[7] For the adequate and correct translation of διάκονος, see Seifrid 2014, 120 n 75: "The term 'emissary' expresses more directly the communicative role of the apostle signified by the term διάκονος than does the usual translation 'minister.'" Later on, he still varies "in rendering διακονία as 'mission,' 'ministry,' or 'administration' according to context." It signifies "agency or communication on behalf of another" (ibid., 151 n 211).

[8] See, e.g., Harris 2005, 269, Johansson 1990, 68, Legarth 2004, 39, Martin 1986, 53, Thurén 2008, 253. For an analysis of 2:16 in light of the wide context in chapters 3 and 4, see Provence 1982.

[9] Guthrie 2015, 195-196, Martin 1986, 53.

[10] Johansson 1990, 69.

6, 8, and 17-18). As a result, the placement and content of v. 6 shows the importance of the whole verse and especially the contrast between the "letter" and the "Spirit." It seems that the meaning and intention of that distinction one way or another permeates the whole of argumentation in chapter 3.[11] For sure, the special theological problem must be dealt with far ahead.

Grammatically, the phrase "not of the letter but of the Spirit" (οὐ γράμματος ἀλλὰ πνεύματος) in v. 6a could be dependent on either "ministers" (διακόνους) or "a new covenant" (καινῆς διαθήκης). In context, the "letter" which kills becomes the ministry (literally, the service) of death (ἡ διακονία τοῦ θανάτου), carved in letters on stone in v. 7, or the ministry (service) of condemnation (ἡ διακονία τῆς κατακρίσεως) in v. 9. Analogously, the Spirit who gives life becomes the ministry (the "service") of the Spirit (ἡ διακονία τοῦ πνεύματος) in v. 8. Already in v. 3, Paul speaks of Corinthians as "the epistle of Christ," the result of our ministry ("service"), written with the Spirit of the living God (διακονηθεῖσα ὑφ' ἡμῶν, ἐνγεγραμμένη . . . πνεύματι Θεοῦ ζῶντος). Besides, Romans 7:6 speaks of the "letter" and the "Spirit" as two different ways of *serving* (ὥστε δουλεύειν ἡμᾶς ἐν καινότητι πνεύματος καὶ οὐ παλαιότητι γράμματος). Consequently, it seems plausible to make the saying "not of the letter but of the Spirit" dependent on the word "ministers" (διακόνους) in v. 6a.[12]

Verses 7-11

In vv. 7-11, Paul unpacks his rather enigmatic theological reasoning in an elaborately drawn set of contrasts. He employs three times the traditional Jewish and rabbinical method of *qal wa-homer* (literally "light and heavy"), known also as *a minore ad maius*, in English: "if then . . . how much more" (πῶς οὐχὶ μᾶλλον in v. 8, πολλῷ μᾶλλον in vv. 9 and 11). If one thing is true, how much more is another related thing true. Hence, if the Sinaitic covenant was glorious, how much

---

[11] See Schneider 1953, 195.
[12] Westerholm 1984, 247 n 32. Similarly, Johansson 1990, 65. Cf. already Schneider 1953, 195, 203. Slightly differently, Harris 2005, 269-271.

more glorious is the new covenant. Paul argues by means of antithetic parallelism. He draws sets of contrast as follows:

death (θάνατος, v. 7)—Spirit (πνεῦμα, v. 8)
condemnation (κατάκρισις, v. 9)—righteousness (δικαιοσύνη, v. 9)
what is disappearing (τὸ καταργούμενον, v. 11)—what is remaining (τὸ μένον, v. 11).[13]

Admittedly, v. 10 appears to interrupt the structure of the antithetic parallelism, standing as it does after the first two contrasts and before the third one. Yet, with regard to the sense, it serves as an explanation of the reference to "abundance of glory" in v. 9.[14]

Also, to be noted is the recurring use of the conjunction "for" (γάρ, occasionally left untranslated) following the explicative statements in vv. 9, 10, and 11.[15] Besides, the emphasis in vv. 7-11 apparently falls on "glory" (δόξα). The word occurs at the end of every protasis and apodosis in the phrases according to the genre of "if then . . . how much more" (twice in v. 7, once in v. 8, twice in v. 9, once in v. 10, and twice in v. 11).[16] The reason for this extraordinary priority is to be postponed to a later exegetical exposition of the text (see below).

In the course of his arguments Paul moves from the shine or glory (δόξα) of Moses' face (v. 7) into "that which has been glorified" (τὸ δεδοξασμένον in v. 10) and into "that which is brought to nothing" or "abrogated" (τὸ καταργούμενον in v. 11). Paul shifts his language slightly, yet significantly: His reference broadens from the feminine form of ἡ δόξα to the neuter form of τὸ δεδοξασμένον encompassing Moses and his shining face within Moses' glorious mission. The transition in thought detaches the assertion from the person of Moses to the institution or, more exactly, the old covenant which he embodies.[17]

---

[13] Martin 1986, 59. See also, e.g., Hickling 1975, 386. Cf. Ulonska 1966, 382.

[14] Thrall 2004, 250.

[15] Martin 1986, 59.

[16] Hafemann 2005, 266. Similarly, Lambrecht 1983, 354. For certain, the second occurrence of δόξα in v. 7 is found in the last expression διὰ τὴν δόξαν τοῦ προσώπου αὐτοῦ τὴν καταργουμένην that forms one composed unit. In addition, the verb δοξάζομαι occurs twice in v. 10.

[17] Seifrid 2014, 159, Thrall 2004, 250.

Verses 7-11 and 12-18—a comparison

The dual perspective of vv. 7-11 makes it easier to follow the argumentation in vv. 12-18 where a subsidiary reference to Moses' shining face (v. 13) is set aside by the notion of Jewish religion (see especially vv. 14-15). The symbol, a straightforward mention of the shining face of Moses, and the thing symbolized, the Mosaic covenant, coalesces into a synthesis, a combination of the symbol itself and the thing symbolized, pointing to the conclusion where the symbol is replaced by the thing symbolized.[18] For sure, the theological implication of the fusion is to be analyzed more in depth below.

There is also another remarkable shift in the interpretation of the glory. Verses 7-11 especially assert the superabundance of glory in terms of degree: there is a lot more of it in the new than in the old covenant. Verses 12-18, on the other hand, particularly affirm the superabundance of glory in terms of extent: it reaches farther, not only to Moses but to all believers (especially v. 18).[19]

Verse 12 as a transition

As already seen, Paul's phrasing "having such hope" (v. 12) corresponds to his preceding claim of "having such confidence" (v. 4).[20] Obviously, in v. 12 the content of the hope points back to the previous unit, the implications of the argument from lesser to greater carried out in vv. 7-11,[21] and particularly to v. 11 with emphasis on that "which remains" (τὸ μένον).[22] If it remains, it will surely endure forever and, accordingly, be a matter for hope.

Thematically, the transition instigates a switch in focus from the glory of the two ministries in vv. 7-11 to the veil of Moses and its associations in vv. 13-18 (whereas the theme of glory is not explicitly mentioned

---

[18] Thrall 2004, 258.

[19] Instead of using the language of "how much more" in vv. 7-11 (see above), Paul conveys the contrasts in vv. 13-15 by the means of "not as" (οὐ καθάπερ) and "but" (ἀλλά).

[20] Seifrid 2014, 162.

[21] Guthrie 2015, 217-218.

[22] Thrall 2004 254.

again until v. 18). In addition, vv. 13-18 are set off from vv. 7-11 by their somewhat exceptional mode of argumentation, which is sustained by an extended application of the interpretation of Exodus 34:29-35 (first introduced in v. 7 and then developed in vv. 13-14a and 16).[23]

Further, in v. 12 Paul turns to address the challenge of questioning his apostolic authority or mission: How should he account for the apparent lack of response among his own Jewish compatriots? They fail to adhere to the Gospel, proclaimed by him.[24]

Verses 13-17

In v. 13 the link with v. 12 is broken syntactically. It is necessary to add a verb: "but [it is with us] not as [it was] with Moses who put a veil over his face."[25] That kind of addition seems quite evident. Consistent with v. 7, also v. 13 retells the stunning story of Exodus 34:29-35 in a parallel manner. They both speak about the gazing or rather non-gazing of the Israelites at the abolishing glory of Moses' face.[26] In Greek, the similarity appears more clearly than in many English translations:

v. 7	v. 13
ὥστε	πρὸς
μὴ δύνασθαι ἀτενίσαι	τὸ μὴ ἀτενίσαι
τοὺς υἱοὺς Ἰσραὴλ	τοὺς υἱοὺς Ἰσραὴλ
εἰς τὸ πρόσωπον Μωϋσέως	
διὰ τὴν δόξαν τοῦ προσώπου	εἰς τὸ τέλος τοῦ
αὐτοῦ τὴν καταργουμένην	καταργουμένου

For certain, it is remarkable that both units of vv. 7-11 and vv. 12-18 (if v. 12 is acknowledged as transition) start in a similar fashion. Apparently, the main core of the passage of Exodus 34:29-35

---

[23] Hafemann 2005, 265. See also 274-275.

[24] Martin 1986, 66. Cf. Thrall 2004, 261: "If Paul's gospel was the proclamation of the new covenant prophesied by Jeremiah, the lack of significant response from the adherents of the old covenant was surely strange. Perhaps, after all, his own claim to be διάκονος of this new covenant was invalid, and his ministry unauthentic."

[25] Martin 1986, 67.

[26] Cf. here Hafemann 2005, 353-355.

lies exactly here according to Paul. Bearing this in mind, his exegetical interpretation has to be analyzed more in depth later on (see below).

In v. 14, Paul directly proceeds from text to commentary. He maintains that the minds of Israelites were hardened (v. 14a), and the hardening endures "until this day" (v. 14b). Precisely, the history repeats itself. There is a similarity of fate from the time of Moses to the time of Paul. The "same veil" (τὸ αὐτὸ κάλυμμα) over the face of Moses remains and lies now upon the Old Testament reading of the Israelites. Indeed, their obstinacy was foretold in Scripture. Their hardening that came to pass at some stage in the past brings forth the reason for their unbelief in the encounter with the gospel.[27]

It seems that v. 13 (the Old Testament text) and v. 14b (Paul's exegetical interpretation of it) nicely correspond to each other as follows:

v. 13	v. 14b
Μωϋσῆς ἐτίθει κάλυμμα	τὸ αὐτὸ κάλυμμα μένει
ἐπὶ τὸ πρόσωπον αὐτοῦ	ἐπὶ τῇ ἀναγνώσει τῆς
	παλαιᾶς διαθήκης
τὸ τέλος τοῦ καταργουμένου	ἐν Χριστῷ καταργεῖται

Further, it seems reasonable to understand the sentence "but their minds were hardened" (ἀλλὰ ἐπωρώθη τὰ νοήματα αὐτῶν) in v. 14a as a Pauline transition from text to commentary.[28]

A similar enveloped correspondence, then, prevails also between v. 14b and vv. 15-16, which push forward the line of thought in the passage. Unpacking the spiritual hardness and hardening of Israel, they resume and restate in parallel fashion what has been told so far as follows:[29]

the hardening of Israel as a general theme

---

[27] See, e.g., Harris 2005, 300-302.

[28] Cf. Belleville 1992, 226-247. However, she surprisingly affirms that "vv. 14b-15 are a phrase-by-phrase paraphrase of vv. 13-14a" (ibid., 228).

[29] Guthrie 2015, 223. Cf. Seifrid 2014, 171. He speaks of the "parallel repetition" between v. 14b and v. 15 (but ignoring here v. 16). Similarly, Lambrecht 1983, 360. Pace Belleville 1992, 228 (she will interpret vv. 13-14a in light of vv. 14b-15).

v. 14b	vv. 15-16
time frame	
ἄχρι γὰρ τῆς σήμερον ἡμέρας . . .	ἀλλ᾿ ἕως σήμερον
ἐπὶ τῇ ἀναγνώσει τῆς παλαιᾶς διαθήκης	ἡνίκα ἂν ἀναγινώσκηται
	Μωϋσῆς
problem	
τὸ αὐτὸ κάλυμμα μένει μὴ ἀνακαλυπτόμενον	κάλυμμα ἐπὶ τὴν καρδίαν
	αὐτῶν κεῖται
solution	
ὅτι ἐν Χριστῷ καταργεῖται	ἡνίκα δὲ ἐὰν ἐπιστρέψῃ
	πρὸς Κύριον, περιαιρεῖται
	τὸ κάλυμμα

It should be noted that in v. 14b it is "the same veil"—in a figurative sense, to be sure!—that Moses placed over his face, whereas in v. 15 it is, more generally speaking, simply "a veil," lying upon the heart. The anarthrous construction serves to distinguish the two veils from each other.[30]

The recurrence of thought in clear parallel manner (the first one between v. 13 and v. 14b, the second one between v. 14b and vv. 15-16) avails to shed much more light on the Pauline reading of Exodus 34:29-35. Later on, the well-defined literal structure of the whole passage allows to overcome interpretative problems and difficulties in the text (see below).

Evidently, v. 17 is Paul's commentary on the text of Exodus 34:34 cited in v. 16,[31] making it an integral part of his argument. Therefore, he interprets both verses in relation to each other. Although the line of thought may not be deciphered instantly, the structural simplicity and precision of the text should not be overlooked. Strictly speaking, v. 17 consists of two halves corresponding to the two halves in v. 16 as follows[32]:

conversion to the Lord	who is the Lord?
v. 16a ἡνίκα δὲ ἐὰν ἐπιστρέψῃ πρὸς κύριον	v. 17a ὁ δὲ κύριος τὸ πνεῦμά ἐστιν

---

[30] Belleville 1992, 238.
[31] E.g., Lambrecht 1983, 360.
[32] Cf. Belleville 1992, 256-272.

	(The article ὁ before κύριος is anaphoric.)
the consequence of the conversion	what does the presence of the Lord effect?
v. 16b περιαιρεῖται τὸ κάλυμμα	v. 17b οὗ δὲ τὸ πνεῦμα Κυρίου, ἐλευθερία

Consequently, the statements of v. 16a and b should be examined in conjunction with their respective counterparts in v. 17a and b.[33] As expected, the freedom (ἐλευθερία) suggests the removal of the veil.[34] At the same time, the removal of the veil is an upheaval of blockades to spiritual reading or understanding.[35]

Verse 18

Also, there is a forward-looking element in the notion of freedom. It serves as a bridge to the concept of the unveiled face in v. 18.[36] Remotely, the thought of liberty certainly refers back to the chief issue in the book of Exodus, namely the factual rescue from the slavery in Egypt.[37]

On the whole, vv. 16-18 revolve around the person of the Lord (κύριος). He is the Spirit (πνεῦμα), apparently an allusion back to v. 6

---

[33] Belleville 1992, 257. Cf. also Dunn 2013, 174: "To categorize conversion as a turning to the Spirit is unusual, but entirely appropriate for a mission to the Gentiles that had been marked from the beginning by clear evidence of the Spirit at work in the lives of the converts."

[34] The voice of περιαιρεῖται (v. 16) can be passive or middle. In Exodus 34:34, Moses himself removes his own veil. In 2 Corinthians 3, a divine initiative seems to lie behind the action of unveiling (see 2 Corinthians 4:3-6). In any case, it does not necessarily exclude human action (if human activity, based on merits, is excluded). Cf. Belleville 1992, 253-254.

[35] Belleville 1992, 270, Guthrie 2015, 226-227.

[36] Belleville 1992, 271.

[37] Seifrid 2014, 178: "Paul's declaration of freedom undoubtedly recalls the Lord's liberation of Israel from Egypt [. . .]." For certain, the association of the Spirit with "freedom" is understandable also etymologically. The (Hebrew and) Greek word for the Spirit means "wind" as well. It suggests an idea of an air current that is unstrained: "The wind blows wherever it pleases. You hear its sound, but you cannot tell where it comes from or where it is going" (John 3:8). See the definition of "freedom" further below.

and v. 3 where the new covenant is established and confirmed by and in the Spirit. Thus, 2 Corinthians 3 is rounded off with interpretative pneumatological statements (as *inclusio*).[38] The emphasis of the entire chapter lies exactly here. The Spirit alone is active in transforming the believers to the likeness of their Lord. He, but no one else, "gives life." The "letter" only kills (v. 6).

In addition, v. 18 concludes and sums up the key thoughts in chapter 3:

1) the glory of the Lord (cf. vv. 7-11),
2) the unveiled face (cf. vv. 12-17),
3) the inward working of the Spirit of the Lord (as an *inclusio* to vv. 3 and 6).[39]

Thus, the theological core of 2 Corinthians 3 is found in the three motives, identified and specified in v. 18.

All in all, the notorious chapter of 2 Corinthians 3 seems to include a clear-cut and well-defined structure with five major units, which are as follows: 3:1-3, 3:4-6, 3:7-11, 3:12-17, and 3:18. Still, the theological content of the passage shows itself highly enigmatic. Before moving on to a comprehensive exegetical analysis of the text, there is a real need for a better understanding of the linguistic style in the overall context.

---

[38] Seifrid 2014, 186, Thurén 2008, 257. *Pace* Belleville (1992, 261). She does not take into account the importance of *inclusio* here. Instead, she speaks of "the reference of to 'spirit' in v. 6" as "too distant" (ibid.).

[39] Cf. Harris 2005, 318-319.

4

Textual multiplicity and interplay of scriptural allusions on metaphorical and nonmetaphorical levels in 2 Corinthians 3:1-18

Pauline discourse—characteristics

It is characteristic of Paul's style to take up a word group and use it repetitiously, sometimes from various perspectives and with different implications.[1] His language or understanding of diverse concepts looks a lot like a spectrum of meanings when a beam of his bright thinking passes through his mental prism and the component waves of thought are dispersed and arranged in order. For that reason, a free association of ideas often runs through the text. An interplay of allusions is caused by catchword bonding, in which one sense of a term suggests another or several other ideas, and so the argument proceeds. To a modern reader, accustomed at least for the most part to a mode of intellectual analysis that is either Aristotelian or related to it, the apostolic way of reasoning does not truly proceed logically. It is difficult to follow since neither syllogism nor enthymeme nor any kind of rational scheme is applied.[2]

---

[1] Thrall 2004, 232 n 295.

[2] Fitzmyer 1981, 634. For sure, Paul was able to make use of syllogism or enthymeme in different contexts as well. Yet, he was never "Aristotelian" in his thinking but rather "Jewish" (see below). In reference to Fitzmyer (but slightly differently), see Lambrecht 1983, 365-369.

Yet, the Pauline discourse has its own internal relevance or validation (*raison d'être*). It works on metaphorical and nonmetaphorical levels simultaneously. A multiplicity of conceptual connotations and nuances amount to new terms. The undercurrents of the discussion should be recognized and investigated in order that the linguistic and theological links of the argumentation are identified to the exclusion of their misinterpretations. My reading seeks to unveil the concrete and specific moves of Paul as he evokes an elaborate build-up of free associations between words, ideas, or scriptural allusions. The purpose of the following examples is to specify or implement the theoretical basis of his reasoning.[3]

Verses 1-3 in context

To begin with, Paul starts speaking of some others who need letters or epistles of recommendation to or from the congregation (v. 1). Then, he adds that the Corinthians themselves are his letter as believers. They have been inscribed on his heart. Hence, he will ask for no further credentials (v. 2). It would absolutely serve no purpose. All know and read what is in his heart. In Greek, 'knowing' and 'reading' (v. 2: γινωσκομένη καὶ ἀναγινωσκομένη) go together. Literally, reading denotes 'knowing again': It enables the reader to re-live what was thought and experienced by the author. Understandably, the word order is, thus, knowing and reading but not vice versa (as often in modern language). In addition, the verb 'commend oneself' (συνιστάνειν) strictly designates 'to bring together, namely as friends who know each other (γινώσκω). The goal of the epistles of recommendation (ἐπιστολαί συστατικαί) was accordingly to bring two persons in a very close relationship with each other. They become near friends. In consideration of the many semantic links in Greek, the linguistic jump from the letters of recommendation to knowing and reading as well as to the spiritual union between Paul and Corinthians appears even more intelligible.[4]

---

[3] Cf. Newman 2017, 231: "A surface reading of the text shows that Paul's complex, highly nuanced argument in 3:4-4:6 points to a linguistic-metaphorical war being waged over reading the Moses tradition."

[4] Bauer 2000, *s.v.* γινώσκω, ἀναγινώσκω and συνιστάνειν.

The notion of having been "inscribed (strictly speaking, not written) on the hearts" (ἐνγεγραμμένη ἐν ταῖς καρδίαις) in v. 2 is illuminated in depth in v. 3: "inscribed not with ink but with the Spirit of the living God, not on tablets of stone but on tablets of fleshy hearts" (ἐνγεγραμμένη οὐ μέλανι ἀλλὰ πνεύματι Θεοῦ ζῶντος, οὐκ ἐν πλαξὶν λιθίναις ἀλλ' ἐν πλαξὶν καρδίαις σαρκίναις). To put it simply, the mention of inscribing something and explicitly on the tablets of stone evokes the biblical association with the giving of the Mosaic law. Similarly, a new inscribing with the Spirit and on tablets of fleshy hearts reminds first of Jeremiah 31:33 (LXX 38:33), where the Lord promises to make a new covenant with Israel and write his law on their hearts, and second of Ezekiel 11:19 and/or 36:26, where the Lord promises to give Israel a new heart and put a new Spirit within them. In line with the scriptural allusions, both the old and the new covenant (vv. 6 and 14) as well as the activity and ministry of the Spirit (vv. 6, 8, 17, and 18) are mentioned later in chapter 3.[5] Moreover, the Mosaic law, which is inscribed (ἐνγεγραμμένη) on the tablets of stone, is called "letter" (γράμμα) in v. 6 and the ministry of death, engraved in letters on stone (ἐν γράμμασιν ἐντετυπωμένη λίθοις) in v. 7.[6] On the other hand, the Corinthians as "our letter" of recommendation (v. 2) is tantamount to "Christ's letter, delivered (or ministered) by us" (v. 3: ἐπιστολὴ Χριστοῦ διακονηθεῖσα ὑφ' ἡμῶν). As known, the writing of that letter is undertaken and completed by "the Spirit of the living God" (πνεύματι Θεοῦ ζῶντος). The related use of language continues in the following verses as the emphasis is put on "being the ministers of the Spirit" (v. 6: διακόνους . . . πνεύματος) or "the ministry of the Spirit" (v. 8: ἡ διακονία τοῦ πνεύματος) and how the Spirit gives life (v. 6: τὸ δὲ πνεῦμα ζωοποιεῖ).[7]

Apparently, Paul plays upon scriptural allusions and multiplicity of linguistic associations making use of some kind of concatenation of his assertions and reasons. His text is heavily laden with

---

[5] Johansson 1990, 64-65, 69-70, 75-76.

[6] Thrall 2004, 234: "The term γράμμα must have something to do with the law of Moses, in view of the allusion in v. 7 to the engraving ἐν γράμμασιν on stone which marked the inauguration of the old covenant." For certain, the participle ἐνγεγραμμένη occurs already in v. 2.

[7] See, e.g., Hays 1989, 127. Cf. Lambrecht 1983, 353.

theological afterthoughts and semantic indicators that are expanded
and developed as the argumentation proceeds and draws on them.
The coalescing or fusing of his interpretive statements and insights
reflects the depth and strength of his reasoning but also challenges
the reader with the difficulty of understanding (cf. 2 Peter 3:15-16).

Verses 4-6 in context

By means of v. 4 as transition, Paul moves on and speaks of his competence that comes from God to the exclusion of his own inability. From
within himself, he is not at all competent as a minister of the new covenant (vv. 5-6). Paul repeats himself and makes it very clear by using
a similar terminology in diverse forms: "Not that we are competent
(ἱκανοί) in ourselves (. . .), but our competence (ἡ ἱκανότης) comes
from God (. . .). He has made us competent (ἱκάνωσεν) as ministers
of a new covenant." As already stated, 3:5-6 harks back to 2:16b with
a reference to LXX Exodus 4:10 (see above). It seems that the question
of 2:16b: "Who is competent (sufficient) for these things?" (καὶ πρὸς
ταῦτα τίς ἱκανός;) is answered in LXX Exodus 4:10 as Moses acknowledges: "I am not competent (οὐχ ἱκανός εἰμι)" as a minister of the old
covenant. Now Paul adds that neither is he competent as a minister
of the new covenant, but, as told, his competence springs from God's
power. He fuses his own opinion and experience with the persuasion
of Moses. The juxtaposition of their spiritual standing facilitates the
appropriation of the biblical allusion in the present context.[8]

    The notion of the "letter" (τὸ γράμμα) that kills in v. 6 was antic-
ipated in v. 3 as Paul spoke of the letter (epistle) of Christ (ἐπιστολὴ
Χριστοῦ) that is "not inscribed on tablets of stone" (ἐνγεγραμμένη . . .
οὐκ ἐν πλαξὶν λιθίναις). In v. 7 he expands his thought and speaks
of "the ministry of death" that was "engraved in letters on stone"
(ἡ διακονία τοῦ θανάτου ἐν γράμμασιν ἐντετυπωμένη λίθοις). As it
may be, the verb ἐντυπόω denotes that the inauguration of the killing
"letter" at Sinai functions as a type (τύπος) for the effect of the Mosaic
law in general. The subsequent line of thought in chapter 3 goes in
that direction (see below).

---

[8] Rightly, e.g., Lambrecht 1983, 350-351.

Since v. 6 puts emphasis on God who enables Paul or his coworkers to carry on as "ministers of a new covenant" (διακόνους καινῆς διαθήκης), the following verses revolve around the ministry (διακονία) of the "letter" and the "Spirit." Consequently, the "letter" that kills performs "the ministry of death" (v. 7: ἡ διακονία τοῦ θανάτου), whereas the "Spirit" who gives life pursues his own ministry (v. 8: ἡ διακονία τοῦ πνεύματος).[9]

Verses 7-11 in context

In vv. 7-11 Paul primarily deals with the glory of the old and new covenant in a comparative manner and applies three times the formal expression of "if then . . . how much more" to define their mutual relationship (see above). In consequence, his main interest does not allow him to deepen the polyphonic composition of his scriptural allusions or thicken the multiple senses of his meticulous terminology.

Yet, it is important to take notice of the use and significance of the verb καταργεῖν. It is one of the key words in the chapter and occurs in vv. 7, 11, 13, and 14 (in all cases in present tense). The basic meaning seems quite clear. A compound of κατά (causative) and α (privative) combined with ἔργον ('not working') yields the simple sense: 'to render inoperative' and 'ineffectual,' 'to nullify,' 'to abrogate,' or 'to bring to nothing.' The verb never means 'to fade away.'[10]

It has already been shown that Paul moves from the shine or glory (δόξα) of Moses' face (v. 7) into "that which has been glorified" (τὸ δεδοξασμένον in v. 10) and purposely broadens from the feminine form (ἡ δόξα) to the neuter form (τὸ δεδοξασμένον) encompassing Moses and his shining face within Moses' glorious mission (see above). That is the way his stringent argumentation proceeds in chapter 3. In a similar manner, he first speaks of the glory on Moses' face, which is to be done away: the verb καταργουμένην refers to τὴν δόξαν τοῦ προσώπου αὐτοῦ (v. 7). Later, he widens his use of language through a change of gender and focus on "that which is

---

[9] See above, chapter 3.

[10] Cf. Belleville 1992, 204. Nevertheless, she maintains that the verb here carries the sense of the fading and diminishing light (204-205). Correctly, e.g., Guthrie 212.

done away or brought to nothing:" τὸ καταργούμενον (vv. 11, 13) harks back to τὴν καταργουμένην (v. 7)—yet putting emphasis on the abrogated character of the whole Mosaic ministry instead of the glory on Moses' countenance.[11]

Verse 13—the noun τέλος and the verb κατάργειν

The crystal-clear meaning of the verb κατάργειν as abrogating or nullifying something sheds more light on the near context as well, especially on v. 13. Time and time again, the discussion of the precise sense of the word τέλος has been raised. Numerous suggestions have been made. They could be divided into two main categories: teleological sense (τέλος as goal, purpose, result) or temporal sense (τέλος as end, termination, cessation).[12] I am not sure if the customary and long-established option "either—or" ever has been a sound alternative. Why should we pick out only one to the exclusion of the other? It seems that the Greek word τέλος rather carries both meanings or, at least, combines nuances of both the teleological and temporal senses. In connection with the verb κατάργειν, the teleological interpretation without any temporal limitation appears absolutely simplistic. Indeed, in Pauline usage the focus lies on a bringing-to-an-end but never on an exclusive or restrictive bringing-to-a-goal as is shown in the following set of examples:[13]

> Romans 3:3
> What if some were unfaithful? Will their unfaithfulness nullify (καταργήσει) God's faithfulness?

> Romans 3:31
> Do we, then, nullify (καταργοῦμεν) the law by this faith? Not at all! Rather, we uphold the law.

---

[11] E.g., Hays 1989, 134-135.

[12] See, e.g., Guthrie 2015, 219-220.

[13] Cf. Watson 2004, 293-294 n 42. Cf. further Thrall 2004, 256: "When two terms which may both bear a temporal sense (i.e., τέλος and καταργούμενον) are juxtaposed, this may be a clear hint that the temporal meaning is intended." Still, she prefers the teleological meaning (ibid., 257). Correctly, Baker 2000, *passim* (especially 3-5, 10-12). Similarly, Hamilton 2011, 591.

Romans 4:14
For if those who depend on the law are heirs, faith means nothing and the promise is worthless (κατήργηται).

Romans 6:6
For we know that our old self was crucified with him so that the body ruled by sin might be done away with (καταργηθῇ), that we should no longer be slaves to sin.

Romans 7:2
For example, by law a married woman is bound to her husband as long as he is alive, but if her husband dies, she is released (κατήργηται) from the law that binds her to him.

Romans 7:6
But now, by dying to what once bound us, we have been released (κατηργήθημεν) from the law so that we serve in the new way of the Spirit, and not in the old way of the written code.

1 Corinthians 1:28
God chose the lowly things of this world and the despised things— and the things that are not—to nullify (καταργήσῃ) the things that are.

1 Corinthians 2:6
We do, however, speak a message of wisdom among the mature, but not the wisdom of this age or of the rulers of this age, who are coming to nothing (τῶν καταργουμένων).

1 Corinthians 6:13
You say, "Food for the stomach and the stomach for food, and God will destroy (καταργήσει) them both." The body, however, is not meant for sexual immorality but for the Lord, and the Lord for the body.

1 Corinthians 13:8
Love never fails. But where there are prophecies, they will cease (καταργηθήσονται); where there are tongues, they will be stilled; where there is knowledge, it will pass away (καταργηθήσεται).

1 Corinthians 13:10
But when completeness comes, what is in part disappears (καταργηθήσεται).

1 Corinthians 13:11
When I was a child, I talked like a child, I thought like a child, I reasoned like a child. When I became a man, I put the ways of childhood behind me (κατήργηκα).

1 Corinthians 15:24
Then the end (τὸ τέλος) will come, when he hands over the kingdom to God the Father after he has destroyed (καταργήσῃ) all dominion, authority and power.
(Take a good notice of the instructive correlation of τὸ τέλος and καταργήσῃ as in 2 Corinthians 2:13.)

1 Corinthians 15:26
The last enemy to be destroyed (καταργεῖται) is death.

Galatians 3:17
What I mean is this: The law, introduced 430 years later, does not set aside the covenant previously established by God and thus do away with (καταργῆσαι) the promise.

Galatians 5:4
You who are trying to be justified by the law have been alienated (κατηργήθητε) from Christ; you have fallen away from grace.

Galatians 5:11
Brothers and sisters, if I am still preaching circumcision, why am I still being persecuted? In that case the offense of the cross has been abolished (κατήργηται).

Ephesians 2:15
By setting aside (καταργήσας) in his flesh the law with its commands and regulations.

2 Thessalonians 2:8
And then the lawless one will be revealed, whom the Lord Jesus will overthrow with the breath of his mouth and destroy (καταργήσει) by the splendor of his coming.

2 Timothy 1:10
But it has now been revealed through the appearing of our Savior, Christ Jesus, who has destroyed (καταργήσαντος) death and has brought life and immortality to light through the gospel.

Given all the previous examples, the phrase τὸ τέλος τοῦ καταργουμένου is to be understood temporally notwithstanding a teleological undertone. "The end of the story is, strictly speaking, the goal of the story." In consequence, it is best to translate the closing part of v. 13 as "the end of that which is abolished."[14] No doubt, the verb καταργέω draws τέλος into its own semantic sphere. Nonetheless, one should at the same time bear in mind that "the goal of that which is abolished" is included in the translation as well. The usage of the Greek language involves double aspects which cannot easily be reproduced in English.[15]

On the other hand, the discussion of how to interpret "the phrase εἰς τὸ τέλος as a whole" in v. 13, "a phrase that occurs only here in the NT,"[16] appears utterly unnecessary since there is no expression like that here! Without a shred of doubt, the preposition εἰς is related to the verb ἀτενίσαι as already in v. 7: ὥστε μὴ δύνασθαι ἀτενίσαι τοὺς υἱοὺς Ἰσραὴλ εἰς τὸ πρόσωπον Μωϋσέως. To be sure, in v. 13 the preposition εἰς is once more connected with the same verb ἀτενίσαι exactly in the same form: πρὸς τὸ μὴ ἀτενίσαι τοὺς υἱοὺς Ἰσραὴλ εἰς τὸ τέλος τοῦ καταργουμένου. It follows of necessity that the alleged non-Pauline adverbial phrase εἰς τὸ τέλος does not exist at all.[17]

---

[14] Here, take notice of Grindheim 2001, 111 n 60. He points out: "Assuming this meaning does not make Paul guilty of pleonasm. The qualification τοῦ καταργουμένου is necessary to identify what it was that was ending and the term τέλος is necessary to identify what it was that was concealed from the Israelites." *Pace* Provence 1982, 76 n 62.

[15] In addition, both verbs καταργέω and μένω occur simultaneously in 1 Corinthians 13:8-13 just as in 2 Corinthians 3:11. The strong contrast between them confirms that they primarily have a temporal meaning. *Pace* Hays 1989, 136-140.

[16] Guthrie 2015, 220. See also Hafemann 2005, 356-362, Philpot 2013b, 175.

[17] See especially Thrall 2004, 259. The verb ἀτενίζω, with its intensifying ἀ- added to the verbal stem τείνω (to "stretch," to "draw tight"), takes εἰς and means to "look intently" or to "gaze earnestly" (Seifrid 2014, 154 n 217). The interest lies on an insistent fixing of the attention or an attentive visual observation of an object (Guthrie 2015, 219).

Verse 14—ἐν Χριστῷ καταργεῖται

Aside from that, the verb καταργεῖται in v. 14 still needs to be analyzed and explained more in detail. The real big problem concerns the subject of the subordinate clause ὅτι ἐν Χριστῷ καταργεῖται. There are quite a few attempts at various solutions.[18] Not all of them are to be dealt with here. In any respect, this much is obvious—that the subject is not veil, since the verb καταργεῖται, "is done away," does not go with it; in the context, the veil περιαιρεῖται, "is taken away" (v. 16). That which is done away amounts to the glory or the whole quintessence of the old covenant (vv. 7, 11, 13).[19]

According to another considerable solution, the negative participle μὴ ἀνακαλυπτόμενον is understood as an accusative absolute: "it not being revealed." It follows that the conjunction ὅτι should be interpreted as declarative: "that." In that case, the subject of καταργεῖται is taken from the preceding clause: ἡ παλαιὰ διαθήκη, "the old covenant." Then, v. 14b can be translated as follows: "Not being revealed that the old covenant is abrogated in Christ."[20]

However, the participle μὴ ἀνακαλυπτόμενον is more naturally seen as referring to removal of the veil than to disclosure in a general sense, for which ἀποκαλύπτω would be more suitable. Also, in v. 18 the known phrase ἀνακεκαλυμμένῳ προσώπῳ is seen as relating to the removal of the veil: "with unveiled (open) face."[21] Besides, the absolute participle is virtually absent in the New Testament and ought not be assumed so long as the context contains a possible subject (here, τὸ αὐτὸ κάλυμμα) for the participle.[22]

The subject of the verb καταργεῖται is to be found on the basis of a sound grammatical analysis of the Greek text. I think the most obvious solution has not been taken into account. It is a peculiarity, not so common in modern languages. Hence, it has vanished from sight during the search for a good explanation. In Greek, the subject can be omitted in special cases. The phenomenon occurs since the forms of the verbs leave no doubt as to the number and person of the subject.

---

[18] See commentaries, e.g., Thrall 2004, 263-266.

[19] Martin 1986, 69.

[20] See especially Seifrid 2014, 168-171. Similarly, Grindheim 2001, 108-110.

[21] Thrall 2004, 264 (without any mention of v. 18).

[22] Thrall 2004, 264.

Especially with regard to impersonal expressions (impersonalia), the subject is often implied in the verb as in the two following examples:

ἐκήρυξε (scil. ὁ κῆρυξ): the herald has heralded or

σαλπίσει (scil. ἡ σάλπιγξ): "the trumpet will trumpet" or "the trumpet will sound" (1 Corinthians 15:52).[23]

Further, the subject "might remain unexpressed without any injury to the sense, especially when it is implied from the nature of the verb itself." Accordingly, the "reference to the subject is often very remote and feeble."[24] In other words, Greek is a typical "null-subject" language whose grammar permits omission of an explicit subject (why it is omitted should be understood from the context).

In 2 Corinthians 3, one of the key words is—as already suggested above—the verb καταργεῖν. It occurs in vv. 7, 11, 13, and 14. Theologically, it conveys the main idea in the whole chapter of the abrogation of the old covenant. It has also been acknowledged above that a close correlation exists between the end of v. 13 (τὸ τέλος τοῦ καταργουμένου) and the end of v. 14 (ἐν Χριστῷ καταργεῖται). They correspond to each other. It follows that Paul, as expected, takes the subject of the verb καταργεῖται for granted. His formulation amounts to the notion of τὸ καταργούμενον ἐν Χριστῷ καταργεῖται: "what is done away is done away in Christ." Yet, being aware of the elegant use of the Greek language, he writes much more to the point and in brief: ἐν Χριστῷ καταργεῖται. Given that, the verb καταργεῖται has no twofold meaning but rather a double grammatical function: the predicate subsumes into itself the role of the subject as well.

Verses 13-18—the oscillating meaning of the veil

Another key word in 2 Corinthians 3 is the substantive 'veil' (κάλυμμα). It has no less than a three-dimensional perspective. First, it lies over the face of Moses (v. 13), second, at the reading of the old covenant (v. 14), and third, upon the hearts of the Israelites (v. 15). Then, it is taken away whenever anyone turns to the Lord (v. 16).

---

[23] Blass-Debrunner 1961, §129.
[24] See already Buttmann 1839, 376.

That is one side of the freedom in the presence of the Lord (v. 17). Ultimately, all those, who with unveiled faces behold the glory of the Lord, are being transformed into his likeness (v. 18).[25]

The oscillating meaning of the veil essentially originates from the fact that the minds of the Israelites were hardened (v. 14: ἐπωρώθη). They did not really understand the true purpose or intention of the veil over the face of Moses. It follows that neither do they understand the reading of the old covenant, in other words, the authoritative liturgical reading of Moses in their get-togethers (vv. 14-15). A metaphorical fusion occurs here in which Moses embodies the Torah and represents it.[26] The interplay of the past and the present discloses that the failure of the Israelites was pre-figured in their own Scripture. Literally, the verb πωρόω denotes 'to petrify,' 'turn into callous.' In passive, it carries the sense of becoming hardened.[27] Paul recalls "the hearts of stone" in Ezekiel 36:26 (cf. above): he speaks of the stubbornness of Israel. Their minds were turned to stone. Besides, Paul also seems to have innovated in a persuasive way and assimilated his use of language to "tablets of stone" (v. 3) as an abridged code for the entire Mosaic religion.[28] An analogous association arises when Moses is read and his text epitomizes the "letter" (γράμμα) that kills (v. 6).[29] In addition, the reading of Moses possibly implies that he is literally "recognized" or "known again" (ἀναγινώσκω) through reading, especially on account of the apostolic preaching to or among the Jews (and in his letters to the Corinthians), so that his face is showing up from behind the veil little by little. But alas, now the loathed veil instead lies on the hearts of the Israelites! In conclusion, Paul provides a thought-provoking and razor-sharp reasoning that moves on or rather moves back and forth both on metaphorical and non-metaphorical levels at the same time. He qualifies himself as the master of theological argumentation.

---

[25] See Fitzmyer 1981, 637.

[26] Fitzmyer 1981, 637-638.

[27] Bauer 2000, *s.v.* πωρόω.

[28] Cf. Seifrid 2014, 166-167.

[29] See above the linguistic links between vv. 3, 6, and 7.

Verse 16—the taking off of the veil

In v. 16, Paul prolongs his multidimensional approach. He refers to the habit of Moses to take off the veil in the presence of the Lord (Exodus 34:34). In the light of the context, this is certainly the primary meaning of the story. That makes sense. The verb ἐπιστρέφω, then, denotes the simple movement of the body as one turns round to meet the Lord, Yahweh, and see his eternal glory. Consequently, a Christological interpretation of κύριος is not allowed.[30] However, there is once again a really strange dichotomy of "either—or" but no profound understanding of simultaneous perspectives in chapter 3 (see above). In consideration of chapter 4, a synchronic interpretation of "both—and" is more to the point. Here, the glory of the Lord takes on two seemingly different meanings. On the one hand, Paul speaks about many unbelievers who do not see "the light of the gospel of the glory of Christ, who is the image of God" (v. 4). On the other hand, he talks about all believers who do see "the light of the knowledge of the glory of God in the face of Christ" (v. 6). Thus, Paul does not set apart theological Christology and Christological theology. Obviously, he regards them as the two sides of the one and same coin. Verse 4 asserts that Christ has his "glory" since he is explicitly "the image of God." Verse 6 affirms that God has his glory to be revealed "in the face of Christ." The harmonious distinction (or distinctive harmony) of the two expressions in chapter 4 defines the identity of the Lord in chapter 3 through a multifaceted interplay of semantic simplicity and complexity.[31]

Additionally, Paul does not maintain in plain language who in v. 16 is going to "turn to the Lord." First of all, he, as expected, aims at Moses. Second, he might speak of himself and his experience on the road to Damascus as the divine glory of Christ from heaven unexpectedly flashed around him (Acts 9:3).[32] Third, the subject of

---

[30] See especially Dunn 1970, 317-318 (cf. 318-320). *Contra* his position, correctly, Legarth 2004, 47-48. For my own interpretation, see below.

[31] For the "criss-crossing of language" between v. 4 and v. 6 in chapter 4, see especially Seifrid 2014, 197-198, 201-204. Similarly, Fitzmyer 1981, 638-639.

[32] More for this, see Kim 1981, 11-13. Cf. Legarth 2004, 38: "Og flere forhold giver god grund till at formode, at Paulus former sin skildring af

the verb ἐπιστρέψῃ is obviously generalized and involves everyone who is converted.[33] The verb ἐπιστρέφω, then, designates more than mere human physical activity. It denotes repentance and religious conversion. Nothing less is included in v. 16, a true masterpiece of a multiple and polyphonic texture.[34]

Verse 17—the Spirit as freedom

In v. 17, Paul adds that the Lord is the Spirit. In v. 16, he has already identified the Lord, Yahweh, and Christ through his associative reading of the Old Testament. Yet alongside that, he has also distinguished between them. Now, Paul completes his "trinitarian" theology. He remarks that the Lord, Yahweh, embodied in Christ, is represented through the presence of the Spirit.[35] I think we have here an apostolic solution to the unresolved evident discrepancy in the story of Exodus. On the one hand, God speaks to Moses "face to face, as a man speaks with his friend" (Exodus 33:11). On the other hand, no one can ever see the face of the Lord, Yahweh (Exodus 33:23). Indeed, both statements are valid and in force at the same time! The Lord, i.e., the Spirit, speaks to Moses "face to face," but the Lord, i.e., Yahweh, will not show his face to him. The meaning of Exodus 32-34 in Pauline theology must be postponed and discussed more in depth later (see below).

The being and action of the Lord through the presence and efficiency of the Spirit is characterized and recognized by "freedom"

---

oplevelsen ved Damaskus under bevidst reference till den forudgående omtale af Sinai-åbenbaringen."

[33] Guthrie 2015, 224-225, Legarth 2004, 41-42. Cf. van Unnik 1963, 166.

[34] It seems that Balla (2007, 757-758, 760-761) fails to see the fine art of the Old Testament quotation in 2 Corinthians 3:16. For the Old Testament background of v. 16, see, e.g., van Unnik 1963, 165.

[35] For a more comprehensive analysis of v. 17, see my discussion of it in chapter 6 (with references). Although Paul does not discuss the dogmatic locus of the Holy Trinity, he still affirms plainly and simply that the Lord *is* the Spirit. He confirms the identification of them. Rightly, Seifrid 2014, 175: Paul asserts that "*the Lord* is the Spirit. This identification is obviously not absolute, since Paul distinguishes the Lord from the Spirit in the following clause when he speaks of 'the Spirit of the Lord.' It is, nevertheless, an identification."

(ἐλευθερία). Definitely, it is an immediate result of a person being unveiled. Further, it matches the overall story of Moses and Exodus (as echoed and written in 2 Corinthians 3) extremely well. Freedom is liberty from slavery in Egypt.[36] In a spiritual sense, liberty from slavery is freedom from sin, death, condemnation, and perishability or eternal destruction. The contrasts have already been anticipated in vv. 7-11 and explained more in other Pauline letters, especially in Galatians. However, it should not be overlooked that freedom is not only freedom from an adverse condition but a positive state. The whole interpretation should be related to the motif of glory, the main topic in chapter 3 which is strongly emphasized once again in v. 18.[37]

Verse 18 in context

Thus, in v. 18, Paul expands one major aspect of the freedom of which he wrote in v. 17. Freedom means that he and all Christians are able to behold the glory of the Lord "with unveiled faces" (ἀνακεκαλυμμένῳ προσώπῳ) or without a veil (κάλυμμα) that has been taken away at conversion (see v. 16 above). Here, the verb κατοπτρίζομαι is to be translated as 'to behold oneself' (in a mirror). It remains in the same semantic domain as ἀτενίζω, 'to look at intently' (vv. 7, 13).[38] In chapter 3, the focus lies on the con-

---

[36] In the Septuagint, ἐλευθερία and its cognates are mostly used either in the context of slavery or prisoners of war. "It is striking that it is not found in connection either with the liberation of Israel from Egypt or the return of Israel from exile. The political use of *eleutheria* is apparently foreign to the LXX." In the New Testament, "*eleutheria* is never used in the secular sense of political freedom." It seems that "the recovery of Israel's political freedom no longer played any part in the thinking of the NT writers." See Blunck 1986, 716-717. Neither in 2 Corinthians 3 does ἐλευθερία coalesce into the political freedom. Nevertheless, it is hard not to see any subtle reference to exodus in a context of the giving of the Mosaic law at Sinai. For sure, the focus still lies on the spiritual freedom, gained by Christ and granted by faith. See below.

[37] See Thrall 2004, 274-276 and Grindheim 2001, 103 (with their own emphases). Similarly, Legarth 2004, 42-45.

[38] Guthrie 2015, 227.

trast between the Jews who cannot see as a result of the veil upon their hearts and the Christians who can see with unveiled faces.[39] In the book of Exodus, special attention is similarly drawn to Moses beholding the glory of God, which feature appears as one of the main themes in the whole story.[40]

However, in consideration of the multiple nuances and inter-relating perspectives in 2 Corinthians 3, an intentional ambiguity might not be excluded in v. 18. The verb κατοπτρίζομαι also denotes 'to reflect' (as a mirror). Then, the Christians—after having been beholding the glory of God—reflect his glory to their fellow people. In other words, their own glory is deduced from his glory. The former is secondary, the latter is primary. By and large, the line of thought recalls the experience of Moses in Exodus 33-34. His face was shining (reflecting) since he had been in the presence of God and seen his glory on the top of the mountain (cf. the light motif in 2 Corinthians 4:6).[41]

In any event, the transformation of the Christians takes form and more force "from glory to glory" (ἀπὸ δόξης εἰς δόξαν). The expression includes the time span from the initial glory already received through regeneration to the final glory to be gained at the Parousia.[42] It makes good sense. Tentatively, the text might be assumed as the source of the transformation (ἀπὸ δόξης) and as the outcome of the transformation (εἰς δόξαν). In that case, ἀπὸ δόξης parallels ἀπὸ κυρίου πνεύματος in the end of v. 18 and stands for (the glorious) God since, sometimes, God is called the (Majestic) Glory (see, e.g., 2 Peter 1:17).[43]

Last, but not least: the transformation of the Christians from beginning to end is brought about by the Lord, Yahweh, who is—as shown in v. 16—identified with Christ and whose divine presence is experienced in the Spirit (ἀπὸ κυρίου πνεύματος). The reading of the book of Exodus in the light of his trinitarian self explains how the Spirit gives life (v. 6, *inclusio*).

---

[39] Martin 1986, 71.
[40] Cf. Seifrid 2014, 180 n 293.
[41] Guthrie 2015, 227. Similarly, Kim 1981, 13 n 2, 232, 237.
[42] Guthrie 2015, 229 in reference to Harris 2005, 316.
[43] Cf. Guthrie 2015, 229.

Summary

In sum, the juxtaposition or concatenation of several biblical associations in 2 Corinthians 3 carries with it a radical reorientation toward Scripture. Paul piles up and pulls together diverse Old Testament concepts and metaphors to release them into the semantic agenda of the new covenant where they speak for and from the perspective of the fulfillment. His inspirational reading resists reduction into a one-for-one scheme. Thus, he works in tandem on the metaphorical and non-metaphorical levels of multiple concentric senses. Next in turn, a closer look at the Old Testament texts, elaborated in 2 Corinthians 3, is needed.

5

Old Testament background

Old Testament texts in 2 Corinthians 3:1-18

It is neither necessary nor required to account for an all-encompassing study and analysis of the Old Testament background. It has already been shown that the most relevant source texts of 2 Corinthians 3 are Exodus 34:29-35, Jeremiah 31:31-34, and Ezekiel 36:26-27 alongside 37:1-10.[1] Other biblical references and allusions are taken, if needed, at face value later in connection with a more thorough explanation of Paul's reading of the Scripture and the contrast he asserts between the "letter" and the "Spirit."[2]

The three main scriptural texts in 2 Corinthians 3 belong together through a verbal and non-verbal linking. To begin with, they all speak about the covenant. Moses communicates the law (or "the ten words") and mediates between Yahweh and Israel in the old covenant. On the other hand, Jeremiah foretells the inauguration of the new covenant. Correspondingly, Ezekiel first foresees how the glory of God departs from the temple (chapter 10) and goes up from within the city of Jerusalem to the mountain east of it (11:23). In his eyes, it symbolizes the end of the old covenant. Then, he prophesies the beginning of the Messianic age in the future. As the stony hearts of the Israelites will be removed and new hearts of flesh given (11:19, 36:26), the Spirit will be poured out (36:26-27), and the national revival or restoration will start (37:1-10) under the leadership of the Davidic king (37:22-25)

---

[1] In addition, see Richard 1981, *passim* (especially 358).

[2] See further Balla 2007, 755.

on the basis of an everlasting covenant, called "a covenant of peace" (37:26).[3]

In addition, the story of Exodus (especially with regard to 32:16 and 34:1) stands in contrast to Jeremiah 31:33 through the keyword, "writing:" the old covenant was *written* on the tablets of stone, but the new covenant is *written* on the hearts. Further, the story of Exodus (particularly in the light of 32:16 and 34:1) stands in contrast to Ezekiel 36:26 by use of the catchword, "stone:" the old covenant was written on the tablets of *stone* while the new covenant is written on the hearts of flesh instead of the hearts of *stone*. Accordingly, the common denominator between Jeremiah 31:33 and Ezekiel 36:26 turns out to be the notion of "heart." Those two prophetic texts are set in opposition to an account in the Pentateuch.[4] On closer reflection, how do they more exactly interact with each other in the narrative framework of the Scripture? To learn their different theological nuances and meanings, they are next dealt with in "canonical" order.

Exodus 32-34

Assuredly, Exodus 34:29-35 amounts to the prime and basic text behind 2 Corinthians 3. It rounds off the long episode of the golden calf in chapters 32-34 which are, to be sure, embedded in the larger context of the book of Exodus (see below).[5] The story goes as follows:

> 29 When Moses came down from Mount Sinai with the two tablets of the covenant law in his hands, he was not aware that his face was radiant because he had spoken with the LORD. 30 When Aaron and all the Israelites saw Moses, his face was radiant, and they were afraid

---

[3] Cf. Johansson 1990, 69. In concert with 37:26, also Ezekiel 16:60 and 34:25 speak about an everlasting covenant.

[4] Johansson 1990, 69 and 76.

[5] For the later interpretations of Exodus 32 in Jewish and rabbinical texts as well as apostolic, patristic and Christian sources, see especially Lindqvist 2008, 89-316. In his survey of the New Testament, he does not analyze 2 Corinthians 3 as related to Exodus 32-34. Neither does he discuss, e.g., Romans 1:23 as a possible reference to Exodus 32 (ibid., 89-98).

to come near him. 31 But Moses called to them; so Aaron and all the leaders of the community came back to him, and he spoke to them. 32 Afterward all the Israelites came near him, and he gave them all the commands the LORD had given him on Mount Sinai. 33 When Moses finished speaking to them, he put a veil over his face. 34 But whenever he entered the LORD's presence to speak with him, he removed the veil until he came out. And when he came out and told the Israelites what he had been commanded, 35 they saw that his face was radiant. Then Moses would put the veil back over his face until he went in to speak with the LORD.

Understandably, the main concern of Exodus 32–34 converges on the question of God's stance on the Israelites after their idolatrous service of the golden calf at Sinai and on his willingness to go before them all along the way. The plot remains focused on Moses' role as mediator between God and the Israelites. His constant plea for mercy provides the narrative structure of the whole story (32:11-13, 31-32, 33:12-17). Finally, his intercessions received favorable response. The Lord promises not to forsake his own people but to forgive their sins, not to leave Israelites in the remote wilderness to starve and thirst but to lead them into the land "flowing with milk and honey."[6]

So, the question of the presence of God in the midst of the rebellious Israel is precisely tantamount to a question of the attendance of his "face" (פָּנִים) among them (explicitly 33:14-15). Given the strong emphasis on "face" in chapters 32-34, the more literal rendering seems very reasonable. It echoes in the accounts of Moses' searching the "face" of Yahweh (32:11), Yahweh and Moses speaking "face to face" (33:11), Yahweh's refusal to allow Moses to see his "face" but his "back" in the cleft of the rock (33:20-23), and Moses' shining face ever since he has been in close conversation with Yahweh (34:29-35).[7]

---

[6] Cf. Childs 2004, 562-563.

[7] Watts 2011, 426 n 34. See also Philpot 2013a, 6 n 18. He further writes (ibid., 6): "Moses exclusively knows Yahweh 'face to face,' that is, 'as a man speaks to his friend' (33:11). The theme of 'face' echoed in 34:29-35 no doubt alludes to 33:11-23." Similarly, Hartenstein 2008, 273-277. In reference to Exodus 32, he already points out (ibid., 268): "Es ist bezeichnend, wie die Exposition von Ex 32 mit der Frage nach der *wahren Gottespräsenz* einsetzt."

In the true sense of the word, Moses has to face up to the rebellion of Israel and ask the Lord to take his servant at face value! The ultimate goal is to ensure that grace and iniquity interface in the divine act of acquittal.

Indeed, the focus of the entire narrative in chapters 32-34 lies on the benevolence and compassion of God, notwithstanding his severe aversion to apostasy and idolatry. He shows his furious rage and temper against the stubbornness of Israel but relents from his anger and wrath when confronted with his promises to the patriarchs still in force. The many-faceted and wide-ranging storyline culminates in the last petition of Moses (33:12-18). To begin with, he entreats for favor or mercy toward himself and then, without delay, proceeds to extend it to his people as well. The idiom "to find favor with somebody" occurs no less than five times in vv. 12-17 and brackets the dialogue between Moses and God resulting in the final request of seeing the divine glory (v. 18).[8]

The response ensues instantly, followed by a detailed plan of practical settings (33:19-23, 34:1-5). Then, the astonishing theophany of the Lord comes to pass (34:6-7). In the context, his celestial glory is remarkably defined as "all his goodness" (33:19), accompanied by a divine proclamation of his name (33:19, 34:5) and explained by indication of his mercy (33:19, 34:6-7).[9] It looks reasonable to achieve a liaison between the name of Yahweh, "I am who I am" (3:14), and the ostensible meaning of his name, "I will have mercy on whom I will have mercy, and I will have compassion on whom I will have compassion" (33:19). He is what he is to substantiate and authenticate the permanent truth that his name and inner being are recognized in or through forgiveness.[10] The tautologous phrases in Hebrew are obviously circular reasoning, assuming what they are saying. They require that the conclusion be true. However, in the case of love there is no other motive but the love. To search for any further evidence spoils everything. Therefore, the tautologous self-characterization of God turns out to be absolutely valid. Believe him or not! Later, he repeats

---

[8] Hamilton 2011, 564. Similarly, Hartenstein 2008, 273-283.

[9] Enns 2000, 584.

[10] Childs 2004, 596, He speaks of "the circular *idem per idem* formula of the name." Similarly, Durham 1987, 452, Enns 2000, 584.

who he is by using the same vocabulary as previously: "Yahweh, Yahweh, the compassionate and merciful God" (34:6). Once more, there is no reason for his loving-kindness but his benevolence, based on his own self.[11]

The amazing grace of God comes into view even more with a comparison of the initial making of the covenant and the subsequent renewal of the covenant. In chapter 20, he introduces himself as "a jealous God, punishing the children for the sin of the parents to the third and fourth generation of those who hate me, but showing love to a thousand generations of those who love me and keep my commandments" (vv. 5-6). Since the Israelites soon renounced their love for him and did not keep his commandments but succumbed to the worship of the golden calf, the covenant was broken, and the tablets of stones were crushed. The renewal of the covenant was no more thinkable on the same basis as before. In chapter 34, there is a striking shift in the text. God introduces himself in a different way. He is "the LORD, the LORD, the compassionate and gracious God, slow to anger, abounding in love and faithfulness, maintaining love to thousands, and forgiving wickedness, rebellion and sin. Yet he does not leave the guilty unpunished; he punishes the children and their children for the sin of the parents to the third and fourth generation." (vv. 6-7) There is no talk about the covenantal relationship, based on Israel's love for God or their keeping of his commandments. Rather, it is all about the "compassionate and gracious" God, "slow to anger, abounding in love and faithfulness," who forgives "wickedness, rebellion and sin" of Israel. This alone is the beginning of the new beginning! For sure, the threat to those who break the covenant in the future remains similar in both cases and affects the fate of the children "to the third and fourth generation." Still, the renewal of the covenant stays on the firm ground of the divine mercy.[12]

---

[11] Cf. the discussion about the tautologous name of God (Exodus 3:14) in Enns 2000, 101-108, Hamilton 2011, 63-66.

[12] See Hamilton 2011, 576. Besides, he points out that "34:5-7, unlike 20:5-6, does *not* refer to God as a 'jealous' God." Further, "20:5-6 begins by talking about punishment first (20:5b), then moves to talking about showing love (20:6). The latter passage reverses that. It begins by talking about showing mercy (34:7a), then moves to talking about delayed punishment (34:7b)." In

On the whole, seeing God's celestial glory—together with the proclaiming of his name, Yahweh—reveals that he is ready to grant clemency to the stiff-necked Israel and go with them and bring them to the land of promise. His loving and caring presence with them is thereby guaranteed all along the way.[13] The definite proof for his change of mind shows itself in the arrangements of encampment in the wilderness. As God first in his wrath refused to go with the idolatrous Israel, the so-called Tent of Meeting was pitched "outside the camp some distance away" (Exodus 33:7). Clearly, it stands for his absence from their midst. As he later relented from his fury, the construction of the Tabernacle was instantly launched according to his prior instruction (Exodus 35-40, in reference to chapters 25-30).[14] Then, the entire work was completed. Once the Tabernacle was set up, "the glory of the Lord" filled it and not even Moses could "enter the Tent of Meeting" (Exodus 40:34-35).[15] Why not? He has habitually been together with the Lord and seen his glory, but this time the state of affairs seems absolutely different. The end of the book of Exodus might be understood as a kind of anticlimax.[16] Did Moses at long last fail? Surely not. His inability to "enter the Tent of Meeting" amounts to the culmination of his intercessions for Israel! Now God's full presence among his

---

addition, "all the positive truths about God that 20:5-6 express are put within the larger context of a double prohibition" (20:3-4). However, "there is not even a single prohibition in 34:5-7." Also, "34:7, when speaking of God's forgiveness" is missing "no 'sin' family word—'who forgives *iniquities* and *rebellion* and *sin*.'" Similarly, Olson 1996, 82-83.

[13] See especially Newman 2017, 18-24. He concentrates on those Old Testament texts where God's glory "(both denotatively and connotatively) is used as a symbol of 'divine presence'" (ibid., 18). In the end, he concludes that God's glory "signs Yahweh's presence in ways that other linguistic formulations do not" (ibid., 24). Cf. Friesen 1971, 3-6.

[14] More for this, see, e.g., Hamilton 2011, 560-562.

[15] Cf. Klein 1996, 266-272.

[16] Correctly, Hamilton underscores the end of the book of Exodus as the *climax* of the whole story. He underlines (2011, 451) that "the tabernacle intensifies the Mount Sinai experience." He concludes: "At the summit of Mount Sinai, Moses enters the cloud (24:18). But when the same glory covers the tabernacle, Moses is not able to enter it (40:35)."

people has totally been established. He no longer stays "outside
the camp," but his dwelling place is found in the middle of the
campsite (Numbers 2:1).[17] Moreover, since Moses was not able
to see God's "face," he is not able to see all of God's majesty and
splendor that abides in the Tabernacle either. It follows that his
deepest wish really came true: The Lord himself remains with Israel
in accordance with his vow to them and their patriarchs. Thus, in
the conclusion of the book of Exodus, we are told that "the cloud of
the Lord was over the Tabernacle by day, and fire was in the cloud
by night, in the sight of all the Israelites during all their travels"
(40:38). Put in short, everything Moses was asking for from his
Lord, he was indeed blessed abundantly. As a result, the story truly
has a happy end.[18]

In the overall theology of the Old Testament, the link between
God's glory and his mercy prevails within the framework of the temple service.[19] Primarily, Aaron and his sons are to bless the Israelites
and assert that the Lord may cause his face to shine upon them
and be gracious to them (Numbers 6:25). This resonates with the
storyline of Exodus as established in chapters 32-40 (cf. above). In
addition, it is explicitly maintained that through the Aaronic blessing God's name is put on the Israelites, and he will, therefore, bless
them (Numbers 6:27). That aspect echoes well in the account of

---

[17] For the tabernacle as *the* dwelling place of divine presence, see Hamilton
2011, 447-453. In his own house, God meets with his people, represented by
Moses and the priests (ibid., 447).

[18] Cf. Watts 2011, 246. He writes in reference to Exodus 33: "Verses 7-11
depict the tent outside the camp until Moses protests YHWH's refusal to go
with Israel (vv. 12-16). Once YHWH relents (vv. 14, 17), Moses can see God's
'glory' on Mount Sinai just as Israel will later see that same 'glory' descend in
the cloud onto the new tabernacle (40:34) that will find its place in the middle
of the camp (Numbers 2-3)." Also, Philpot 2013a, 7-8: "[. . .] Moses' shining
face functions as a conclusion to the Sinai story and as a fitting transition to
the continued construction of the tabernacle. The glory of Yahweh is one way
in which Yahweh discloses himself to Israel." Exodus 34:1-9, 29-35 looks back
to 24:15-18 and forward to 40:34-38.

[19] See, e.g., Hartenstein 2008, 279: "Der 'Ort' der in Ex 33,18 erbetenen
Gottesschau wäre also normalerweise der *Tempel* bzw. die mit der
Tempelsymbolik verbundene mentale *Szenerie der Thronsphäre Gottes.*"

proclaiming the name of Yahweh in connection with the benevolent renewal of the covenant (see Exodus 33:19, 34:5).[20]

Further, it is later told that the glory of the Lord "filled" the temple with the purpose of dedicating the holy dwelling to him and devoting it to a stronghold of his gracious compassion. At the ceremony of the feast, the Israelites rejoiced in singing the traditional psalm: "For he is good, for his mercy endures forever" (2 Chronicles 5:13-14 and 7:1-3, 6 introducing Psalm 136). The settings of the whole story resemble the historical account of Exodus in chapters 33-34. Once more, the common details appear apparent. The glorious revelation of the Lord accompanies his merciful presence in the temple dedicated to his name. All of his goodness abounds there just as on the top of Sinai (Exodus 33:19). Also, the Israelites knelt with their faces to the ground and worshiped the Lord as Moses did (see Exodus 34:8 and 2 Chronicles 7:3). After the ceremony of the feast, they went home "joyful and glad in heart for the good things (or literally: the goodness) the Lord had done for David and Solomon and for his people Israel" (2 Chronicles 7:10).[21]

Conversely, the fall of the temple and Israel ending up in exile were preceded by the departing of God's glory from the temple. It symbolized the cessation of his covenantal lenience and long-term tolerance with them (Ezekiel 10).[22] At that point, there was nothing left but waiting for a national crisis to happen. Judgment was going to fall upon wicked sinners. They were all utterly damned

---

[20] The two central motives in Exodus 34:6-7 (the proclamation of the name of the Lord and his glorious presence) are thus included in the Aaronic blessing. That connection is widely overlooked in the commentaries on the book of Numbers. Cf. Brown 2002, 57-58.

[21] The commentaries on the book of 2 Chronicles usually (and correctly) refer to Leviticus 9:23-24 as a parallel passage to 2 Chronicles 7:1-3. Mostly, some sparse references to Exodus 40:34-38 are added. Nevertheless, the underlying connection with Exodus 33-34 is overlooked. See, e.g., Dillard 1987, 56-57, Japhet 1993, 609-610, Klein 2012, 105-106.

[22] See, e.g., Block 1997, 314-327. Nicely, Newman 2017, 21. He speaks of God's glory "outside the temple and the city" in Ezekiel 10. He maintains that "the 'absence' should be related to Yahweh's regular 'presence' in the 'normative' sacred space of the Jerusalem temple."

and cursed (Ezekiel 11:1-12 and 21-23).[23] Ominously, God pronounced a similar threat to Moses as he prophesied of Israel after their worship of the golden calf that "when the time comes for me to punish, I will punish them for their sin" (Exodus 32:34). It is not fully revealed what exactly he does have in mind here.[24] We may well at least assume that the manifestation of the glory of the Lord as a gracious sign for his presence among his stubborn people must have come to a close by then. As long as he dwells among them in his majesty and grants them his amnesty, they are safe from every sort of hostile oppression.[25]

Taking into consideration the near and more distant context, the story of the shining face of Moses in Exodus 34:29-35 looks back to his unique and distinct experience with the splendid revelation

---

[23] See, e.g., Hummel 2005, especially 325. He speaks of Jerusalem as follows: "It is no longer 'Zion,' the elect holy city, inviolable because of the divine presence, as Isaiah had preached so forcefully a century earlier." Similarly Block 1997, 360: "From Ezekiel's perspective, the turning point in Israel's history came not with the accession of Zedekiah or even the Babylonian capture of Jerusalem, but with the departure of the glory of the King of heaven from his temple." Many other commentaries argue in a similar way. *Pace* Balla 2007, 755. He rightly emphasizes that Ezekiel 11 "contains a reference to God's glory." Then, he concludes that Paul "does not polemicize with *this* 'glory' in 2 Corinthians 3, but only with the 'glory' that shone on the face of Moses." Surely, it is about the same gracious glory of God in Exodus 33-34 as well. In fact, it anticipates the proclamation of the gospel in 2 Corinthians 3. See below.

[24] Cf. Hamilton 2011, 556. "The language of vv. 34b-35 ("And on the day of my visiting . . .") is not easy to interpret, but its ominous tone is clear enough." Similarly, Childs 2004, 572.

[25] For the great religious importance of Exodus 34:6-7 in Israel's history, see Saleska 2021, 202: "Because of the theological significance of this event [Exodus 32-34] in shaping Israel's life with Yahweh, Israel's prophets and poets frequently allude to this text [Exodus 34:6-7] in their writings." Similarly, Larsson 1997, 299. Bizarrely, Longman and Dillard in their excellent survey of Exodus do not at all deal with Exodus 34:6-7 (2006, 63-80). Neither does Hagelia (2017, 75-91) address the issue. For the Old Testament references, see Numbers 14:18, Nehemiah 19:17b, Psalm 86:15, 103:8, 145:8, Joel 2:13, Jonah 4:2, Nahum 1:3. Cf. further Deuteronomy 4:31, 2 Chronicles 30:9, Nehemiah 9:31, Psalm 78:38, 86:5, 111:4, 112:4, 116:5 (in reference to Hamilton 2011, 576, cf. Durham 1987, 453-454).

of Yahweh in Exodus 34:1-9.[26] Consequently, it clearly functions to emphasize God's goodness and grace to the Israelites. There is no indication of his glory as a negative image, emblematic of his wrath and judgment on them. To be sure, the reminiscence of the worship of the golden calf with mighty horns as a substitute for the one and only Lord remains just beneath the surface of the narrative. Hence, Moses is "horned" (קָרַן) with a divine radiance (Exodus 34:29) that dismisses every kind of animal idolatry and claims superiority over all erroneous devotions. Staring him in the face, the Israelites were extremely overwhelmed with fear. Besides, their trepidation derived from their encounter with transcendental reality, a characteristic feature for most of the theophanies in the Old Testament. Still, there is no more any trace of verdict against them. They are now totally forgiven and restored to the covenantal relationship with their heavenly Benefactor.[27]

In view of the story itself and its context, it seems rather embarrassing that Exodus 34:29-35 in general is understood in terms of disapproval and reprimand of Israel. In the end, they nevertheless fail. The repeated need for the veil indicates the wrath of God that threatens the stubborn people. Therefore, his glory, shining on the face of Moses, must be veiled. Total destruction will follow if not.[28] However, the difference between God's supreme presence in his majesty and his gracious presence as he reveals himself in a compassionate manner must be remembered. The former indeed destroys, but the latter saves. That kind of distinction explicitly shows itself in Exodus 33:19-34:9. Further, the Israelites initially *did* see the radiant face of Moses. They *did* see it every single time he came down from Sinai (Exodus 34:33-35). Yet, they did not die.[29]

---

[26] Precisely, e.g., Philpot 2013a, 5: "The shining of Moses' face is no doubt the result of his unique experience with Yahweh's glory in 34:1-9, for this is the only difference in terms of exposure to Yahweh between his first stint on Sinai and his second one. This 'glory' Moses bears back with him as he returns to the camp of Israel."

[27] See Hamilton 2011, 589. Cf. Philpot 2013a, 3-8.

[28] Hafemann 2005, 231. Similarly, Beale 2008, 79.

[29] *Contra* Balla 2007, 756. He writes on Exodus 34:33-35 that "we are first told that Moses put a veil on his face only after he had spoken to the people (34:33)," but nonetheless "from the rest of the passage it is clear that later he

Even if the gracious outlook of God's revelation in Exodus 33:19-34:9 is truly acknowledged, the veiling of Moses' face is still interpreted in quite negative terms. It indicates Israel's "inability" to grasp the content of God's preceding revelation, his divine goodness. They fail to know him.[30] Alternatively, "Moses' veiling of his face was an act of judgment that prevented the sons of Israel from looking upon its glory."[31] But why should Moses accomplish "an act of judgment" since he has diverted God from fulfilling it? Or for what purpose has he made his plea for mercy if he is straight away ready to take his first opportunity to condemn his people?

Obviously, Moses' veiling appears to be relatively unmotivated in Exodus 34:29-35. No explanation is given for his custom. The emphasis simply lies on his practice. Time and again, he veils and unveils his face.[32] The unexpected or unrelated fact would naturally evoke midrashic explanations.[33] Paul has his own in 2 Corinthians 3. He suggests an insight consistent with his Christological reading of the Old Testament. Yet, an in depth analysis of his view must be postponed and dealt with in a later connection.

Jeremiah 31:31-34

The second major passage in the Old Testament that 2 Corinthians 3 relies on relates to Jeremiah 31:31-34 where we read:

---

always put on the veil when he was speaking to his people and took it off when he went in before the Lord." Cf. Baker 2000, 10-11.

[30] See Philpot 2013a, 11. He maintains: "[. . .] if Moses' shining face signifies God's 'goodness' before the people, the veil signifies the inability of the people to grasp that goodness. To be part of covenant is to 'know God.' Thus, that the glory in Moses' face was veiled means that the Israelites failed to grasp the core of the covenant—knowing God." Cf. Balla 2007, 756.

[31] Seifrid 2014, 155 (see also 161-164).

[32] Watson 2004, 292. In reference to him, Guthrie 2015, 210 n 18. See already Hickling 1975, 390: "What is the purpose of this veiling? The narrative of Exodus, as is well known, gives no reason."

[33] Childs 2004, 623: "The fact that the text itself does not offer a motivation for the wearing of the veil would naturally evoke a midrashic interpretation."

31 "The days are coming," declares the LORD, "when I will make a new covenant with the people of Israel and with the people of Judah. 32 It will not be like the covenant I made with their ancestors when I took them by the hand to lead them out of Egypt, because they broke my covenant, though I was a husband to them," declares the LORD. 33 "This is the covenant I will make with the people of Israel after that time," declares the LORD. "I will put my law in their minds and write it on their hearts. I will be their God, and they will be my people. 34 No longer will they teach their neighbor, or say to one another, 'Know the LORD,' because they will all know me, from the least of them to the greatest," declares the LORD. "For I will forgive their wickedness and will remember their sins no more."

The wonderful vision of the new covenant in terms of putting the law in the minds of the Israelites and writing it on their hearts collides with the harsh reality of the present situation as "Judah's sin is engraved with an iron tool, inscribed with a flint point, on the tablets of their hearts" (Jeremiah 17:1). As a matter of fact, the Jeremianic contrast nicely squares with the opposite poles of writing on tablets of stone or on tablets of human hearts in 2 Corinthians 3:3. The similarity is palpable. Paul follows the prophetic guidelines for his reasoning. He does not only refer to the book of Ezekiel (the frequently quoted replacement of the stony hearts with the fleshly ones, cf. below) but that of Jeremiah as well.[34]

The opposition of the new promised covenant to the terminating Sinaitic covenant further emerges in the explicit polarity of the historical description in Deuteronomy 4:13 and the prophetical prediction in Jeremiah 31:33. In accordance with the former passage, God "wrote them (= ten words)" on two stone tablets but, in line with the latter passage, God will "write it (= his law)" on the hearts of his own people. It seems that the linguistic similarity in way of speaking

---

[34] Cf. Hafemann 2007, 51. However, he does not go into an analysis of the parallel Pauline thought in 2 Corinthians 3:3. In reference to Jeremiah 17:1, Lundbom (1999, 776) rightly assumes: "We see here the background for Jeremiah's new covenant prophecy of 31:31-34, which will be written on a heart substantially transformed from the one Judah now possesses." Similarly, Brueggemann 1998, 157: "This record on the heart is the very antithesis of the torah on the heart (31:33)."

truly underscores the theological dissimilarity in way of thinking. Still, the divine will does not alter with the times. On the contrary, it remains the same all the time. God's law is in essence not changed. It is in charge of conducting people to live a righteous life also in the new covenant.[35]

Jeremiah's promise of the new covenant stands out all the more since in his days the lost "book of the law" was found, and the old covenant took a new lease on life as a result of the religious reformation in Judah. King Josiah read and reaffirmed the Mosaic commandments and orders as he renewed the divine treaty with his people (see 2 Kings 22:8-23:25 and 2 Chronicles 34:14-35:19). It was indeed a new beginning but, in the end, only with some skin-deep effects and without any transforming bearing on the human heart (cf. Jeremiah 3:6-10). The impending national catastrophe was no longer to be averted in the future. The full-scale devastation loomed large far ahead. Thus, the new covenant is not simply the renewal of the old covenant like Josiah's reform was. Rather, it suggests a totally new dealing of God with his people, even though his will, as once attested in the Mosaic law, remains unchangeable.[36]

---

[35] See Meyer 2019, 552.

[36] Cf. Martin 1986, 54: "The new covenant does not entail a notion of a renovated Judaism but of a new chapter in God's dealing with humankind." Similarly, the critical evaluation of the lip-service of Judah during Josiah's religious reformation in Jeremiah 3:6-10 does not usher in a requirement of a better renewal of the old covenant. Quite the opposite, it results in a totally new beginning and an utterly different state of affairs to the exclusion of every memory of "the ark of the covenant." See v. 16: "Men will no longer say, 'The ark of the covenant of the Lord.' It will never enter their minds or be remembered; it will not be missed, nor will another one be made." Put it simply, the question is about the new covenant of Jeremiah 31:31-34. Rightly, Lundbom (1999, 308) writes on Jeremiah 3:6-11 that Israel's "return was insincere." He then concludes that "the audience may now perceive that a negative judgment is being made on Josiah's reform." Later, he (2004, 466) writes on Jeremiah 31:31-34 as follows: "In my view, the new covenant cannot be reduced to a renewed Sinai covenant" such as took place "in Jerusalem at the climax of the Josianic Reform (2 Kings 23)." He points out: "Although this new covenant will have admitted continuity with the Sinai covenant, it will be a genuinely new covenant, one that marks a new beginning in the divine-human relationship . . ."

The far-reaching and wide-ranging disparity of the new covenant from the old one shows itself also in Jeremiah 32:37-41, which
perfectly compares to 31:31-34. They look to be parallel in content as
well as in style. Gerhard von Rad reads them "almost as two targums
to one and the same text." Consequently, he allows them to explain
each other.[37] They both belong as integral parts to a larger setting,
namely the so-called "Book of Consolation" (Jeremiah 30-33), further
referred to as the "Book of Comfort" or "Book of Restoration." It is
composed of a cycle of poetic units in chapters 30-31 and a series of
prose sections in chapters 32-33.[38] Jeremiah 32:37-41 predicts the
time of the new covenant as follows:

> 37 I will surely gather them from all the lands where I banish them in
> my furious anger and great wrath; I will bring them back to this place
> and let them live in safety. 38 They will be my people, and I will be
> their God. 39 I will give them singleness of heart and action, so that
> they will always fear me and that all will then go well for them and
> for their children after them. 40 I will make an everlasting covenant
> with them: I will never stop doing good to them, and I will inspire
> them to fear me, so that they will never turn away from me. 41 I will
> rejoice in doing them good and will assuredly plant them in this land
> with all my heart and soul.

The new covenant is characterized as God's everlasting covenant with his people. He will not turn away from doing good to
them and he will put the fear of himself in their hearts so that they
will not depart from him (v. 40). The promise of the future is based
on God's mercy. He will give his people "singleness of heart and
action" (or literally: "one heart and one way"), so that they will
always fear him and prosper in their own land (v. 39). In a similar
manner, Jeremiah 24:7 maintains that God will give his people "a
heart to know" him, namely that he is the Lord. Then, they will
return to him "with all their heart." Therefore, writing the law on
the hearts of the Israelites in Jeremiah 31:33 suggests creating a new
heart where the fear of the Lord prevails. As anticipated, it inevitably

---

[37] von Rad 1987, 222: "fast wie zwei Targume zu einem Text."

[38] See the discussion, e.g., in Lundbom 2004, 368-376. Similarly, Brueggemann
1998, 268.

follows that the new covenant does not amount to the renewal of the old covenant but to the recreation of the human heart to the exclusion of sins and transgressions. On that condition, it will truly turn out that the broken relationship between the Lord and Israel is restored forever. They will be his people, and he will be their God. This particular expression of the mutual bond of love occurs in all three texts (Jeremiah 24:7, 31:33, 32:38) and ties them together into a meaningful harmony.[39]

On account of his overall theology, Jeremiah defines and refines the salvation from strong anthropological perspectives. He lays his emphasis on total human depravity and the need for divine intervention in accomplishing deliverance from corruption to the freedom of the new covenant where the spiritual heart transplantation has taken place.[40] Obviously, his thought resembles the crucial point of focus in the book of Ezekiel, who, however, underscores the role of the Spirit in the act of re-creation more (see below).[41]

Interestingly, Jeremiah seems to know the story line in Exodus 32-34 well. He speaks about Moses and Samuel who have stood before the Lord and fervently interceded for Israel. However, not even their earnest supplications would turn the impending destruction and disaster away from Jerusalem and Judah this

---

[39] Cf. von Rad 1987, 222-223. For the similarities between Jeremiah 31:31-34 and 32:37-41, see the somewhat sparse and sporadic comparisons and references in Lundbom 2004, 518-521. A little bit more clearly, Allen 2008, 370.

[40] See von Rad 1987, 222-223. He rightly concludes: It is very remarkable that "der vergleichsweise schon späte Jeremia das Heilswerk Jahwes so stark nach der Seite des Anthropologischen hin bestimmt" (222). Similarly: "Kein Prophet hat vor ihm das göttliche Heilsgeschehen nach der antropologischen Seite hin so sorgfältig unterbaut." (225) The new covenant is characterized by an "exceptional" interest in "eschatological man" (226 footnote 35): "Dieses eigentümliche prophetische Interesse an dem—man könnte sagen—eschatologischen Menschen, der vor Gott recht ist [. . .]." For more, cf. 277-282: "Das Neue wird sich allein im Bereich des Anthropologischen ereignen, nämlich in einer Wandlung des menschlichen Herzens." (279) See also, e.g., Hafemann 2007, 54.

[41] von Rad 1987, 223.

time (15:1, cf. Psalm 99:6-9).[42] Besides, it looks as if Jeremiah has begged for mercy on behalf of his wicked kinsmen three times just like Moses did before (see Exodus 32:11-13, 31-32, 33:12-18; cf. above). However, the many petitions of the prophet were to no avail. On every occasion, God told him *not* to pray for his people (Jeremiah 7:16, 11:14, 14:11). All hope for a better tomorrow was already gone. No mercy was ensured any more. The sinners have to leave and go into exile.[43]

In addition, the promise of the new covenant in Jeremiah 31:31-34 involves features that are included in Exodus 32-34. First, the problem of God's presence in the midst of the idolatrous Israel at Sinai turns into a confident conviction that "I am their God and they are my people" (Jeremiah 31:33). Second, the near relationship between God and Israel for sure results from the truth that the Israelites know their God (Jeremiah 31:34) just as Moses asked to know God's ways and God himself (Exodus 33:13 that literally reads: "let me know your ways so that I may know you") and, alternatively, whom God will send with him (Exodus 33:12). Indeed, the whole discourse between Moses and God speaks of their mutual knowing of each other (Exodus 33:12-17). Third, knowing God indicates the knowledge of his mercy: "I will forgive their wickedness and will remember their sins no more." (Jeremiah 31:34) As shown, the theophany at Sinai culminates in a similar self-manifestation of God (Exodus 34:6-7a). Fourth, God's grace is accompanied with a constant proclamation of his name, the name of the Lord or Yahweh (Exodus 33:19, 34:5-6). In Jeremiah 31:31-34, every single verse or every distinct fact is bolstered with the repeated formula "says the Lord" (נְאֻם־יְהוָה). For that reason, the new covenant is the everlasting fulfillment of God's compassionate love that Moses *had* already gazed at. He got a foretaste of the

---

[42] Hafemann 2007, 50.

[43] Cf. Allen 2008, 98. On account of Jeremiah 7:16, he maintains: "In this case the people's religious offenses are judged to be so flagrant that the normal prophetic service had to be suspended, letting Yahweh's anger take its destructive course, as v. 20 will affirm—in striking contrast to Moses' successful pleading after the golden calf incident (Exodus 32:11-14)." In a similar way, Lundbom 1999, 720.

impending messianic days.[44] Simply put: Exodus 33-34 foreshadows Jeremiah 31:31-34.[45]

Accordingly, Jeremiah 31:32 is not first and foremost a common reproach of breaking the covenant: "It will not be like the covenant I made with their ancestors when I took them by the hand to lead them out of Egypt, because they broke my covenant, though I was a husband to them." Rather, it takes as read that Israel, right from the beginning, sinned against their own God at Sinai through the worship of the golden calf. That is the bad precedent for all their coming transgressions and the poor pattern they have followed ever since.[46]

In general, Paul's discussion of Exodus 32-34 in the context of the new covenant makes sense in 2 Corinthians 3. His reading chimes perfectly well with the one in Jeremiah 31:31-34, the only passage in the whole Old Testament where the concept of "the new covenant" appears.[47] To be sure, he does not explicitly cite his source text, but

---

[44] In Jeremiah 32:37-41, a parallel passage to 31:31-34 (see above), and in the following verses, there is one quite subtle similarity to Exodus 32-34 that might be of certain interest. God promises never to stop doing "good" to his people (Jeremiah 32:40). He rejoices in doing them "good" (Jeremiah 32:41). He will give them all prosperity (more precisely: "all the good") he has envisioned them (32:42). Similarly, God promised at Sinai that "all his goodness" will pass in front of Moses (Exodus 33:19). In both cases, Israel will win divine goodness despite their recent idolatrous apostasy.

[45] The parallels between Exodus 33-34 and Jeremiah 31:31-34 are mostly overlooked in the commentaries. Still, in the Jewish triennial lectionary cycle, Exodus 32-34 and Jeremiah 31:31-34 were read together. For instance, see Hays 1989, 132. He affirms: "Interestingly, Jeremiah 31:31-39 was the *haftarah* correlated with the Torah reading of Exodus 34:27-35 in the Palestinian triennial lectionary cycle. Thus, the linkage of these texts might already have been traditional in the Judaism of Paul's time, though his distinctive interpretation of the texts was certainly far from traditional." Also, Lambrecht 1983, 371, Legarth 2004, 51 n 123.

[46] Cf. Lundbom 2004, 467. He interprets Jeremiah 31:32 against the background of Exodus 32 as follows: "The seeds of destruction for the Sinai covenant were sown at the very beginning, when the people made a golden calf in the Wilderness (Exodus 32)" as Moses, in his anger, broke "the tablets on which the Ten Commandments were written (v. 19)."

[47] Lundbom 2004, 465-466. He underlines that the concept of "the new covenant" occurs "only here in the OT, denoting the basis on which a future relation

there are no two ways about it. Yet, the meaning of "putting the law in the minds of the Israelites" and "writing it on their hearts" still needs to be explained in simple terms. Exactly, how to get to the point? Apparently, Jeremiah 31:31-34 does not offer a clear-cut answer. The verses do not directly envision sinlessness. Rather, they focus on the forgiveness of sin. As he continues, it seems that Paul addresses the question of being a Jew "inwardly" and not only "outwardly" (Romans 2:28-29), or, alternatively, Spirit performing his transforming power through faith (2 Corinthians 3:1-6). An examination of his thinking (with some allusions to Jeremiah 4:4 and 9:26) is not to be prolonged here. It has to be postponed for later.[48]

Ezekiel 36:24-28

Another Old Testament text that is consistent with Jeremiah 31:31-34 and pertains to the imminent expectation of the new covenant is Ezekiel 36:24-28. It reads as follows:

> 24 "For I will take you out of the nations; I will gather you from all the countries and bring you back into your own land. 25 I will sprinkle clean water on you, and you will be clean; I will cleanse you from all your impurities and from all your idols. 26 I will give you a new heart and put a new Spirit in you; I will remove from you your heart of stone and give you a heart of flesh. 27 And I will put my Spirit in you and move you to follow my decrees and be careful to keep my laws. 28 Then you will live in the land I gave your ancestors; you will be my people, and I will be your God."

The passage portrays the time of the new covenant whereupon the heart transplant of the Israelites will take place. God will then remove their "stony" hearts. Instead, he will give them hearts of flesh. As already shown, the book of Jeremiah ends up in a similar vision. Obviously, his prophesies function as a model for later eschatological expectations.

---

between God and his people will rest following the collapse of the Mosaic covenant and Israel's loss of nationhood in 586 B.C."

[48] See the next chapter.

The close theological proximity between the prophesies of Ezekiel and Jeremiah shows itself even more through an analysis of their contextual framework in Jeremiah 32:37-41 and Ezekiel 37:21-28. A comparison of both the texts corroborates that they have much in common. The former passage has been quoted above. The latter passage goes like this:

> 21 This is what the Sovereign LORD says: I will take the Israelites out of the nations where they have gone. I will gather them from all around and bring them back into their own land. 22 I will make them one nation in the land, on the mountains of Israel. There will be one king over all of them and they will never again be two nations or be divided into two kingdoms. 23 They will no longer defile themselves with their idols and vile images or with any of their offenses, for I will save them from all their sinful backsliding, and I will cleanse them. They will be my people, and I will be their God. 24 My servant David will be king over them, and they will all have one shepherd. They will follow my laws and be careful to keep my decrees. 25 They will live in the land I gave to my servant Jacob, the land where your ancestors lived. They and their children and their children's children will live there forever, and David my servant will be their prince forever. 26 I will make a covenant of peace with them; it will be an everlasting covenant. I will establish them and increase their numbers, and I will put my sanctuary among them forever. 27 My dwelling place will be with them; I will be their God, and they will be my people. 28 Then the nations will know that I the LORD make Israel holy, when my sanctuary is among them forever.

On reflection, the prophetic vision in Ezekiel 37:21-28 seems to bear upon the eschatological scenario in Jeremiah 32:37-41. First, the Israelites will return from exile (Jeremiah 32:37, Ezekiel 37:21). Second, unison will abound in the land as they will have "one heart and one way" (Jeremiah 32:39) and as they will come together and form "one nation" under the supervision of "one king" or "one shepherd" (Ezekiel 37:22, 24). Third, the Lord will once more be their God and they will be his people (Jeremiah 32:38, Ezekiel 37:23, 27). Fourth, the joining of mutual love between them indicates "an everlasting covenant" (Jeremiah 32:40, Ezekiel 37:26). Fifth, every kind of former idolatry has vanished (Jeremiah 32:33-35, Ezekiel 37:23). Sixth, the

Israelites, instead, will then follow the law and keep the commandments (Jeremiah 32:39-40, Ezekiel 37:24). Seventh, they and their children and grandchildren will prosper in their own land and constantly
live in peace and harmony (Jeremiah 32:39, Ezekiel 37:25). Taken as
a whole, Ezekiel, for sure, puts some added emphasis on the national
unity (37:16-22) and the royal institution (37:22, 24-25)[49] and especially
on the future construction of the end-time temple (37:26-28 and chapters 40-48).[50] Nevertheless, he still follows the line of reasoning in the
book of Jeremiah. They, as it were, speak in concert with each other.[51]

   The specific focus in the prophecies of Ezekiel lies on God's ultimate promise that the heart transplant of the Israelites will be followed
by the putting of his Spirit within them. Both features belong together
in Ezekiel 36:26-27 (as already in 11:19, see also 18:31; cf. further
Psalm 51:12). But exactly, how do they relate to each other? Here,
D. I. Block argues:

> "Concomitant with the heart transplant, Yahweh will infuse his
> people with a new spirit, his Spirit. On first sight, the present juxta-
> posing [. . .] suggests that 'spirit' and 'mind/heart' should be treated
> as virtual synonyms. However, the synonymity is seldom exact in
> Hebrew parallelism, and here the terms are associated with different
> prepositions. The new heart is given to [. . .] the Israelites, but the
> spirit is placed *within* [. . .] them."[52]

   Yet, the different prepositions obviously do not make a difference. If the new *heart* is given to the Israelites, it is indeed placed

---

[49] However, see also, e.g., Jeremiah 23:5-6 and 33:14-16.

[50] Cf. Jeremiah 3:16. However, the whole city of Jerusalem will in the future
be rebuilt "for the Lord" (31:38). Then, it "will be holy to the Lord" (31:40) just
like the holy place of the sanctuary in days gone by. At that time, the Levitical
priests will always stand before the Lord and offer their sacrifices to him (33:18,
see also vv. 20-22).

[51] Cf. the feeble links in Block 1998, 419-420. A little more clearly,
Brueggemann 1998, 308-309. He (ibid., 308) speaks of Jeremiah 32:38-41 as "a
series of theological statements reflective of Israel's best exilic faith, statements
which find important parallels in exilic Isaiah and in Ezekiel (vv. 38-41)." See
also Greenberg 2004, 736-740.

[52] Block 1998, 355-356. Cf. Guthrie 2015, 192.

within them! That conclusion stringently follows from the fundamental meaning of the semantic data in any language. Nonetheless, for another reason it seems that the synonymity in Ezekiel 36:26a does not provide a full-scale balance but, rather, bears some resemblance to a synthetic parallelism where the second line echoes and expands the sense of the first line, then develops and completes it. The relationship is more precisely supplementary. The thought reaches culmination in the final statement. In this case, Ezekiel 36:26a is explained in 36:26b-27 as follows:

> I will give you a new heart =
> I will remove from you your heart of stone and give you a heart of flesh.
> and put a new Spirit in you =
> and I will put my Spirit in you and move you to follow my decrees
> and be careful to keep my laws.[53]

Taking into consideration the textual evidence, it turns out that neither removing the heart of stone nor receiving the heart of flesh as such does bring about obedience to the divine orders. Both are necessary but not sufficient causes for a real transformation. More is absolutely needed. Submission to the requirements of the new covenant comes about only through the Spirit who indwells the inmost part of the believers. His power and energy entrust them to fulfill the law. In light of chapter 37, it becomes totally clear that the Israelites, without God's Spirit upon and within them, are as dead as ever. They do not live, though they are recreated as to their bones, flesh, and skin. Rather, they look like the figures in a modern wax cabinet! Death ends once God's Spirit animates and vivifies the recipients. He draws closer and abides in them. At that moment, everything changes for the better or for the best.[54] The relevant passage of Ezekiel 37:1-10 reads like this:

---

[53] Allen 1990, 179: "The two statements of v 26a are unpacked in v 26b and v 27." Similarly, Greenberg 2004, 730.

[54] *Pace* Richardson 1973, 210-211. He insists on the following contrast: "But in Ezekiel the word *pneuma* is used anthropologically (it is that which is put in man), whereas for Paul, in this passage, the word is used in a distinctive theological sense (he who works in man by writing on the heart is the Spirit of the living God)." The whole argument is based on an artificial analysis of the

1 The hand of the LORD was on me, and he brought me out by the Spirit of the LORD and set me in the middle of a valley; it was full of bones. 2 He led me back and forth among them, and I saw a great many bones on the floor of the valley, bones that were very dry. 3 He asked me, "Son of man, can these bones live?" I said, "Sovereign LORD, you alone know." 4 Then he said to me, "Prophesy to these bones and say to them, 'Dry bones, hear the word of the LORD! 5 This is what the Sovereign LORD says to these bones: I will make breath [Spirit] enter you, and you will come to life. 6 I will attach tendons to you and make flesh come upon you and cover you with skin; I will put breath [Spirit] in you, and you will come to life. Then you will know that I am the LORD.'" 7 So I prophesied as I was commanded. And as I was prophesying, there was a noise, a rattling sound, and the bones came together, bone to bone. 8 I looked, and tendons and flesh appeared on them and skin covered them, but there was no breath [Spirit] in them. 9 Then he said to me, "Prophesy to the breath [Spirit]; prophesy, son of man, and say to it [the Spirit], 'This is what the Sovereign LORD says: Come, breath [Spirit], from the four winds and breathe into these slain, that they may live.'" 10 So I prophesied as he commanded me, and breath [Spirit] entered them; they came to life and stood up on their feet—a vast army.

On the whole, the hearts of flesh are indeed "the *result* of God's saving work"[55] but no more than a *partial* result of his saving actions. He has not *finished* salvation simply with a heart transplant since the pouring out of his Spirit is missing. The new life has not been born before that decisive moment; neither the religious regeneration of the entire nation or a single national has taken place. Incidentally, whatever the *terminological* differences between the use of language in Ezekiel and Paul, they do agree on the fundamental anthropological premise: human beings, even at their very best, are not involved in any divine dominance but are, instead, doomed under the dominion of death. Absolute depravity prevails in the world. It distorts the

---

data. In Ezekiel 36-37, the word *pneuma* certainly refers to God's own Spirit just as in 2 Corinthians 3. He is he and not only "it" (that is put in man)!

[55] Seifrid 2014, 117. He maintains: "In Ezekiel the 'hearts of flesh' are the *result* of God's saving work. Paul, in contrast, speaks of 'fleshly hearts' as the place of human fallenness *upon which* God performs his saving work."

most honest efforts to escape the vicious circle of failing constantly. It follows that Paul, in contrast to Ezekiel, calls the *corrupt* human condition "flesh" and Ezekiel, in contrast to Paul, calls the *incorrupt* human heart "flesh," but, in both cases—whether it is a matter of the lowest or highest level of personal activity—people, without exceptions, have no life in themselves, and death does not lose control of them. Therefore, they need help from outside, and it comes from God's Spirit who alone vivifies them (cf. Genesis 2:7).[56]

As in the case of Jeremiah 31:31-34, there are also in Ezekiel 36:24-28 and the nearby context features that are included in Exodus 32-34.[57] First, the sin of idolatry is the most abysmal one of all transgressions that urgently needs to be atoned for or "cleansed" (Ezekiel 36:25). Second, the Lord reveals himself as a forbearing and forgiving God who is ready to show his incomprehensible compassion and mercy to his idolatrous people (Ezekiel 36:21-38). Definitely the emphasis lies on his benevolence as once at Sinai in his self-manifestation (Exodus 34:6-7a). Third, the Lord comes to grips with the future salvation of Israel only for the sake of his holy name which has been profaned by them among the nations. The repetition of his own reputation stands out in the whole story (especially in Ezekiel 36:20-23). Similarly, the book of Exodus concerns the honor and integrity of God. The theophany after the profanation of his name through the worship of the golden calf is related to a constant proclamation of the name of Yahweh (Exodus 33:19, 34:5-6). Fourth, the restoration of Israel results in a new covenantal relationship as they together with the other nations will know that God is the Lord (Ezekiel 36:23, 36, 38 and 37:6, 13). As already shown above, the conversation between Moses and God as well revolves about their

---

[56] In Ezekiel 36-37, the Spirit gives life. Hence, "no one would have doubted that it is the life-giving Spirit of God that is in view" (Dunn 2013, 165). Accordingly, it is not correct to translate the Hebrew word with the lower-case s as a reference to human spirit. Rightly, Schreiner 1998, 143. He further emphasizes that πνεῦμα in the γράμμα-πνεῦμα contrast "refers to the Holy Spirit." For the Pauline use of language in general and especially in 2 Corinthians 3, see below. *Pace* Hughes 1962, 101, 115-116.

[57] As in the case of Jeremiah 31:31-34, the links with Exodus 32-34 are mostly overlooked in the commentaries on Ezekiel 36:24-28.

mutual knowing of each other (Exodus 33:12-17). Fifth, God's gracious presence in the midst of Israel is reinforced due to the cessation of idolatry. It is based on and established in the new covenant liaison ("Bundesformel"): "I am their God and they are my people" (Ezekiel 36:28). The same formula is true for the reestablishment of the broken bond of love in the narrative of Exodus 32-34.[58]

Conclusion

In conclusion, the numerous intercessions of Moses in Exodus 32-34 relate to the restoration of the *old* covenant whereas both the prophecies in Jeremiah 31:31-34 and Ezekiel 36:24-28 refer to the completion of the *new* covenant. Despite the difference, the three Old Testament texts have much in common and speak in concert about the abundance of God's amazing grace. Whatever sins there are, they are all wiped out by his incomprehensible loving kindness. It seems that the account of Exodus 32-34 in actual fact anticipates the future visions of Jeremiah 31:31-34 and Ezekiel 36:24-28. Certainly, this does *not* mean that the old covenant simply turns into the new covenant. It still makes sense to differentiate them. No doubt about that! The old one has led and leads to shame, curses, and death. Moses once told Israel that "cursed is the man who does not uphold the words of the law by carrying them out." They said: "Amen!" (Deuteronomy 27:26). In the same way, Jeremiah told the people of Judah that "cursed is

---

[58] For the concept of "Bundesformel," see von Rad 1987, 245-247 *et passim*. He further puts emphasis on the importance of the "knowing" in the book of Ezekiel: Israel viz. the nations will "know that I am the Lord." There, the phrase occurs no less than 86 (!) times (247 n 26 in reference to W. Zimmerli). Concerning the covenant formula ("I am their God and they are my people"), Hafemann (2007, 52) concludes: "This pledge picks up and underscores the covenant relationship of the Bible, occurring in various forms around twenty-five times in the Bible. More important than its frequency is the fact that the covenant formula unpacks in summary form the covenant relationship ratified in the redemptive covenants of the Scriptures, from the covenant with Abraham (Genesis 17:7) to the Sinai covenant (e.g., Exodus 6:7; 29:45-46), and from the summaries of Deuteronomy (e.g., Deuteronomy 4:20; 29:12-13) to the promise of the new covenant (Jeremiah 24:7; 31:33; 32:38-40; Ezekiel 36:26-28; 37:26-28)."

the man who does not obey the terms of this covenant" (11:3). Since they have discarded his orders, he himself answered: "Amen, Lord!" (11:4). Further, Ezekiel maintains that "the man who obeys them (the commandments) will live by them," but they have been abandoned by the fellow Jews, children who rebelled against their Father (20:21). Hence, the old covenant is indeed "the ministry of death" (2 Corinthians 3:7).[59] Yet, it has its own glory, not least in the story of Exodus 32-34 (2 Corinthians 3:7-18).

All things considered, the three main Old Testament texts in and behind 2 Corinthians 3 obviously belong together. They should not be interpreted in isolation from one another. Paul really seems to have understood that basic fact. He reads and explains them together. Nevertheless, much more light should be shed on their meaning in the context of 2 Corinthians 3. For sure, it is worth studying next.

---

[59] Cf. Watson 2004, 288. He concludes that "Moses' advent with the first pair of stone tablets issues in the death of three thousand of the people of Israel, who had earlier flouted the divine prohibition of idolatry." See Exodus 32:27-28. Still, Watson seriously errs as he writes with regard to Paul's strong reinterpretation of Exodus 32-34: "The two pairs of stone tablets represent two sides of the single event of the giving of the law. The second pair is associated with the glory of Moses' transfigured face, the first with Moses' deadly vengeance on the idolatrous people; and, just as the pairs of inscribed stone tablets are essentially the same, so the glory and the killing belong together." In Exodus 33-34, God's glory does not pertain to the killing but his gracious presence in the midst of the idolatrous Israel. Paul thinks along those same lines. For his line of reasoning, see below.

6

The ministry of Moses versus the ministry of Paul

Corinthians as letters of recommendation and the apostolic competence of Paul

From start to finish, 2 Corinthians 3 in some form or other revolves around or gets across the badly aggravated relationship between Paul and the Corinthians. He tries to explain the divine authority of his apostolic ministry to them, devoid of any human control of their carnal superiority. In his apology, he refers to the figure of Moses and the giving of the Mosaic law in the book of Exodus. Critical evidence for the support of this already stands out convincingly (see chapters 3, 4, and 5 above).

At the beginning of his stern confrontation, Paul moves on to the problem of self-recommendation and the imagery of recommendation letters (v. 1). He promptly asserts that he has no use of external written witnesses to his credit. They show themselves as futile. In this context, they are moreover associated with the "letter" (γράμμα) as an outward codification of the hoped-for behavior. Therefore, they do not validate or substantiate a real inner transformation (v. 6).[1]

Yet, recommendation of another kind is not excluded. 2 Corinthians 10:18 maintains that "it is not the one who commends himself who is approved, but the one whom the Lord commends." God does not accept a superficial only conformity to his law. In contrast,

---

[1] For the meaning of the "letter" (γράμμα) in Pauline theology, see especially the next chapter.

he insists on a wholehearted submission to his will. Then, recommendation does not turn into measuring "oneself by oneself," neither into comparing "oneself with oneself" (2 Corinthians 10:12). As a result, Paul does not boast "beyond proper limits" but confines his boasting "to the field God has assigned" to him (2 Corinthians 10:13). He is certainly not going too far in his rejoicing because he does not boast of work done by others (2 Corinthians 10:14-15) but of the Lord who enables his mission impossible (2 Corinthians 10:16-17).[2]

Thus, Paul does *not* reject letters of recommendation in 2 Corinthians 3. He *does* have them, but his letter of recommendation rather relates to the Corinthians themselves (v. 2). His notion establishes a well-thought-through reinterpretation of recommendation. According to a common way of thinking, there are the ones who recommend and, then again, the others who are recommended (or not recommended). The Corinthians considered themselves as spiritual, devout outsiders who have the right to recommend (or not to recommend) the apostle and his coworkers (and his adversaries). They evaluate them and rank them in proportion to their preferences. In their arrogance, they often show contempt, contemn, and condemn. Yet, their maneuver of judging is backfiring since it finally falls upon themselves! If they boo and, so to speak, refuse to raise their hands up to give their master "the highest of fives," they are not able to win themselves applause hands down. They should definitely acknowledge that it is not at all about what they write *in* their letter of recommendation but what they are *as* a letter of recommendation. In other words, if they do not recommend their apostle, they actually do not recommend themselves. In that case, their judging obduracy discloses that they have not taken his gospel at face value and, as a result, *they* now lose face.[3]

Paul forges ahead as he speaks of the Corinthians not only as his letter of recommendation but also as Christ's letter of recommendation, ministered by the apostle and his coworkers (v. 3). To put it very simply: the apostle represents and embodies Christ. "He who listens to you listens to me; he who rejects you rejects me; but he who rejects me rejects him who sent me." (Luke 19:16) Thus, Paul does not act

---

[2] See, e.g., Harris 2005, 258-261.
[3] Cf. ibid., 261-266. Similarly, Seifrid 2014, 111-115.

as a private person. He serves his Lord as he functions as a servant (or slave) of the Corinthian congregation (2 Corinthians 4:5). The feedback he gets will be forwarded to his Master. The feedback he gives likewise originates from his Master. Their interests and intentions, aims and ambitions are entangled. They pull together and in the same direction. If the Corinthians fall short in front of the apostle, they have flopped miserably in the presence of his Sender. At last, they should realize the gravity of the situation and draw the right conclusions from it.[4]

Further, Paul accelerates his defensive measure as he discusses his own credentials but negates his own competence. What is left of his recommendation in that case? Very much—many positive things and notions! Paul affirms that his competence "comes from God" (v. 5), who has made him competent as a minister of a new covenant (v. 6). Thus, the Corinthians who disapprove of the apostle have failed to approve the first-rate qualifications he has from his Superior. They boast of their exclusive understanding of the spiritual wisdom but blurt out sheer stupidity. Supposing to be wise, they act and behave like fools. In the divine test of their human cognitive ability, do they—I regret to say—perhaps have the intelligent quotient of a dinner plate? They seem to like a "no top of the head"-look. No wonder; Paul sarcastically admits that he has made a fool of himself since they drove him to it (2 Corinthians 12:11). He became ensnared by boasting of himself even though he should have been commended by them, especially with regard to all of his apostolic signs that were wrought among them (2 Corinthians 12:12).[5]

On the whole, the dispute about the letters of recommendation between the Corinthians and Paul does not concern an internal and immanent exchange of ideas but pertains to a transcendent reality where the apostolic ministry is integrated into authorization of Christ and related to skills acquisition in accordance with the empowerment of God. In that context, various human standards and criterions are out of place. They usher in a fatal misunderstanding that will end up in a total loss for all eternity.

---

[4] Cf. Seifrid 2014, 112-115.
[5] Ibid., 119-120.

Besides the vertical dimension of the apostolic ministry, 2 Corinthians 3 shows also a horizontal aspect of the divine commission in a very profound fashion. As already made known, the letter of recommendation is not a piece of paper (papyrus) but living persons—Corinthians themselves, as far as they are really transformed since their conversion. Equally, this exceptional letter of their recommendation is written not as an outward proof of the excellent quality of the apostolic proficiency but as an inward confirmation in the heart of Paul of his loving involvement for their spiritual best (v. 2). Further, the reading of an ordinary letter of recommendation is conditional on the literacy and distinct interest of the recipients. They either take a look at it or perhaps they do not. In contrast, Corinthians *as* a letter of recommendation will be examined by everyone who meets them or their apostle in their ability to verbalize and communicate a corporate letter of recommendation in and through their innermost being. Accordingly, it will be "known and read by all people" (γινωσκομένη καὶ ἀναγινωσκομένη ὑπὸ πάντων ἀνθρώπων, v. 2). The phrase particularly refers to all those people who get in touch with the Corinthians and/or Paul. Without exception, they get insight into the special form of the "incarnate" letter of recommendation. They do not decide if they will read it or not. It is written in a material manner by means of embodied contents with the result that they have to read it. It follows that Paul does not make use of a hyperbolic expression (as seldom insisted) as he speaks of a letter of recommendation that all are familiar with.[6] Moreover, the letter of recommendation, "known and read by all people," does not convey a superficial influence on the recipients. In biblical language, "to know" (γινώσκω) rather involves a deep-seated acquaintance and relationship with the others.[7] Respectively, "to read" (ἀναγινώσκω) indicates "to re-know" inherently the views and experiences of the author.[8] In Greek, reading thus comes after knowing but not vice versa (as in many modern languages).[9] On the whole, Paul effectively promotes his apostolic ministry and ensures that his letter of recommendation bears upon a personal and personified

---

[6] Cf. the discussion in Lenski 1963, 910-912.

[7] See Bauer 2000, *s.v.* γινώσκω.

[8] Ibid., *s.v.* ἀναγινώσκω.

[9] See above, chapter 4.

character to the exclusion of a static data. He does not issue bureau-cratic reports of his mission accomplishments. Instead, he calls for internal rapports, based on an inside transformation of an individual or the entire congregation. Nothing less matters.

The former three aspects of the letter of recommendation are all put closely together in v. 2 as follows:

1) Corinthians themselves are Paul's letter of recommendation (ἡ ἐπιστολὴ ἡμῶν ὑμεῖς ἐστέ).[10]
2) This letter is written in the heart of Paul (ἐνγεγραμμένη ἐν ταῖς καρδίαις ἡμῶν).[11]
3) It is known and read by all people (γινωσκομένη καὶ ἀναγινωσκομένη ὑπὸ πάντων ἀνθρώπων).

It is worth recalling that every aspect of the former three points puts weight on the letter of recommendation not as a written docu-ment but as a living testimony in person.

The how of writing spiritual letters of recommendation

For understandable reasons, more attention in v. 3 turns on the writ-ing process of the special letter of recommendation. How is that to come about? It is not just about a simple paperwork or ink stains on

---

[10] To the point, Dunn (2013, 172) nicely writes: "The other missionaries based their authority and appeal on letters of recommendation written from afar (3:1), whereas Paul cites *them*, the Corinthians themselves, as his letters of reference."

[11] The textual variant of ὑμῶν is not so strongly attested as the more common alternative of ἡμῶν. I prefer the latter reading that makes good sense in the con-text (see above). The former reading puts emphasis on the hearts of Corinthians (as in v. 3, see below). Pace Martin 1986, 51 and Thrall 2004, 223-224. Correctly, Guthrie 2015, 202. Further, Hays (1989, 127) nicely comments on the letter of recommendation, "inscribed on our hearts" (v. 2), as follows: "The turn of phrase is a little confusing because it makes two points at once; it emphasizes both Paul's love for the Corinthians and the fact that they themselves are the proof of Paul's legitimacy."

papyrus. Much more is needed. A letter of recommendation in person is written with the Spirit of the living God, not on tablets of stone but on tablets of fleshly hearts (οὐκ ἐν πλαξὶν λιθίναις ἀλλ᾽ ἐν πλαξὶν καρδίαις σαρκίναις). Accordingly, both the means (*materia qua*) and sphere (*materia in qua*) of the writing, namely the divine Spirit and the human heart,[12] relate to the fulfillment of the prophetic visions in Ezekiel 11:19 and 36:26-27.[13] Neither the removing of the heart of stone nor the receiving of the heart of flesh completes the salvation. It comes to pass through the reviving work of the Spirit as soon as he animates those who previously have undergone a heart transplant. Whatever the terminological differences between Ezekiel and Paul, they agree on the ultimate necessity of God's Spirit in his recreative activity.[14] The notion of the spiritual reality then permeates the line of thought in the whole chapter of 2 Corinthians 3 (see vv. 3, 6, 8, 17-18). It amounts to a characteristic facet of the new covenant.[15]

The writing itself refers back to the prophecy of Jeremiah 31:31-34 where God promises to write his law on the hearts of Israel. It suggests creating a new heart where the knowledge of his will prevails and abounds (cf. also Jeremiah 24:7, 32:39). The future vision is called the new covenant that relies on recreation. Currently, "Judah's sin is engraved with an iron tool, inscribed with a flint point, on the tablets of their hearts" (Jeremiah17:1). The harsh contrast between the two texts speaks volumes. The two hearts of adversative impetus nicely squares with the usage of language in 2 Corinthians 3:3. Further, the notion of the new covenant in Jeremiah 31:31 (occurring nowhere else in the Old Testament) is then employed later in 2 Corinthians 3:6 (and the antonym, the old covenant, in 2 Corinthians 3:14).[16]

Thus, the writing of the recommendation letter in a Pauline sense does not rest on human efforts but solely depends on the creative work of the divine Spirit. He animates and vivifies those who receive him as a gift from above. The prophetic visions of Jeremiah and Ezekiel stand in contrast to the Mosaic nomism within the

---

[12] See above, chapter 3.

[13] See above, chapter 5.

[14] See above, chapter 5.

[15] See above, chapters 3, 4, and 5.

[16] See above, chapter 5.

Sinaitic treaty, even though the core and content of the law basically remain the same. At any rate, the stony tablets of the commandments still correlate with the stony tablets of the hearts. Therefore, the old covenant fails while the new covenant enters into force. The antithesis between them continues in the opposite poles of the "letter" and the "Spirit" in 2 Corinthians 3:6 and further permeates the line of reasoning in the whole chapter (see below).

On the other hand, the study of the Old Testament background (see chapter 5 above) demonstrates that the prophetic visions of Jeremiah and Ezekiel stand in an unbroken continuity with the *figure* of Moses (as opposed to the *law* of Moses) and particularly the account of his intercourses for the idolatrous Israel in Exodus 32-34. In a certain sense, he has indeed anticipated the dawn of the new covenant as his petitions moved God to show mercy against all odds and beyond all understanding. Accordingly, the three interrelated narratives should be read and interpreted together. In addition, many verbal and theological links coalesce Jeremiah 31:31-34 and Ezekiel 36:24-28 with the spectacular theophany in Exodus 33-34. Obviously, the texts converse and engage with each other.

Hence, it comes as no surprise that Paul first applies the prophetic visions of Jeremiah and Ezekiel about the new covenant to his own theological outline in 2 Corinthians 3 and then proceeds to delve into the narrative about the shining face of Moses in the rest of the chapter. This is accurately what might be expected from the one who knows the Sacred Scripture inside out! For sure, there is utterly no absolute need to assume that Paul appeals to Exodus 32-34 since he calls into question the Judaizing interpretations of his adversaries who misconstrue the respective text. Rather, he sets forth his reading as an endorsement for his gospel and explains the meaning of it for his apostolic ministry. Too much time and energy have been wasted in the "mirror-reading" of the views of the opponents from an analysis of 2 Corinthians 3. At best, it remains pure guesswork. Here, this sort of speculation is shrugged off.[17]

---

[17] Cf. especially Seifrid 2014, 100-110. He argues for a similar conclusion but from another perspective. For sure, Paul's interpretation of Ex 32-34 in 2 Cor 3 (as well as the whole letter) reflects the problems he faces in Corinth. Still, there is no evidence that he here reads his Old Testament text against the background

Even prior to his revision of Exodus 34:29-35, Paul promptly after his mentions of Jeremiah 31:31-34 and Ezekiel 36:24-28 compares his person or personal experience to that of Moses. Actually, he had already in 2 Corinthians 2:16 asked "who is sufficient" (καὶ πρὸς ταῦτα τίς ἱκανός;) for the proclamation of the end-time salvation. Now in 2 Corinthians 3:5, he adds that "our sufficiency comes from God" (ἀλλ' ἡ ἱκανότης ἡμῶν ἐκ τοῦ Θεοῦ). For certain, his use of language recalls the obstructive resistance of Moses to the mission of God: "I am not sufficient" (οὐχ ἱκανός εἰμι, LXX Exodus 4:10).[18]

---

of the misreading of his alleged opponents or adversaries. *Pace* Georgi 1986. Cf. also Hulmi 1999. Similarly, Ulonska 1966, 388: "Die Exegese von 2. Kor. 3 kann nur dann sachgemäß genannt werden, wenn sie das nachzusprechen vermag, was Paulus damals in der Auseinandersetzung mit seinen Gegnern sagen wollte." Correctly, Hays 1989, 126: "Whatever his opponents may have taught, Paul's discourse in this chapter [sc. 2 Cor 3] has its own internal metaphorical logic, which can be described in terms of its unfolding tropes, without recourse to hypotheses about external sources or influences on the discourse." Likewise, Hickling 1975, 380: "It is perhaps fair to say that these studies, from Georgi's influential treatment of this chapter onwards, indicate great ingenuity on the part of their authors (as well as claiming an even greater ingenuity for Paul himself, and attributing remarkable exegetical sensitivity to his readers in Corinth), but leave one with the impression that the wrong questions have been asked of the text." In his article, he then substantiates his claim in a careful manner (ibid., 380-395). Similarly, van Unnik (1963, 156) speaks of solving no riddles, but only creating new ones. He avows: "There is not a shred of evidence that the apostle is commenting upon a previously existing document or teaching nor is it clear why Paul himself should have been unable to make this application of the Exodus-story. Before setting out on hypothetical reconstructions behind the given text, we should first try to understand the text as it stands." Last but not least, Provence (1982, 55) writes as follows: "The great difficulty with the theory that this chapter opposes false teaching at Corinth is its circularity. It first assumes the identity of the opponents and then seeks to find evidence in the passage to support this identification." More cautiously, Nathan 2020, 144-146, Stockhausen 1989, 7-8, 12-13. Cf. Vegge 2008. In his thorough study of (human) reconciliation in 2 Corinthians, he does *not* in any more detail deal with the alleged opponents in chapter 3.

[18] See chapter 3 above. Cf. further Seifrid 2014, 120. He comments on 2 Corinthians 3:6a: "His unusual language should not be overlooked. One was not normally judged as 'sufficient' or 'competent' as an 'emissary' or 'agent' of another. As he already has reminded the Corinthians, 'stewards'

It seems that Paul, not only keeps the lexical similarity in mind, but he also hints at the historical setting of the succeeding story line in the Pentateuch. There we learn that Moses was not eloquent. He got into various troubles with Israel. They protested against him and threatened him, along with lots of other concerns and conflicts or woes and worries. Accordingly, at the moment, Paul faces similar problems. His speaking amounts to nothing (2 Corinthians 10:10). His authority comes next to naught (2 Corinthians 10:1-11). And to top it all off, he should just disappear and not step in and intervene in various controversial issues (*passim*). On the whole, Paul easily finds himself and his controversial hullabaloos in the biographical data of Moses. Hence, he refers to his Old Testament paragon on purpose.[19]"

Just as in the Old Testament God entrusted Moses with "sufficiency" or "competence," so he does also now in the New Testament as he appointed Paul to be his apostle. He empowers his servants to his work. Every sort of ability and skill comes from him (2 Corinthians 3:5-6). On occasion, God is called "the suffi-cient one" in varied Jewish texts (a common title for the Lord in Aquila, Symmachus as well as in Philo; see already LXX Ruth 1:20, Job 21:15, 31:2, 40:2, and Ezekiel 1:24 [the attestation of the so-called manuscript A]). Since ἱκανός functions as a divine name, best-owing of ἱκανότης amounts to a divine gift.[20] In context, it relates to the "know-how" of performing the ministry of the new covenant (2 Corinthians 3:6). Paul, in himself and out of himself, is not able to accomplish anything like that. He puts his trust in God alone through Christ (2 Corinthians 3:4-5). Only then, does his preaching transmit the recreative power of the Spirit in agreement with the prophecies in

---

and 'underlings' are examined not for their adequacy but for their *faithfulness* (1 Cor 4:1-5)."

[19] Without a doubt, Paul compares himself with the figure of Jeremiah as well. See Hafemann 2007, 57: "Paul's ministry of the Spirit in fulfilment of Jeremiah's promise (2 Cor. 3:8) leads him to allude to the call of Jeremiah himself in 2 Corinthians 10:8 and 13:10 in order to underscore his call to be a servant of the new covenant." Cf. Jeremiah 1:9b-10. Similarly, see the correla-tion between Galatians 1:15-16 and Jeremiah 1:5.

[20] See Harris 2005, 269, Martin 1986, 53, Thrall 2004, 230.

Ezekiel and mediate the making of the new covenant in accordance with the prophecies in Jeremiah (2 Corinthians 3:3, see above).

Moses and his ministry

In a sense, Moses (as already told) has anticipated the eschatological turning point in the salvation history through his intercessions for the idolatrous Israel in Exodus 32-34. As a *person*, he stands for the abundance of God's benevolence and on the same side as the former patriarchs Abraham (Romans 4:1-5, Galatians 3:6-18), Isaac (Romans 9:7-9, Galatians 4:21-31), and Jacob (Romans 9:10-13). He further confirms what David writes about the justification of the ungodly (Romans 4:6-8) and the prophets about the future of Israel's conversion (see the whole argumentation in Romans 9-11). In contrast, the *ministry* of Moses is without a shred of doubt that of death and condemnation (2 Corinthians 3:7-11). Seen from that perspective, he truly represents the "letter" that kills (2 Corinthians 3:6).[21] Therefore, the obvious dichotomy of the entire text in 2 Corinthians 3 needs to be explained to the exclusion of fatal misinterpretations before the antithesis between the "letter" and the "Spirit" is analyzed more in depth. In consequence, an analysis of v. 6b will be postponed in the next chapter. Here, the focus apparently lies on the reading of what follows in vv. 7-18.

The transition from the antithesis between the "letter" and the "Spirit" in v. 6b to the ensuing contrast between the ministry of death and its arrival in glory in v. 7a adheres to the same syntactic pattern. In both cases, the conjunctive particle δέ occurs. It has an adversative force. Just as the "letter" and the "Spirit" stand in opposition to each other, so also the ministry of death and its arrival in glory are loaded with opposite features. Thus, the conjunctive particle δέ does not effect "a mild transition to the new unit."[22] Rather, it provides a more serious antagonism between the two poles.

---

[21] As is well-known, Paul speaks of the Mosaic law very negatively with regard to its accusing and condemning function in the case of justification. On the other hand, he speaks of it very positively as far as it testifies to the "righteousness of God" that is manifested in the gospel (see, e.g., Romans 3:19-21). A related dichotomy occurs in 2 Corinthians 3 (see below).

[22] *Pace* Guthrie 2015, 205.

The thought of the ministry of death that was engraved in letters of stone (ἡ διακονία τοῦ θανάτου ἐν γράμμασιν ἐντετυπωμένη λίθοις) in v. 7 resumes the notion of the letter that kills (τὸ γὰρ γράμμα ἀποκτείνει) in v. 6. On that basis, it turns out that v. 7 explains and expands the language and meaning of v. 6. They fall into one and the same category of theological conception and interpretation.[23]

In simple terms, the ministry of death (v. 7) and condemnation (v. 9) aims at the Sinaitic covenant (Exodus 19-20). At the giving of the law, anyone who would go up the mountain, touch the foot of it and cross the boundaries around it should die (Exodus 19:12). The offence against the prohibition of idolatry through the worship of the golden calf ushers in the slaughter of the guilty by the Levites (Exodus 32:27-28, 34). Many commandments are attended by severe sanctions. Sentence of death is pronounced as the most extreme punishment for a wide variety of transgressions (see Exodus 21:12, 14-17, 28-29, 22:2, 19, 31:14-15).[24] On the national level, death is associated with exile just like in the overwhelming vision of Ezekiel 37.[25] Expulsion from the Promised Land proves that the promise of "living by doing" in Leviticus 18:5 has been brought to naught. The passage is quoted repeatedly in the Old Testament to corroborate the judgment over Israel as a result of their religious decay and heinous sins. They are the ones. They are to blame (Nehemiah 9:29, Ezekiel 20:11, 13, 21).[26] In Pauline theology, the threat of death and condemnation further relates to the law that convicts (Romans 3:19-20) and kills the sinners (Romans 7:9-11). On the whole, the Sinaitic covenant really amounts to a ministry of denunciation and destruction already in the Old Testament as well as in the proclamation of the gospel.

Strikingly, the antithesis between the "letter" and the "Spirit" in v. 6 changes into a contrast *inside* the old covenant in v. 7: the ministry of death "came with glory" as an indication of the shining face of Moses. He has acquired amnesty for his people after their idolatrous worship of the golden calf at Sinai. The reference to Exodus 32-34 remains beyond all reasonable doubt. As already founded, the two

---

[23] See above, chapter 4.
[24] Guthrie 2015, 207, Hafemann 2005, 283-284, Watson 2004, 288-289.
[25] See above, chapter 5.
[26] See Laato 2021, 56-57.

successive units in 2 Corinthians 3, namely vv. 7-11 and vv. 13-18
(v. 12 functions as a transition), speak of the shining face of Moses
at the outset of the respective section.[27] Hence, the emphasis lies on
the divine compassion and mercy that came to pass also in the old
covenant as the stubborn Israel was restored to God's own people.
The particle δέ with an adversative force in v. 7 (see above) underlines
the paradoxical fact that the ministry of death, nonetheless, came with
that kind of glory.[28] In the following juxtaposition of the ministry of
Moses and that of Paul (vv. 7-11), there must be some element common to the glory of Moses and that of Paul, otherwise the argument
falls to the ground.[29] They are in unison on the benevolence of God.
He demonstrates his amazing grace out of his goodness and God-
ness. Moses also knows perfectly well that salvation does not depend
on the Mosaic law! Indeed, he consents to the preaching of amnesty
without any merits.[30] By his ardent intercessions, he has anticipated

---

[27] See above, chapter 3.

[28] *Contra* Provence 1982, 71. He asserts: "Paul's intention, then, is to illustrate
the hardening effect that the glory of God may have upon those whose hearts
have not been changed by the Spirit." Hence, he concludes: "Thus Paul's exegesis of Ex. xxxiv supports his contention that his ministry is, at least in part,
a ministry which leads to destruction (ii 15)."

[29] The suggestion of Thrall (2004, 246) turns out to be correct. She presents
various alternatives of "the basic meaning of δόξα" (ibid.). Cf. Hafemann 2005,
269: "In 3:7f. Paul simply *asserts* that Moses' ministry possessed the δόξα needed
to provide the *similarity* between the two ministries, *and* that it was nevertheless a ministry 'of death,' the point of *dissimilarity* upon which the argument
turns." Later, he (ibid. 272) speaks of "the contradiction which appears to exist
between Paul's pronouncement that Moses' ministry came in glory *and* that
it brought death." He concludes: "Its participation in glory apparently negates
the attempt to associate it with death." For another interpretation, see below.
Cf. Legarth 2004, 40 and 50 with regard to 2 Corinthians 4:1-6. He (ibid., 40)
affirms: "Paulus ser en analogi mellem teofanien på Sinai og kristofanien ved
Damaskus." *Pace* Lambrecht 1983, 354. He maintains: "The relation between
these two types of δόξα is one of opposition." Instead, the opposition prevails
between the *ministry* of Moses and that of Paul.

[30] See above, chapter 5 (especially the difference between the initial making
of the covenant with the subsequent renewal of the covenant in Exodus 20:5-6
and 34:6-7). Cf. Kim 1981, 235-238. He speaks of "an antithetical typology"
between Moses and Paul (ibid., 236). He affirms (ibid. 238): "The parallels

the dawn of the new covenant in accordance with Jeremiah 31:31-34 and Ezekiel 36:26-27.[31] In the Old Testament, the two latter passages coincide with the account in Exodus 33-34. They all synchronize well together.[32] Since Paul has been dealing with both prophetic texts (see above), he now sheds more light on the paragon of their visions. He puts God's glorious theophany to Moses in Exodus 33-34 on the side of his gospel but still regards the *Mosaic ministry* precisely as that of death and condemnation.[33]

---

between the Sinai theophany and the Damascus Christophany enable Paul to see a typology between the old covenant and the new, between Moses and himself. But the particular circumstances and content of the Damascus revelation lead him to make it an antithetical one." However, the glory of Moses or his experience of the gracious theophany in Exodus 33-34 exactly anticipates the glorious Christophany of Paul on his way to Damascus. There is no "antithetical typology" here, but, rather an analogy even if the manifestation of the divine splendor in the new covenant widely exceeds that in the old covenant. The strong contrast in 2 Corinthians 3 prevails between the *ministry* of death/condemnation and the *ministry* of life/righteousness (cf. above). Utterly, my modification of Kim's interpretation corroborates his conclusion of the central meaning of Christophany behind many Pauline texts (and especially in Corinthian correspondence).

[31] See above, chapter 5, especially the common traits between the three passages.

[32] See above, chapter 5.

[33] *Pace* Seifrid 2014, 157: "We presently encounter God's glory in two forms: the glory that accompanies the mission of Moses and brings death, and the glory of God that belongs to the distribution of the Spirit and brings life." In one sense, this holds true given the systematic (Lutheran) distinction between the law and the gospel. However, the notion of glory in 2 Corinthians 3 relates to the theophany in Exodus 33-34 where God's glory reveals his *benevolence*. Therefore, it definitely anticipates the glory of the gospel. The whole argumentation takes for granted that there is no basic and principal difference between the two glories (see above) despite many other weighty differences (see below). In other words, the ministry of Moses is that of death and condemnation, but the story of God's glorious theophany invokes his mercy and indicates the dawn of the new covenant. *Contra* Watson 2004, 290 as well. He writes that the ministry of death "is illuminated by the radiance of Moses' transfigured face." He overlooks the adversative force of the particle δέ in v. 7 (see above) to the exclusion of the paradoxical fact that the ministry of death, nevertheless, came with the glory of God's gracious presence.

To be sure, God shows his glory and is glorious whenever he makes himself known, also as he revealed his mighty power in front of the whole Israel at Sinai (Exodus 19:16-25, 24:9-17) or sent his consuming fire against Nadab and Abihu in their rebellion to offer "unauthorized (strange, profane) fire before the Lord" (Leviticus 10:1-3). Furthermore, his glorious appearance instills much fear in those who see it, as manifest in the cases of Gideon (Judges 6:1-24), Manoah and his wife, the parents of Samson (Judges 13:1-23), and Isaiah (6:1-7).[34] Despite their fear and trembling, they received his unearned compassion and mercy. Therefore, the human condition of dread and horror do *not* necessarily indicate that the divine judgment falls upon them. Quite the opposite. God "saves those who are crushed in spirit" (Psalm 34:18); he revives "the spirit of the lowly" and "the heart of the contrite" (Isaiah 57:15); he esteems the one "who is humble and contrite in spirit" and trembles at his word (Isaiah 66:2). Bearing in mind their sin of idolatry, the Israelites definitely "were afraid to come near" Moses owing to his radiant face (Exodus 34:30), but the fact remains that they were nevertheless forgiven and granted amnesty. Their broken covenant relationship was restored with an immediate effect on their religious position as the chosen ones. Since then, they moved on and continued on their way to the Promised Land.[35]

Moses' placement of a veil over his face

At this point, a serious confusion and a vast array of improbable interpretations commonly prevail in the mainstream exegesis. After all, "sad story, happy ending" turns into "sad story, unhappy ending" in Exodus 32-34. Despite the fact that the astonishing abundance of God's generous benevolence in largest measure fell on Israel, they nevertheless failed or flopped totally. Moses' placement of a veil over his face indicates their inability to grasp God's goodness.[36] It

---

[34] Cf. the case of Moses in Exodus 3:1-10 as well!

[35] Cf. chapter 5 above, primarily the difference between God's presence in his majesty as he convicts and his presence in his benevolence as he acquits. For sure, at the Final Judgment (and even before), both sides of his being coincide (as he destroys those who are against him and saves those who are for him).

[36] Philpot 2013a, 11. See already my reference to him in chapter 5.

"becomes symbolic of a dull heart that does not grasp God's purpose" and, therefore, functions as a "barrier standing between the people and the manifestation of God's presence."[37] It marks "the continuing judgment of God upon his people, who remain 'stiff-necked.'"[38] Moses "effects condemnation and death: his veil cuts off access to the glory of the Lord."[39] His action as "an act of judgment"[40] compares to "an effective parable, much like the prophetic signs performed by Jeremiah or Ezekiel." In other words, what he does to himself comes upon Israel.[41] More strikingly, "it does seem that some degree of intentional deception is attributed" to Moses.[42] He conceals the

---

[37] Guthrie 2015, 221-222: "The veil then becomes symbolic of a dull heart that does not grasp God's purpose nor enjoy the outcome of being a people who know God's presence. In short, the people fail to embrace the fullness of the glorious relationship that God desires with them [. . .]. A key here is to understand the veil as barrier standing between the people and the manifestation of God's presence." See also pp. 224 and 229.

[38] Hafemann 2005, 280: "He [Moses] must then replace the veil, however, as an expression of the continuing judgment of God upon his people, who remain 'stiff-necked.'" Cf. Hofius 1989, 95: "Paulus erwähnt das verklärte Angesicht des Mose und das Unvermögen der Israeliten, den Strahlenglanz zu ertragen, vielmehr deshalb, weil er den in der Tora ergehenden und sich auf dem Angesicht des Mose widerspiegelnden δόξα-Erweis als eine richtende und für den Sünder tödliche Manifestation göttlicher Macht verstanden wissen will."

[39] Seifrid 2014, 163: "Moses acts as the Law does and effects condemnation and death: his veil cuts off access to the glory of the Lord."

[40] Ibid., 159: "This inability has its counterpart in Moses' placement of a veil over his face, which Paul subsequently interprets as an act of judgment (v. 13)."

[41] Ibid., 163: "Paul understands Moses' action as an effective parable, much like the prophetic signs performed by Jeremiah or Ezekiel. What Moses does to himself comes upon 'the sons of Israel.'" Consequently, Seifrid widens the focus of his exegetical analysis beyond the story of Israel's worship of the golden calf in Exodus 32: "The shift in the Exodus story from God's direct address to Israel by his own voice (Exod 19:16-20:21) to the mediation of God's word through Moses (20:22-24:8) and finally to the commandments written on stone tablets (24:12-18) is of far greater significance to Paul's account than is the story of Israel's idolatry." Then, he concludes: "This fundamental change in the Lord's dealings with Israel is not precipitated by any particular event." (ibid., 154)

[42] Thrall 2004, 258: "[. . .] it does seem that some degree of intentional deception is attributed to him [Moses]. But since he is co-operating in some way with the divine purpose for Israel, his moral responsibility is lessened."

fact that the old covenant performs "only an interim function until its supersession by the Christ-event."[43] For sure, his "culpability is mitigated" since he "is seen also as co-operating with the purpose of God."[44]

With regard to the preceding and corresponding theological reflections or speculations of the most sophisticated art, growing skepticism is arising, reasonable suspicions are abounding and confounding, considerable doubts are creeping in. It seems that recent exegetical explanations evoke perplexity and complexity rather than perception and comprehension. In truth, for what reasons should Moses presume to judge the Israelites if he, just a short time ago, convinced God to relent from judging them? Seriously, did he really intend to deceive them after not allowing God to go back on promises to them and wipe them out? It does not sound very plausible to make the veil like a "barrier" standing between the people and their Lord! We never read anything about this and that in Exodus 32-34. Modern interpretations end up next to nonsense.[45] Here, if ever, a better knowledge of the new perspective on Judaism adds up to a more accurate alternative or approach.

---

[43] Ibid.

[44] Ibid., 261: "[. . .] the element of deception does remain, but its culpability is mitigated since Moses is seen also as co-operating with the purpose of God." Cf. Hanson 1980, 16. He affirms that Moses "wished to hide the glory of the pre-existent Christ whom he had seen in the tabernacle." Else, "there is little point in the contrast between what Moses did and what Paul and his companions do." Later, he (ibid., 17) adds: "As long as Moses lived, the veil could be described as a means by which the Israelites were prevented from seeing the glory of the pre-existent Christ." The whole reading of Hanson sounds very strange. He seems to make Moses as a representative of "the god of this age" who prevents unbelievers from seeing "the glory of Christ" (2 Corinthians 4:4)! Contra Hanson, see also Baker 2000, 8.

[45] For a vast array of modern interpretations, see Belleville 1992, 206-208. In the end, she concludes quite promptly: "Indeed all Paul explicitly says is that Moses was not public about the old covenant ministry and its glory, fading though it was. The reason for Moses' act of veiling, according to Paul, was to prevent further gazing. [. . .] Paul does not give the reader the information necessary to draw any further conclusion—if he, in fact, intended the reader to take this step at all." (ibid., 208) Similarly, Lambrecht 1983, 359-360. See my own analysis below.

As already indicated in the reading of Exodus 34:29-35, the passage does not spell out any explanation for Moses' veiling of his face.[46] The disclosure of God's glory denotes his presence among the Israelites and his readiness to lead them to the Promised Land. Their offense in terms of the sacrilegious worship of the golden calf has been eradicated by his mercy. Now, his gracious commitment is reflected on the face of Moses. No doubt, that aspect captures the essence of the story. Presumably, other motives have a bearing on the text as well. It appears most likely that the glorification of Moses has increased his authority. It has further authenticated his message.[47] Yet, the renewal of the covenant has the primary meaning in the context. Does Moses' placement of the veil over his face one way or another call into question the sincerity or validity of the relationship between the Israelites and their Lord?

At least, God kept his promises. His glorious presence "filled the Tabernacle" (Exodus 40:34). As Moses was not able to see the face of the Lord on the top of the mountain, so neither can he now "enter the Tent of Meeting" because of the divine splendor remaining there (Exodus 40:35). The immense construction project started immediately after the renewal of the covenant. All energy was put into that job. It signals that God will find his dwelling place among the Israelites in his own transportable house. Then, his glorious presence follows (or rather leads!) them during their various travels and journeys (Exodus 40:38).[48] Until then, it shows itself "only" on the face of Moses. Through his constant conversations with Yahweh, he had to "recharge" the shining skin of his countenance. It was not permanent. It seems, therefore, plausible that Moses did not veil himself the rest of his life. After some time, he got back his natural appearance. At any rate, Paul evidently reads the text like this. He speaks about the fading away or, more accurately, abolishing of the glory. He does not affirm the Jewish speculations of the enduring character of the shining face of Moses (2 Corinthians 3:7-11). In addition, he speaks of "the end of that which is abolished" (v. 13: τὸ

---

[46] See above, chapter 5.

[47] Klein 1996, 268: "His glowing face indicated his direct contact with the deity and gave authority to the message he delivered." Cf. Hafemann 2005, 280.

[48] See above, chapter 5.

τέλος τοῦ καταργουμένου), meaning in the first place the declining and disappearing of the divine splendor shortly after the succeeding theophanies in Exodus 34:29-35.[49]

Further, an analogous approach prevails in the Old Testament concerning the temple in Jerusalem. It mediates God's grace since his glory abides there. As once at Sinai, he reveals his goodness to the Israelites, "for his mercy endures forever" in accordance with their inaugural Psalm 136 at the dedication feast (2 Chronicles 5:13-14 and 7:1-3, 6). The alluring story continues like this until they abandoned him and collapsed morally. At that point, his glory departed from the Temple, and they were deported to exile (Ezekiel 11:1-12). Then, his horrible threat came true: "However, when the time comes for me to punish, I will punish them for their sin" (Exodus 32:34).[50] It follows that, in one sense, the shining face of Moses and the fading away of his glory anticipates the future fate of Israel. To put it very simply: His story becomes their history!

Exodus 34:29-35, read through the lenses of Paul and in light of the overall view of the Old Testament, shows that Moses veiled himself in order to prevent the Israelites from seeing the end of God's grace. He persists in his loving caring for them. No talk about *his* alleged judgment of them—despite the fact that the Sinaitic *law* amounts to the ministry of death and condemnation (2 Corinthians 3:7-9)! Thus, Moses was aware of the impermanence of the old covenant. He also knew that only the revelation of God's gracious glory protects and saves the Israelites from total destruction. In the midst of the national crisis because of their idolatry, he did everything in his power to avoid the slightest hint of the loss of divine benevolence. That was the deepest reason for his veiling himself. At least, Paul reads the whole

---

[49] See above, chapter 4. For the Jewish notions of the permanent character of the shining face of Moses, see Hofius 1989, 96-101. Cf. also Cover 2015, especially chapters 3-6, where he analyzes a wide series of Jewish homiletic and commentary traditions as well as some other relevant texts. He indicates: "As many commentators have lamented, the search for parallel exegeses of Exod 34:29-35, which might throw some light on Paul's interpretation, yields few positive results." (ibid., 262-263). Cf. also Stockhausen 1989, 21-31 *et passim*.

[50] See above, chapter 5.

story along these lines. His reading complies with the intention of the Old Testament: the theophany or the recurring theophanies in Exodus 33-34 anticipate the commencement of the new covenant as prophesized in Jeremiah 31:31-34 and Ezekiel 36:26-27.[51]

Hence, Moses' placement of the veil over his face was not an act of disapproval. Rather, it warded off all doubts of the diminishment of the mercy his intercessions for Israel had acquired. The setting up of the Tabernacle (and the later erection of the temple) has then substituted his role as a mediator and "officialized" the sacrificial economy of divine forgiveness (Exodus 35-40). Remarkably, not in that case either does the "veiledness" of God's glory suggest any judgment of his own people.[52]

The permanence of the glory in the new covenant

Yet, things and conditions change ever since the commencement of the new covenant. Now, there is a much better hope (2 Corinthians 3:12). "The Lord of glory" has been crucified (1 Corinthians 2:8). His glorious grace will last forever. It never ends. Thus, Paul proclaims his gospel with great boldness and confidence (2 Corinthians 3:12). He knows the superabundant plus of his preaching. He absolutely needs no veiling of himself in opposition to Moses (2 Corinthians 3:13) who acknowledged the temporary element of the old covenant. In contrast, Paul proclaims his gospel with the full awareness of the eternal validity of his message. He enjoys the unsurpassed privilege of his celestial mission and does not lose his courage in the midst of his tribulations (cf. the meaning of παρρησία in v. 12 that derivates from "pas" + "rhésis" and denotes the audacity to "tell everything" vis-à-vis "to hide oneself behind the veil").[53]

---

[51] See above, chapter 5.

[52] In the Tabernacle as well as in the temple, God's glory was hidden or concealed not behind the "veil" but the "curtain" (correctly, Philpot 2013a, 9). In any case, the "veiledness" of his true self does not imply any act of condemnation. That same discernment applies to the story in Exodus 34:29-35.

[53] The association between "to tell everything" and "to hide oneself behind the veil" in Greek language very easily clears up the connection between v. 12 and v. 13. The linguistic equivalence might go back to Aramaic idioms "to

It follows from the previous reading of 2 Corinthians 3 that the overall line of reasoning becomes easier to understand. The meaning of "glory" remains constant and does not alter from the condemning glory to the forbearing and forgiving glory (even though the intensity and permanency of the glory greatly varies). As already indicated, without some element common to the glory of Moses and that of Paul, the juxtaposition of them or comparison between them completely falls to the ground. The *a minore ad maius* argument ("if then . . . how much more") in vv. 7-11 precisely "depends for its cogency on the presupposition that what is stated in the protasis is agreed to be true," both by the one advancing the argument and by the one obtaining it.[54] Consequently, God's glory as an expression for his benevolence is taken for granted. It reveals his inner being in line with Exodus 34:6: "The Lord, the Lord, the compassionate and gracious God, slow to anger, abounding in love and faithfulness."[55]

---

uncover the face" resp. "to uncover the head" which mean confidence and freedom. See van Unnik 1963, 160-162. Yet, he interprets the covering of face or head only in pejorative sense as "a sign of shame and mourning." Further, the "strange" behavior of Moses in veiling himself becomes a "sign of shame and bondage" (ibid., 161). At least in Corinthian correspondence, head coverings are a matter of *honor* and *glory* in the case of female attendance in Christian worship (see 1 Corinthians 11:2-16 with a similar vocabulary as in 2 Corinthians 3). They show the right attitude of modesty and humility. Godly women have the right to pray and prophesy. However, they should not preach or proclaim (see 1 Corinthians 14:33b-40). In this sense, they truly have no παρρησία! On the other hand, the same head coverings are indeed a matter of shame and dishonor in the case of male attendance in Christian worship (see 1 Corinthians 11:2-16). Taken as a whole, van Unnik overlooks the evidence of the ancient habits of veiling oneself in Corinthian correspondence. Neither does he properly discuss the purpose and function of the veil of Moses on account of the story in Exodus 34 as explained by Paul in 2 Corinthians 3.

[54] Thrall 2004, 240.

[55] *Pace* Seifrid 2014, 159. He writes as follows: "Yet the glory of the mission of righteousness is so bright that it eclipses and eliminates the former glory. There is no line of continuity that may be drawn between them. They meet in the crucified and risen Lord alone." Once again, the deep-rooted and well-established inquiry of Seifrid holds true given the proper distinction between the law and gospel in Lutheran theology. To be sure, Paul speaks for it! Yet, he does not suggest that the glory of Moses stands for the law but for the purest

Despite the basic consistency or coherence of divine glory in the Old and New Testament, various weighty differences stand out between them. In 2 Corinthians 3:7-11, the focus lies on the following central aspects:

1) The use of the *a minore ad maius* argument shows that as already the Mosaic ministry came with glory so also and with even more convincing *certainty* the Pauline ministry is attended with glory.
2) Since there was glory in the Mosaic ministry, then the Pauline ministry possesses an incomparably *greater* glory.
3) The glory of the Mosaic ministry was done away but the glory of the Pauline ministry remains or *endures forever*.
4) In the Old Testament, the divine glory relates to Moses alone. In the New Testament, it even pertains to Paul and *each believer* (see especially v. 18).[56]

All in all, the superiority of the Pauline ministry in comparison with the Mosaic ministry has been proven beyond any doubt. However, it should not be overlooked that the glory of the Mosaic ministry was outward and visible, but paradoxically the glory of the Pauline ministry at present is inward and invisible. Currently, it remains hidden under the opposite. It becomes manifest on the Last Day. Only then and not before, the truth of the gospel will appear obvious in the sight of everyone.[57]

The question then arises whether the verb ἔσται in v. 8 has either a logical or eschatological sense: "How much more will the ministry of the Spirit be in glory?" Does the future tense refer to a consequence that has already now taken place, or does it relate to a result that will come to pass first at the Parousia? Here, the opinions in the commentaries widely differ and split. No unison ensues.[58] At any

---

gospel (Exodus 34:6-7). Therefore, the line of continuity prevails in salvation history.

[56] For instance, cf. Seifrid 2014, 151 and Thrall 2004, 239. Similarly, Hays 1989, 143.

[57] Seifrid 2014, 151 and 157.

[58] See, e.g., Martin 1986, 62-63, Seifrid 2014, 157, Thrall 2004, 245.

rate, it does not seem obvious that the whole debate on the logical
or eschatological sense is on the right track at all. The artificial alternative "either—or" casts serious doubt on the rationale of the two
mutually exclusive options. Indeed, the atomistic method of exegesis
does little to convince. In another context, it has turned out that the
future tense, more to the point, simply assumes a *prospective* function
setting aside further restrictions.[59] Thus, the permanent glory (v. 11)
pertains forward to the consummating of the enduring state of glory
at the Parousia. It depicts the object of the *hope* (v. 12). As such, it
has not yet become manifest.[60] On the other hand, the permanent
glory prevails at the present time since it holds sway at any time. It
abounds or exceeds (v. 9: περισσεύει in the present tense) already
now.[61] The eschatological age has truly begun. Christians behold the
glory of the Lord and see more and more of it until they will finally
perceive it perfectly. They progress "from glory to glory" (v. 18).[62]
Hence, the logical and eschatological aspects blend into each other.
They fuse together into the prospective approach. Proceeding from
the age of the covenant making at Sinai, the fact remains that the
succeeding time span, say, from the impending days of the Messiah
to the consummation in eternal bliss lies in the future.[63]

Paul and his ministry

The more glorious ministry of the new covenant is characterized as
the ministry of the Spirit (v. 8) and righteousness (v. 9). They form the

---

[59] Laato 2013, 111-113 (relating to the future tense in Romans 6). Cf. Martin
1986, 63. He writes on 2 Corinthians 3:8: "More likely, [. . .] the two meanings [the logical and eschatological senses of the future tense] are not to be
divorced, yet with the eschatological dimension predominant [. . .]." See further
Johansson 1990, 81 and Thrall 2004, 245.

[60] Thrall 2004, 245 n 376. See also Seifrid 2014, 157.

[61] Lambrecht (1983, 356) rightly speaks of "a rising tone, a crescendo, a
Steigerung" of the glory.

[62] Thrall 2004, 245.

[63] Guthrie 2015, 212 n 26: The form of the verb in 2 Corinthians 3:8 "is future
tense, given with the time of Moses as its point of reference, since the new
covenant would come, from the perspective of Moses's day, in the future."

sharp contrast to the reign of death (v. 7) and condemnation (v. 9) in the old covenant (see the historical outline from exodus to exile above). Moreover, the two poles on the opposite sides account for the weighty tenet in v. 6: "The letter kills, but the Spirit gives life." It then follows from that specification that the "letter" kills because of condemning people, but the "Spirit" gives life because of justifying people.

The specific contrast of death and Spirit discloses a sort of imbalance since the mission of death is not set against that of life. Paul puts emphasis on the source of life. He wittingly speaks of the Giver of the life.[64] For sure, he alludes to the prophecy of Ezekiel 37 where the Spirit of God vivifies the dead persons. Therefore, 2 Corinthians 3 does not generally deal with human existence. Rather, it defines the true life as a close relationship and communion of the Creator with his creatures. Above and beyond, the Spirit amounts to a "down payment" (ἀρραβών in 2 Corinthians 1:22 and 5:5), a deposit or an earnest that is offered in advance as a security that the whole sum of money will be paid afterwards.[65] It constitutes the present possession of that which is to come, explicitly the eternal bliss. Concisely, it is about the celestial glory. For that simple reason, the ministry of the Spirit is "even more glorious" (v. 8) given that he already represents the heaven on earth.

The close connection or correspondence between the Spirit and righteousness as representative attributes of the apostolic ministry shows that salvation does not in the slightest rest on any human efforts and merits but solely on divine mercy. All alleged abilities, inborn or inherent, do not make the difference. They are in vain and a forlorn hope. The Spirit alone brings forth the vivification of dead persons (Ezekiel 37). He alone causes the recreation of stony hearts into the fleshly ones (Ezekiel 36:26). God "let light shine out of darkness." He forwarded the bright beams of the gospel into the inner being of believers (2 Corinthians 4:6).[66] Regarding the absolutely marvelous

---

[64] Seifrid 2014, 156: "[. . .] the gift of life is no mere possession of the human being that can be isolated from the Giver."

[65] In reference to the definition of ἀρραβών in Greek dictionaries. See also, e.g., Seifrid 2014, 67-68, 229.

[66] Cf. Kim 1981, 236. Interestingly, he draws a parallel between the "Jewish conception of the Sinai revelation as a second creation, as the restoration of

phenomenon of salvation, Paul affirms his own total insufficiency and incompetence in his apostolic ministry. He is really not able to accomplish his mission. His qualification for his commission originates from the power of the Spirit (2 Corinthians 3:5-6). Otherwise, he fails. On the whole, his teaching on the right righteousness ushers in a strong doctrine on salvation *sola gratia* from the bottom up.

On closer examination, the content and meaning of the righteousness crystallize in light of the Old Testament setting. As known and shown, Paul orients his whole discussion to the story of Exodus 32-34. His chief interest lies in the disclosure of divine glory. In the context of that glorious theophany, the focus turns to LXX Exodus 34:6-7. The concept of "righteousness" occurs there (the only use of it in the framework of the narrative). God declares of himself that he is "compassionate and merciful, patient and full of mercy and true, and maintaining righteousness (δικαιοσύνην διατηρῶν) and accomplishing mercy for thousands, taking away lawlessness (ἀνομίας) and injustice (ἀδικίας) and sins." G. H. Guthrie maintains that righteousness mostly implies "that form of life which is the Israelite's appropriate response to the covenant" and becomes attainable only in the new covenant.[67] Still, Exodus 34:6-7 differs from Exodus 20:5-6 where the covenant is really based on human love in response to divine love: God promises to show his "love to a thousand generations of those who love me and keep my commandments." As a consequence of the incident with the golden calf at Sinai, the relationship of mutual keeping of treaty stipulations was ominously broken. The national destruction was right around the corner. What remains is God's undeserved love, his righteousness. The renewal of the covenant is based solely on his amazing benevolence.[68] It anticipates the new covenant. It predicts the preaching of the gospel. It substantiates the core of justification. To be sure, it also results in a new way of life since the Spirit at the same time effects

---

the primeval glory" and "Paul's conception of the Damascus revelation of the gospel as a new creation, as the restoration of the primeval light of glory" in 2 Corinthians 4:6.

[67] Guthrie 2015, 213-214 (relating to Moo who, however, does not directly comment on 2 Corinthians 3:9).

[68] See above, chapter 5.

vivification and recreation (see above). In any event, the main thing is that the main thing remains the main thing. God's glory amounts to his mercy, his justification of wretched sinners who glorify false gods. To tip the scale in favor of them over him and to put emphasis on them becoming more and more glorious in their own achievements of sanctification run the risk of misunderstanding totally the new covenant as well as the renewal of the old covenant.[69] Moses did not misunderstand. Neither did Paul. They both, personally, had seen the glory of the Lord who forgives and forgets. His glorious presence was a present to them.[70]

The juxtaposition of righteousness with condemnation in v. 9 further corroborates that it primarily unfolds God's saving work, his activity to restore sinners to a right relationship with himself. Clearly, condemnation denotes his announcement of a hard judicial verdict against them while righteousness similarly designates his assertion of a legislative acquittal of their transgressions. The heavenly Supreme Court fairly decides whether anyone is guilty or not guilty. It will put the divine judgments into effect. Therefore, salvation amounts to the vivification of dead persons or the recreation of nonexistent people as well as damnation results in eternal punishment.[71] To top it all off, the present justification revolves, in one sense, around the theology of glory in Paul's thinking! Somewhat surprisingly, he asserts in Romans 8:30 that those God "justified, them he also glorified" (ἐδόξασεν). The glorification has already taken place. The ministry of justification really exceeds in glory even now and not only on the Last Day (2 Corinthians 3:9). However, this special aspect meanwhile remains hidden under the theology of the cross.[72]

---

[69] Cf. Guthrie 2015, 228. Once again, he interprets God's glory mainly as a power of effecting (moral) transformation.

[70] For the notion of God's glory as his presence in the Old Testament, see above, chapter 5. Paul follows a similar line of reasoning. In his theology, δόξα "relates to a field of words like 'spirit,' 'power,' 'word,' 'gospel' and 'presence,' words which sign the presence of God" (Newman 2017, 163). Cf. Friesen 1971, 16-24.

[71] Cf. Seifrid 2014, 157-158.

[72] On purpose, in relation to the well-known contrast between "the theology of the cross" and "theology of glory" in Luther's overall thinking.

The abolition of the glory in the old covenant

In the structural analysis of 2 Corinthians 3, it has already been set out that the line of thought moves from the vanishing glory of Moses' face (ἡ δόξα τοῦ προσώπου αὐτοῦ ἡ καταργουμένη in v. 7) into "that which has been glorified" (τὸ δεδοξασμένον in v. 10) and "that which is vanished" (τὸ καταργούμενον in v. 11).[73] The shift from the feminine to the neuter form detaches the biography of Exodus 34:29-35 from the historical scenery to the theological sense and significance of the text in the Old Testament framework of salvation. The ancient account of the past distinct event becomes a prophetic vision of the future explicit development. It is no more particularly about the shining face of Moses but, more generally, his glorious mission or the whole moral and cultic institution he embodies. The great promise of the renewal of the old covenant was intertwined with him and his intercessions for the Israelites at Sinai. In this sense, the divine grace, as known, had a Mosaic prototype. For sure, it was not nearly as bright as the divine grace is now in the face of Christ (2 Corinthians 4:6). The latter surpasses and outshines the former completely (2 Corinthians 3:10). Besides, the latter remains forever while the former only prevailed until the dawn of the sunny day from the blue sky (2 Corinthians 3:11).[74] Accordingly, the old covenant was going to be superseded by the new one with the result that the divine benevolence will be superabundant in every respect.

The interplay of the historical meaning of Exodus 34:29-35 and the prophetic use of the same narrative in Pauline thinking[75] blend together in 2 Corinthians 3:13-14. Moses put a veil over his face so that the Israelites would not see the end of the glory on his

---

[73] Without any doubt, the phrase in v. 7: "the glory of his face which (glory) is done away" (ἡ δόξα τοῦ προσώπου αὐτοῦ ἡ καταργουμένη) relates to the vanishing shine of Moses' face. However, an intended reformulation occurs already in v. 11: "that which is done away was glorious (through glory)" (τό καταργούμενον διὰ δόξης). To be sure, the glory is even now passing since it bears on something that is done away. But the notion of the vanishing shine of Moses' face does no longer receive some special attention.

[74] See above and cf. chapter 3.

[75] More for the multiplicity and interplay of scriptural allusions in 2 Corinthians 3, see chapter 4 above.

countenance.[76] He knew that his glory was the glory of the divine benevolence towards them. It was absolutely crucial for the survival of them! Accordingly, he "kept putting a veil" over his face (ἐτίθει as an iterative imperfect in v. 13)[77] to stop them from gazing at the possible end of their amnesty (the kind of threat in Exodus 32:34). Later, the celestial glory in the Tabernacle reassured that Yahweh will show compassion for his people. The same scene with his gracious presence reoccurs in the temple. Yet, it did not last forever. As God and his glory in the long run departed from Jerusalem, the city was destroyed, and its inhabitants were obliged to go into exile (see above). Moses did everything to save his people from that fate. He never abstained from his intermediate role for them. He veiled himself in the hope that they would not mistrust God's glorious and gracious presence among them even if the glory on his face was finally abrogated. He also provided instructions for the construction of the Tabernacle to prepare a place for God's glory to reside in the midst of the desert during the wandering in the wilderness. Last but not least, he certainly yearned for the imminent coming of the Messiah who will incarnate and embody the mercy that was promised in the theophany at Sinai (see the former study of Exodus 33-34 and the survey of the Old Testament context).[78]

The hardening of Israel until the present day

The turn of thought in v. 14 to the response of the Israelites has initiated the notorious difficulty in determining the force of the

---

[76] For the primary meaning of τέλος as end, termination, cessation, see chapter 4 above.

[77] Guthrie 2015, 219.

[78] *Contra* Watson 2004, 287: "As Paul reads this passage, the 'glory' is associated not just with Moses' face but also and above all with the text that he bears in his hands." He finally concludes that "the glory on Moses' face is the glory of the text" (ibid.). Yet, the text that Moses bears in his hands is the law (or the decalogue), written "on tablets on stone" (v. 3) and identified with his ministry of death and condemnation (vv. 7 and 9). Surely, it does not reflect the gracious glory of God's presence. Later, Moses himself, but *not* exactly the glory on his face is associated with the text and the reading of the old covenant (see vv. 14-15).

introductory conjunction "but" (ἀλλά): "But their minds were hard-ened." Some scholars consider it in an intensive sense ("indeed"). Others construe it in an ascensive sense ("still more").[79] However, neither of the two renderings holds true. They both involve that the action of Moses in v. 13 takes aim at condemning the Israelites. Supposedly, he veils himself in order to mark the austere judgment of their stubbornness. As shown, the interpretation of that kind is far from the truth. Accordingly, the conjunction ἀλλά should be under-stood in its normal adversative sense (it is a stronger adversative particle than δέ).[80] A contrast lies between the intention of Moses and the outcome of his earnest commission. He did everything in his power to grant amnesty to his people. He succeeded in his efforts. But nevertheless, the Israelites failed in their faith. They should have put their trust in God's amazing grace. They should have seen it as a temporary or transitional anticipation of the much greater grace in the new covenant. Their reading of the old covenant (ἡ ἀνάγνωσις τῆς παλαιᾶς διαθήκης) did not and does not help them to recognize their need for the gospel. Worse still, although they themselves were right from the outset engaged in idolatry, they do not allow the idola-trous Gentiles to receive forgiveness in common with them. On the con-trary, they reserve their right to a covenantal relationship with God themselves. That is why they oppose the apostolic preaching. They simply do not welcome the indisputable fact that the old covenant

---

[79] For the two alternatives, see Belleville 1992, 218-219. Van Unnik (1963, 163) slightly criticizes both the intensive and ascensive sense of ἀλλά but does not perceive the adversative force of it. Without a doubt, the aorist passive ἐπωρώθη is ingressive (it denotes the beginning of the hardening), not gno-mic. Otherwise, the link between vv. 13-14a and the Exodus narrative is lost (Belleville 1992, 221, especially n 2).

[80] Rightly, Belleville 1992, 219-225 (even if her overall interpretation of the intention of Moses' action in v. 13 goes too far and also results in the divine judgment of the Israelites at odds with Exodus 33-34). *Pace* Martin 1986, 68: "Even so, there is a hiatus, because ἀλλά, on this view, has to open a fresh sec-tion of thought, and cannot provide a reason for it by contrast with v 13." Thrall (2004, 262) concedes that the opening ἀλλά "normally functions as a strong adversative particle, but it is not obvious here what it relates to." By necessity, she then supplements the text with an addition: "And they did not, in fact, see the τέλος . . ." but, on the contrary, their minds were hardened (ibid., 263).

is done away in Christ (ἐν Χριστῷ καταργεῖται).[81] The permanent bright glory on his face supersedes overwhelmingly the shine of all other lights in fulfilling what they stand for (cf. 2 Corinthians 4:4-6).

In the mixture of the argumentation, v. 14a functions as a transition from text to commentary. The sentence "but their minds were hardened" sets apart the Old Testament story in v. 13 from the interpretative usage of the holy writing in v. 14b. The contrast between the two poles stands firm. Moses put a veil over his shining face to prevent the Israelites from seeing the abrogation of the glory, the very sign of God's gracious presence among them. Now, "the same veil" (to be sure, in a non-literal sense) lies upon the reading of the old covenant (a non-personal substitution for Moses) and obstructs them from perceiving the abrogation of the glory that has taken place in Christ who has initiated a much better and greater glory as he subsumed in himself the former revelation(s) of the divine splendor. As a result, the corresponding expressions τό τέλος τοῦ καταργουμένου (v. 13) and ἐν Χριστῷ καταργεῖται (v. 14b) explain each other. That means that τό τέλος primarily takes the temporal meaning ("end"), including in itself also a teleological undertone ("goal").[82] The adversative sentence "but their minds were hardened" (v. 14a) between the action of Moses and that of the Israelites shows that the former falls under the side of the positive and the latter under the side of the negative. Accordingly, Moses' placement of a veil over his face does *not* indicate any symbolic performance of a strict judgment of the Israelites (cf. my criticism of the common misinterpretation of the whole passage above).[83] The

---

[81] For the construction and sense of the Greek phrase, see above chapter 4. In Greek as a typical "null-subject" language, the predicate subsumes into itself the role of the subject as well: "what is done away is done away in Christ."

[82] See above, chapter 4. Similarly, v. 7 speaks of the shining face of Moses and the abrogation of his glory. Further, v. 10 speaks of the glory that is no more glorious. It follows that the expression τό τέλος τοῦ καταργουμένου primarily relates to the *end* of the old covenant. However, Christ has ended the old covenant by fulfilling all the promises in Scripture. In this sense, he is not only the end but even the goal of it. See Romans 10:4 (Laato 2021, 54-55).

[83] *Contra* Watson 2004, 291-296. He speaks of "the deceptive veil" (ibid., 291). Later, he (ibid., 296) underscores: "Paul uses the scriptural image of the veil to speak not just of some 'Jewish misunderstanding' but of a problematic feature of the scriptural text itself. In the story of Moses' veil, the text

well-balanced parallelism of opposite outcomes precludes all far-fetched conclusions of exegetical imagination.[84]

In the form of parallel repetition, vv. 15-16 resume and restate v. 14b. It is like a phrase-by-phrase paraphrase that increases and improves the clarity of thought. Both passages speak of the development of hardening "right up to the present time," the remaining hindrance of the veil, and the Lord Christ as the one who removes the spiritual obstacle or obtuseness.[85] The lack of understanding from the side of the Jews and their outright misunderstanding of Scripture (v. 14b: the veil upon the reading of the old covenant), more exactly, stem from their self-delusion (v. 15: the veil upon their own hearts). They are to blame for their errors. They do not see though they have eyes to see (cf. already the descriptions in Isaiah 6:9-10 and 29:10-12 as well as the quotation in Romans 11:8). The veil in front of their sight will be taken away only if they turn to their Lord (v. 16). He is Yahweh who reveals himself in Christ. Moses encountered him at Sinai given that theological Christology and Christological theology blend together (cf. 2 Corinthians 4:4 and 6: "the glory of Christ" who is the image of God and "the glory of God" that shines in the face of Christ).[86] As "Moses is read" (ἀναγινώσκηται), he is literally "recognized" or "known again" (ἀναγινώσκω) through that reading, explicitly in consequence of the apostolic preaching. In a sense, his face is showing up from behind the veil. The true meaning of this text is thus exposed with the emphasis on the messianic interpretation of

---

acknowledges that it conceals the truth about the revelation at Mount Sinai, which is also the event of the text's own origin: and what it conceals is the fact that the definitive, unsurpassable manifestation of the divine glory is to be found not at Mount Sinai but elsewhere." In fact, Paul reads Exodus 34 with no sense of "a problematic feature of the scriptural text itself" (as already shown). For his interpretation, see below as well.

[84] Here, the precise literal structure of 2 Corinthians 3 allows to overcome interpretative problems and difficulties in the text. See my tentative suggestion in chapter 3.

[85] For the structural similarity between v. 14b and vv. 15-16, see chapter 3 above.

[86] See above, chapter 4. As told there, the one who turns to the Lord is in the first place Moses. However, he functions as a model for everyone who puts his trust in Yahweh. In the end, it is all about a religious conversion.

Scripture. Therefore, unbelief and distrust arise from inside out. In other words, they result from the veil covering the hearts of the Jews.[87] Therein lies the reason for their failure. It was foretold or prefigured in their own writings long ago.[88]

Turning to the Lord

Next, Paul more accurately explains his Old Testament quotation in v. 16. He particularly expands on two theological issues in v. 17. The focus first lies on the identity of the Lord, and second on the outcome of a personal communion with him. Since the entire argumentation is very dense and compact, it is indeed no simple task to find out the true meaning of the text.

Most obviously, Paul draws the subject of v. 17 from his preceding quotation of Exodus 34:34. Hence, the Lord equals Yahweh Sabaoth in the reading of the Old Testament history. In the New Testament context, the subject remains the same but receives a further innovative dimension in terms of a messianic identification of the Lord with Christ (see above). In addition, the pneumatological identification of the Lord with the Spirit stands out. Paul explicitly writes: "The Lord is the Spirit." In his use of language, "is" is "is" without any restrictions, alterations, or modifications. Accordingly, the trinitarian structure of his *theology* crystallizes in a brief and brilliant manner here: The Lord is Yahweh who is represented by Christ and embodied in him and who is present and operative through his Holy Spirit in love and truth.[89] Yet, the identification of the three persons is

---

[87] See above, chapter 4.

[88] *Pace* Belleville 1992, 241-241. To a certain extent, she tries to minimize the absolute mysterious character of Scripture and/or the total human depravity in spiritual matters. She asserts: "The veil, then, would not completely conceal or mask the gospel realities, and the diligent observer could penetrate the veiling."

[89] *Pace* Bauckham 2008, 187 n 10. According to him, "3:17 means that in this case, uniquely, Paul took the *kurios* of the text (Exod. 34:34) to be the Spirit, not Christ." However, the linguistic interplay of multiplicity of the language in 2 Corinthians 3 (see above, chapter 4) rather speaks for a "fusion" of subjects in vv. 16-17. Accordingly, the Lord originally stands for Yahweh Sabaoth but simultaneously represents Christ and appears as the Spirit. All divine persons

evidently not absolute. Paul differentiates between God and Christ as he speaks of God's glory and Christ's glory in 2 Corinthians 4:4, 6 but does not regard them as different forms or categories of the celestial shine (see above).[90] Similarly, he distinguishes between the Lord and the Spirit as he speaks of "the Spirit of the Lord" in 2 Corinthians 3:17 but does not regard them as essentially distinctive persons.[91] It follows that the unity and diversity in deity are in force at the same time.[92]

---

are intertwined without being mixed together. For certain, Bauckham himself finds a similar multiplicity in Pauline theology. In his very insightful analyses of the data, he (ibid., 191) later underlines: "But it is equally significant that he [Paul] clearly does not simply equate YHWH with Christ, but can take the divine name to designate either God or Christ, occasionally even in the same text cited on different occasions (Rom. 11:34; 1 Cor. 2:16; Isa. 40:13)." Cf. also Romans 8:9-17 where the Spirit, the Spirit of God, the Spirit of Christ, God and Christ are interchangeable but surely not reduced to one person only. Cf. further the discussion in Stockhausen 1989, 9-10 against my own interpretation.

[90] For the parallel expressions of 2 Corinthians 4:4 and 6, see, e.g., Savage 2004, 127-129.

[91] Cf. 2 Corinthians 3:3-4 where the work of the *Spirit* leads to "confidence . . . through *Christ* before (or toward) *God*" (see Philpot 2013b, 162), or alternatively, 2 Corinthians 3:3 where "the letter of (or from) *Christ*" is written "with the *Spirit* of the living *God*" (see Schneider 1953, 192). *Contra* Hermann (1961, *passim*) who artificially argues for an identification of Kyrios and Pneuma in Christian experience but not in divine substance. His interpretation of v. 17a is only functional (ibid., 28-31, 49-57). Similarly, Dunn 1970, 319. However, he then asserts: "This does not mean that they are identical in all their functions (far less their 'beings'), as though, for example, the Spirit had been crucified and raised from the dead. It only means that they are identical in experience." In reference to Hermann (1961), see also Friesen 1971, 73 and 135.

[92] Cf. Seifrid 2014, 175. Contra Belleville 1992, 256-267. After a quite lengthy analysis, she concludes: "This means that Paul need not be construing κύριος in v. 17a in any personal sense. It is merely a term [!?] in his text that finds its meaning and application in his contemporary situation." *Pace* Martin 1986, 71 as well. He writes: The Spirit "is usually taken as the Holy Spirit, but it is a case of his dynamic action rather than the person of the Spirit that is in view." In my understanding, his quite unusual interpretation derives from his analysis that the copulative ἐστιν should be "treated as the exegetical *significat*" ('it represents') in the phrase: "The Lord is the Spirit" (ibid.).

The Lord and the freedom

Remarkably, the ensuing result of the presence of God's Spirit amounts to freedom. A wide series of meanings arises in the overall context through numerous allusions and associations. The Old Testament setting revolves around the book of Exodus. Therefore, the factual rescue from the slavery in Egypt shimmers in the background. Equally, the removal of the veil indicates another kind freedom. At the same time, it suggests an upheaval of blockades to spiritual understanding. Further, it implies release from sin, death, and condemnation (vv. 7-11). In addition, the free entrance into the celestial bliss gains attention. At that time, the saved will behold the glory of the Lord "with unveiled faces." Already at the present, they experience something of that marvelous splendor in advance as they are transformed "from glory to glory" (v. 18).[93]

Accordingly, there are several elements in freedom. At any rate, it originates from the Spirit and is carried out in the realm of glory that manifests the divine mercy and reaches the final culmination in the eternal consummation. The whole train of thought resembles the argumentation in Romans 8. Here, Paul speaks of "the glory that shall be revealed to us." Literally, he speaks of "the glory that shall be uncovered in us" (v. 18: ἡ μέλλουσα δόξα ἀποκαλυφθῆναι εἰς ἡμᾶς). He also adds that the eager expectation of the creation is awaiting "the revelation (or the uncovering) of the sons of God" (v. 19: ἡ ἀποκάλυψις τῶν υἱῶν τοῦ Θεοῦ). At that time, "the creation itself shall be set free from the bondage to decay into the freedom of the glory (inexactly: the glorious freedom[94]) of the children of God" (v. 21: αὐτὴ ἡ κτίσις ἐλευθερωθήσεται ἀπὸ τῆς δουλείας τῆς φθορᾶς εἰς τὴν ἐλευθερίαν τῆς δόξης τῶν τέκνων τοῦ Θεοῦ). The future freedom in the celestial glory will come to pass due to the Spirit who works out the transformation even in the midst of the present tribulations and sufferings (vv. 14-25). Already now, the divine

---

[93] See above, chapters 3 and 4.

[94] Freedom that has its origin in the Spirit reigns in the sphere of glory, already now in consequence of the apostolic ministry that is encompassed by the divine glory, and finally in full measure as the heavenly glory will be manifested on the last day. The translation "the glorious freedom" (see, e.g., NIV) misses the point.

glory concerns all those whom God has justified and, therefore, "also glorified" (v. 30: ἐδόξασεν).[95] It really seems that Paul in Romans 8 elaborates his teaching in 2 Corinthians 2:14-4:6 where he combines the glory of the Lord with his proclamation of the gospel in a hostile environment and looks forward to the visible fulfillment (or the unveiling) of it first on the last day. In his theology, both texts ultimately explain each other.

Similarly, Galatians 4:21-31 bears more than a passing resemblance to the main lines in 2 Corinthians 3. In both cases, there are two covenants that stand in opposition to each other. The latter chapter speaks of the old and new covenant. The former passage talks about Hagar and Sarah as they personify and represent the Sinaitic covenant respectively the promise to Abraham that has been fulfilled in Christ and become an everlasting covenant. In contrast to Hagar, the slave woman, who brings forth her children in and into slavery, Sarah is the free woman who brings forth her children in and into freedom. In addition, they embody the present Jerusalem under the yoke of the law respectively the heavenly Jerusalem that lives a life in divine presence (given the assumption of the celestial glory). The shift from the subservient condition to the privileged position and preferential status is accomplished by the Spirit of God who indwells Christians (Galatiansl 4:1-7). They have received him as they put their faith in the message of the gospel they heard (Galatians 3:1-5). That involves the removal of all obstacles to true understanding.[96]

Thus, the texts in Romans and Galatians corroborate and substantiate the meaning of ἐλευθερία in 2 Corinthians 3:17. The verse with the emphasis on the Spirit as the guarantee of freedom refers back to the opening of the entire discourse in vv. 3 and 6 with the scriptural allusions to the creative and recreative work of the Spirit in the new covenant as told in Jeremiah 31:31-34 as well as Ezekiel 36-37 (*inclusio*).[97] Paul suggests that the new Christian life with release from every sort of inherent corruption and evil powers does not in the slightest depend on any human efforts and accomplishments. Rather, he concludes that it is solely the result of the divine intervention. His

---

[95] Cf. Thrall 2004, 276.

[96] Cf. Thrall 2004, 275-276. See also Grindheim 2001, 103.

[97] See above, chapters 3-5.

distinctive "localization" of the Spirit and freedom presupposes that no one is innately free, but all are bound.[98] His pessimistic anthropology permeates his line of reasoning from beginning to end.[99]

Moreover, the notion of the Spirit as freedom explains the idea of the Spirit as contrast to the "letter" since 2 Corinthians 3:17 in terms of *inclusio* obviously bears upon v. 6. The "letter" that "was engraved in letters on stone" (v. 7) is for understandable reasons anything but "freedom." Definitely, it is precisely fixed and sternly restricted. It does not make provision for discretion. What it describes, is indeed inscribed, prescribed, and circumscribed on the stone tablets. No luxury of choice. The impetus of that aspect to the interpretation of the "letter" calls for more attention, but meanwhile the question has to be postponed to the next chapter.

Beholding the Lord

To end with, v. 18 extends more an in depth one characteristic of freedom. It speaks of beholding the Lord "with unveiled faces" or without the veil that covers the hearts of the unbelieving Jews (v. 15). In his time, Moses was the only one who saw God's glory. No one else was like him, but that is different now. In the new covenant, *all* Christians (ἡμεῖς δὲ πάντες) behold the Lord's glory. In fact, they see the superabundant glory in Christ that exceeds the glory of the previous theophanies. In the overall context, they are related to Moses and, just as he himself, are opposed to the Israelites. Thus, the point of comparison is neither Moses nor the Israelites but both of them.[100]

---

[98] Seifrid 2014, 176: "Here, for the only time in the letter, Paul describes salvation as *freedom*, which necessarily finds its definition in opposition to slavery to condemnation and death, as is clear in Paul's use of this metaphor in his other letters, especially Galatians and Romans. His 'localization' of the Spirit and freedom presupposes that the human being is *not* inherently free, but bound." He further adds that "the freedom of the Spirit is a freedom of hearing and responding to God." Yet, it "is not limited to exchange and communication with God but extends to communication with our neighbor" (ibid., 177).

[99] For Paul's pessimistic anthropology, see Laato 1991, 1995, 2004, 2008, 2019.

[100] *Pace* Thrall 2004, 282-283. She writes that Christians should not be contrasted with Israelites. In that case, "one would expect their hearts, rather than

The object of beholding is "the glory of the Lord" that in view of vv. 16-17 denotes the Old Testament glory of Yahweh that amounts to the splendor of Jesus Christ that shines in the gospel through the presence of the Spirit.[101] For sure, the divine "trinitarian" structure of seeing has an intense impact on those who see. Literally, they are being transformed "from glory to glory" (ἀπὸ δόξης εἰς δόξαν). The present tense of the verb (μεταμορφούμεθα) expresses the idea of a continuing event. The focus obviously lies on the gradual and progressive movement.[102] In vv. 7-11, Paul has already spoken of the glory in the new covenant that exceeds the glory in the old covenant. Then, he asserts that the preceding glory has no glory at all in comparison with the current surpassing glory. Now, he further adds that the transformation continues and increases "from glory to glory" until it will be completed in the most splendid glory in eternity.[103] At

---

their faces, to be unveiled." Quite the reverse, "they are contrasted with Moses, who both veiled and unveiled his face" (ibid., 283). At any rate, Moses is contrasted with the Israelites. Therefore, Christians are likewise contrasted with them. Admittedly, faith enables believers to behold God's glory. They see it just like Moses did. In that sense, they are not *contrasted* with him but follow his example. On the other hand, Belleville supposes that "we all" (ἡμεῖς δὲ πάντες) should denote "all true gospel ministers" (1992, 276). Her suggestion does not convince. It appears inevitable to conclude that "we all" are truly "we all Christians." Paul speaks of himself and Christians in a context where he relates their current situation to that of Moses and the Israelites. Belleville knows perfectly well the exceptional peculiarity of her reading: "Virtually all modern commentators maintain that by ἡμεῖς πάντες Paul is broadening his reference to include all believers." See ibid., 275. Rightly, e.g., Lambrecht 1983, 347-348.

[101] See above.

[102] *Pace* Seifrid 2014, 183-186. Correctly, he concludes: "The glory of the crucified Christ is nothing other than the glory of the eschaton, which has broken into the present age. The transformation it brings is the projection of the eschaton into the present, fallen world." However, it does not follow from that argumentation that every thought of progress really loses relevance. The crucified Christ "was raised up from the dead by the glory of the Father" and, therefore, Christians should "walk in newness of life" (Romans 6:4). Indeed, they should "work out" but not "work for" their own salvation. See Philippians 2:12.

[103] Cf. Kim 1981, 236. On the basis of some Rabbinic sources, he first affirms that "the image of God (or some aspects of it) which had been lost or reduced in mankind through Adam's fall" was restored to Israel through "the revelation

that moment, Christians will receive and put on the "body of glory" (Philippians 3:21) that initiates the last phase of their transformation. Surprisingly, the differences in their glory still seem to endure in heaven as well (cf. 1 Corinthians 15:40-41)!

The Spirit who enables the transformation through beholding the glory of the Lord reaches toward the goal for the inner change and development as he presides and pursues the whole process or progress into "the same image" (τὴν αὐτὴν εἰκόνα). It is, however, not immediately evident what the peculiar Greek expression involves. What does it refer to? There is no preceding mention of the "image" and the like in the text. The verb κατοπτρίζομαι contains within itself the idea of a reflecting mirror (and mirror-image). It stands for "beholding in a mirror." Therefore, "the same image" comprises what is seen in the looking glass, a piece of polished brass for which the ancient Corinth was so famous.[104] In addition, the "image" and "glory" are often synonymous or closely related terms. The apostle juxtaposes "the image of God" and "the glory of Christ" (2 Corinthians 4:4) just as he, on the other hand, locates "the glory of God in the face of Christ" (2 Corinthians 4:6).[105] It follows that Christians who behold the glory of the Lord are being transformed into "the same image" they see in him or in his face in the light of his glory. For certain, they are not changed into "the same image as each other," even less into "carbon copies of one another."[106] Here, every modern mode of social gospel fails to carry conviction as a primary meaning of an antique writing.

---

of the law," though "she later lost it again through sin." Then, he concludes that this kind of reasoning is "to be compared with Paul's idea of the believer's transformation into the image of Christ" in v. 18 (ibid.).

[104] See especially Thrall 2004, 285. Similarly, Johansson 1990, 86. Cf. also Belleville 1992, 299.

[105] In 1 Corinthians 11:7, the man is at the same time "the image and glory of God." In Romans 1:23, the sinners "exchanged the glory of the immortal God for the likeness of the image of mortal man." In Romans 8:29-30, those whom God predestinated to be conformed to the image of God, he also has glorified. See Johansson 1990, 86. Cf. Thrall 2004, 285. For a more cautious interpretation, see Seifrid 2014, 184 n 309.

[106] Contra Belleville 1992, 290. Rightly, Guthrie 2015, 228. See also Thrall 2004, 285 n 669: "There is no reason, in the context, to emphasize that the process of transformation is identical for each believer."

As already taken into consideration, an intentional ambiguity might unfold in v. 18. The verb κατοπτρίζομαι does not only entail "to behold in a mirror" but also "to reflect as a mirror." In that case, Christians first behold the Lord's glory, and then, they reflect his glory just as Moses did in the past. The two aspects belong together, whether or not they coalesce here. As to their theological content, they are combined in 2 Corinthians 3 (as well as in other Pauline letters).[107]

In the end, Paul repeats his crucial argument that the transformation takes place due to the activity of the trinitarian God (καθάπερ ἀπὸ κυρίου πνεύματος): the Lord, Yahweh Sabaoth, who is incorporated in Christ and identified with the Spirit, makes the big difference. He alone is able to enable vivification.[108] The theological conclusion harks back to v. 6. It expands on the life-giving power of the Spirit.

---

[107] See above, chapter 4. For the interaction between "indicative" and "imperative" (grace and works) in Pauline theology generally, see, e.g., Laato 1995, 155-162 and 2018, 167-176. Cf. LXX Exodus 33:16 where Moses supplicates God earnestly and asks him to go along with Israel. Then, they shall be *glorified* above all the nations that are on the earth: καὶ πῶς γνωστὸν ἔσται ἀληθῶς ὅτι εὕρηκα χάριν παρὰ σοί, ἐγώ τε καὶ ὁ λαός σου, ἀλλ᾽ ἢ συμπορευομένου σου μεθ᾽ ἡμῶν; καὶ ἐνδοξασθήσομαι ἐγώ τε καὶ ὁ λαός σου παρὰ πάντα τὰ ἔθνη, ὅσα ἐπὶ τῆς γῆς ἐστιν. In other words, God first reveals his gracious glory to Moses. In consequence, Moses and Israelites show or reflect that glory to other people.

[108] For the different interpretations of the Greek expression καθάπερ ἀπὸ κυρίου πνεύματος, see in particular Thrall 2004, 287. Belleville (1992, 293-294) summarizes the various options very succinctly: "Some claim that the exact meaning of the phrase καθάπερ ἀπὸ κυρίου πνεύματος is in doubt. The primary difficulty is in determining the relationship between κυρίου and πνεύματος. Older commentators [especially Church Fathers] and versions tended to take πνεύματος as the subject. A few today still invert the word order but understand κυρίου in an adjectival sense: 'the Spirit who is sovereign'. The majority of recent interpreters, however, follow the given word order and take κυρίου as the subject. Those that do gravitate toward one of several solutions. Some construe the genitive as possessive, 'the Lord of the Spirit', or subjective, 'the Lord who sends the Spirit'. Others take πνεύματος in a qualitative sense: 'the Lord who is spirit', or 'the Lord who is Spirit'. The large majority support an appositional relationship, 'the Lord, that is, the Spirit'." Here, suffice it to say that ἀπὸ κυρίου πνεύματος resumes the thought of v. 17: "The Lord is the

Summary

On the whole, v. 18 sums up the main points in chapter 3:

1) The *glory* of the Lord relates to his gracious benevolence in forgiving sins.
2) To behold the glory of the Lord with *unveiled* faces denotes the outcome of conversion, the act of putting one's trust in his mercy.
3) The Lord as the *Spirit* effects the transformation through faith.

In view of the three main points in chapter 3, the "letter" (v. 6) apparently fails in every respect. It forms the harsh contrast by killing and convicting (v. 7: "the ministry of death" and v. 9: "the ministry of condemnation"). Besides, it does not evoke any freedom (v. 17) but slavery. In short, it represents the opposite of what the Spirit stands for and brings forth. Hence, the argumentation so far cogently leads to a more in depth analysis of the content and meaning of the "letter" in Pauline theology (the question of the following inquiry) since, figuratively, black is seen better on the white background.

Spirit." Cf. for instance Seifrid 2014, 186: "Out of the various possibilities, it is most likely that Paul speaks of 'the Lord who is the Spirit.'"

7

The antithesis
of the "letter" and the "Spirit"

Basic outlines

Following the reading of 2 Corinthians 3 thus far, the "letter" (γράμμα) in contrast to the "Spirit" obviously stands for the Mosaic legislation that was "inscribed" (ἐνγεγραμμένη) "on the tables of stone" (ἐν πλαξὶν λιθίναις) in v. 3 or "engraved in letters on stone" (ἐν γράμμασιν ἐντετυπωμένη λίθοις) in v. 7 (cf. Exodus 24:12, 31:18, 34:1; Deuteronomy 9:10-11). On the other hand, there is no talk of the law *per se* in the entire chapter, nor, for that matter, in the letter as a whole. Besides, Paul nowhere takes up the question of the works of the law. Neither does he mention Jewish rules for circumcision, temple festivals, and kosher food (cf. Galatians).[1] Apparently, his appeal to the account of Exodus 32-34 does not serve to ward off the threat of Judaizing. His adversaries are not promoting that kind of excessive adherence to the Mosaic law. Those who wish to find advocates of legalistic casuistry or rationalization in the Corinthian correspondence must read them into the text.[2]

---

[1] Seifrid 2014, 98. Paul once refers to "lawlessness" (ἀνομία) in 6:14. In his first letter to the Corinthians, he briefly and secondarily deals with the question of circumcision. For the interpretation of 1 Corinthians 7:19, see below.

[2] Seifrid 2014, 102 (cf. also161). He maintains: "[. . .] Paul finds the defining pattern of Christian experience in the story of Moses, the exodus, and Israel's sojourn in the wilderness (1 Cor 10:1-13). We need not suppose, then, that Paul's appeal to the story of Moses in 2 Cor 3 is directed against adversaries

1 Corinthians 7:19—Galatians 5:6—
Galatians 6:15—2 Corinthians 5:17

It follows that the exact meaning of the "letter" merges into the wide-ranging understanding of the law in Pauline theology. Hence, a more in depth analysis of the data is needed. A good place to start is 1 Corinthians 7:19. The verse speaks of circumcision and uncircumcision along with keeping God's commandments. In addition, it resembles two other verses in Galatians where the freedom from the Mosaic law deserves much attention. No doubt, the three passages explain each other:

> 1 Corinthians 7:19 ἡ περιτομὴ οὐδέν ἐστιν καὶ ἡ ἀκροβυστία οὐδέν ἐστιν, ἀλλὰ τήρησις ἐντολῶν θεοῦ.
> Circumcision is nothing and uncircumcision is nothing. Keeping God's commands is what counts.
> Galatians 5:6 ἐν γὰρ Χριστῷ Ἰησοῦ οὔτε περιτομή τι ἰσχύει οὔτε ἀκροβυστία
> ἀλλὰ πίστις δι' ἀγάπης ἐνεργουμένη.
> For in Christ Jesus neither circumcision nor uncircumcision has any value. The only thing that counts is faith expressing itself through love.
> Galatians 6:15 οὔτε γὰρ περιτομή τί ἐστιν οὔτε ἀκροβυστία ἀλλὰ καινὴ κτίσις.
> Neither circumcision nor uncircumcision means anything; what counts is the new creation.

It very much looks that the three equivalent indications that really count in Christian life make use of different words for the same thing. Thus, keeping God's commands comes into effect in faith that expresses itself through love as evidence that the new creation has already taken place. Then, it does not matter if that person is circumcised or not. He is, nevertheless, the one who proves himself to be a true believer.[3]

---

promoting Judaizing, nor even against the apostolic claimants who have made their way to Corinth." Rather, "Paul sets forth the apostolic mission as he finds it in Scripture and directs this exposition to the Corinthians" (ibid., 107-108).

[3] The similarity between 1 Corinthians 7:19, Galatians 5:6 and 6:15 has been widely accounted for in several commentaries. See, e.g., Gardner 2018, 327 and Garland 2003, 305.

Further, it is worth noticing that the three passages, taken as a whole, corroborate and demonstrate the fulfillment of Jeremiah 31:31-34 and Ezekiel 36:26-27 (combined with chapter 37), the two fundamental Old Testament prophecies concerning the inauguration of the new covenant that lie beneath 2 Corinthians 3. As shown, God's law and commandments will be written on the hearts of the Israelites. They will know and love him. They will be recreated, resuscitated, or revivified and enjoy a new life by the power of his Spirit. Here, the "letter" avails nothing (but death).[4]

Besides, the words that are added at the outset of Galatians 5:6 (ἐν γὰρ Χριστῷ Ἰησοῦ) and at the end of Galatians 6:15 (καινὴ κτίσις) assert the core of 2 Corinthians 5:17: εἴ τις ἐν Χριστῷ, καινὴ κτίσις. "If anyone is in Christ, he is a new creation." Accordingly, the verse refers back to the prophecies of Ezekiel. At the same time, it relates to 2 Corinthians 3 where the main focus lies on the activity of the Spirit in resuscitation of all converts. In addition, there are many other traits in the context of 2 Corinthians 5:17 that resume some central lines of thought from the previous disapproval of the adherence to the "letter." The most important ones are as follows:

1) Paul denies once again that he is trying to commend himself to the Corinthians (3:1, 5:12).

2) He speaks of his ministry of the Spirit or righteousness (3:8-9), respectively, his ministry of reconciliation (5:18) that brings forth righteousness (5:21).

3) He strives to ensure that people know Christ or what Christ has accomplished in the congregation (the verb γινώσκω in 3:2 and 5:16).

4) Paul's competence in his apostolic ministry; his "everything" truly comes from God (ἐκ τοῦ θεοῦ in 3:5 and 5:18).

5) He emphasizes that the old covenant (ἡ παλαιὰ διαθήκη in 3:14) has become obsolete; it has been replaced by the new covenant (ἡ καινὴ διαθήκη in 3:6). In other words,

---

[4] See above, chapter 5. That kind of specific Old Testament background is overlooked (or maybe taken for granted) as a common denominator between 1 Corinthians 7:19, Galatians 5:6 and 6:15 in many commentaries.

he underscores that "the old (τὰ ἀρχαῖα) has gone, the new (καινά) has come" (5:17).

6) In his apostolic ministry, he promotes mission among the Jews (chapter 3) as well as in the world (chapter 5).[5]

Strikingly, Paul emphasizes "keeping the commandments of God" while he in the same breath denounces or at least depreciates the absolute necessity of physical circumcision. Indeed, 1 Corinthians 7:19 is "one of the most amazing sentences that he ever wrote."[6] In Galatians, Paul argues similarly. He denigrates the explicit requirement for physical circumcision in 5:6 and 6:15. Still, in 5:14, he indicates that the one who loves has fulfilled the law. But once again, he "does not explain *how* one who does not accept circumcision can fulfill the entire law." He simply asserts his own opinion.[7] Accordingly, more light is to be shed on that kind of discrepancy.

Romans 2:26-29

Interestingly, Paul devalues the "outer" and "fleshly" circumcision in Romans 2:26-29 as well. Nonetheless, he speaks of "following the requirements of the law" (τὰ δικαιώματα τοῦ νόμου φυλάσσειν) in v. 26 or "keeping the law" (τὸν νόμον τέλειν) in v. 27. His use of language resembles what he has written in 1 Corinthians 7:19

---

[5] To be sure, the comparison between 2 Corinthians 3 and 5 could be drawn out much more. However, here it is sufficient to detect a close correlation between the two chapters. In general, the commentaries fail to deal more thoroughly with the obvious shared features that integrate 2 Corinthians 3 and 5 into a meaningful whole.

[6] Sanders 1983, 103. Correctly, Gardner (2018, 327) underscores in regard to the phrase "keeping the commandments of God" (1 Corinthians 7:19) that such or similar phrases "were used in the Pentateuch to refer broadly to the commands God gave the Israelites" or "in the Psalms to refer to the whole Mosaic law." Further, he considers that "many argue this cannot be Paul's intention here." It would imply something like: Circumcision (a prominent part of the commandments) "does not count but keeping the commandments does." To overcome the problem, see below.

[7] Sanders 1983, 97.

regarding "keeping the commandments of God" (τήρησις ἐντολῶν θεοῦ).[8] Additionally, he resumes the concept of "letter" and disqualifies every form of religious engagement or involvement on that basis. Accordingly, circumcision in "letter" avails nothing (v. 29). The one who transgresses the law suffers the harsh consequences from his wickedness despite his potential adherence to the "letter and circumcision" (v. 27). Further, it appears that the law's external "embodiment of knowledge and truth" (ἡ μόρφωσις τῆς γνώσεως καὶ τῆς ἀληθείας ἐν τῷ νόμῳ) introduces or substantiates the reason for the ultimate inadequacy of the "letter" (v. 20). It only remains on the superficial level.[9]

On the other hand, a true circumcision amounts to the circumcision of the heart. It comes about by the power of God's Spirit who prompts his creative work in the innermost of mortals. His divine activity or action forms and shapes a real Jew "inside" (ὁ ἐν τῷ κρυπτῷ Ἰουδαῖος) who fulfills the law and keeps the commandments (Romans 2:28-29). Once again, both Jeremiah 31:31-34 and Ezekiel 36:26-27 are echoed here as in 2 Corinthians 3.[10] The new

---

[8] *Pace* Grindheim 2001, 100-101. He writes about "keeping the law" by some Gentiles in Romans 2:29: "This is not an ability to keep the Mosaic law as such, however, as is seen from the fact that the Gentiles in question are uncircumcised in flesh (v. 27), contrary to the requirements of the Mosaic law." Nevertheless, Paul *does* say that the Gentiles indeed fulfill the law in conformity with the Torah (notwithstanding that they are uncircumcised). That is exactly his point! More for this, see below. In consequence, Schreiner (1998, 139) fails to carry conviction with his following (in itself logical) conclusion: "Since the Gentiles keep the law apart from circumcision, the text implies that the Gentiles keep the moral norms of the law." Similarly, Dunn 1988, 122, 127-128. The sharp line of reasoning here is ultimately not the one that Paul allegedly takes for granted in Romans. No, he simply thinks differently—and even much more effectively.

[9] The exact meaning of ἡ μόρφωσις has been much discussed. Paul follows the usage of *koine* ("embodiment" resp. "expression") rather than that of classical Greek ("summary" resp. "structure"). Apparently, he draws on "existing formulations taken from the Diaspora synagogue." See, e.g., Käsemann 1980, 70-71. At any rate, it should be taken much better into account that the ultimate inadequacy of the "letter" in v. 29 correlates with the external "embodiment of knowledge and truth" of the law in v. 20. See below.

[10] No doubt, πνεῦμα in Romans 2:29 refers to God's Spirit (and not human spirit). See, e.g., Schreiner 1998, 143.

covenant ushers in a fresh start, a different set of circumstances on account of Christian faith. Now the law is written on the human hearts by the Spirit who initiates the change of times.[11]

Philippians 3:3

In concert with Romans 2:26-29, Philippians 3:3 points the argument in the direction intended by Paul. Even if he, as expected, rejects the necessity of physical circumcision, he still maintains that Christians do not fail in their sober commitment to fulfill the law. Rather, he proclaims that they are the ones who "are the circumcised" (ἡ περιτομή, literally: "the circumcision"). They "serve God by his Spirit" (or simply: "serve by God's Spirit") as they "boast in Christ Jesus" and "put no confidence in the flesh" (καυχώμενοι ἐν Χριστῷ Ἰησοῦ καὶ οὐκ ἐν σαρκὶ πεποιθότες). In other words, Philippians 3:3 nicely harmonizes with 1 Corinthians 7:19. Christians who are physically uncircumcised are truly circumcised since their service of God comes about as a result of his Spirit. They keep his commandments under that condition.[12]

On closer examination, it seems that Paul does not only deal with the question of circumcision but more broadly of the Jewish cult or religious practice. He speaks of those who are "serving by God's Spirit" (οἱ πνεύματι θεοῦ λατρεύοντες). The Greek verb λατρεύω means "to render holy service and homage" or "to worship."[13] It surely stands for

---

[11] *Pace* Seifrid 2014, 117. He writes on 2 Corinthians 3:3 like this: "Yet in contrast to Jeremiah 31:33, Paul does not speak of the Law being written on the heart. It is Christ, the Law's goal (*telos*), who is written there (v. 13; cf. Romans 10:4)." However, Seifrid later on *does* speak of "the Law being written on the heart" in the new covenant (ibid., 121-123). He rightly demonstrates the different character of that writing from the writing on tablets of stone in the old covenant. Since Christ has already fulfilled the whole law, he brings with and within himself the law he has fulfilled for sinners. In a sense, he represents and embodies God's everlasting will. For that very reason, he is called the Savior of the world. Simply put: On the cross, he is for us. By our faith, he is in us. In our loving care for each other, he is through us. Hence, it follows that "the law being written on the heart" stands for Christ living in Christians. For the fulfillment of the law in love, see below.

[12] See already Laato 2021, 83-84.

[13] Bauer 2000, *s.v.* λατρεύω.

the temple worship in Jerusalem (λατρεία), one of the benefits Israel at that time possessed (Romans 9:4). Since Christians are the only ones who are "serving by God's Spirit," they, in contrast to the priests in the sanctuary, really inaugurate a divine ceremony and perform a celestial ritual in the midst of their ordinary circumstances as they willingly live up to their faith. As a consequence, they also fulfill the cultic aspects (alongside the festal calendar) of the law without being involved in any sacerdotal incumbencies in Jerusalem.[14]

Philippians 2:17

In Philippians 2:17, Paul sets himself as an extreme example of his most radical fulfillment of the sacrificial liturgy. He speaks of his own death and refers to his blood as a drink offering which will finally be poured out on the sacrifice (σπένδομαι ἐπὶ τῇ θυσίᾳ) as his body has been slaughtered by the Roman authorities! Here, he explicitly comments on his "temple service" (λειτουργία) for the Philippians and in their place. As it were, he functions as their "liturgist" since they have so generously supported and sponsored his missionary journeys (4:10-20).[15] Their donations are distinguished in sacrificial language as well. Their gifts are characterized as "an odor of a sweet smell, an acceptable sacrifice, well-pleasing to God" (v. 18: ὀσμὴ εὐωδίας, θυσία δεκτή, εὐάρεστος τῷ Θεῷ). Consequently, they have made financial sacrifices whereas their apostle shows his willingness to offer himself as a living sacrifice *in persona*.[16]

Romans 12:1-2

Also in Romans, the question of true circumcision (2:25-29) easily widens into the broad question of fulfilling the cultic aspects of the

---

[14] Laato 2021, 83-84.

[15] Ibid., 83.

[16] In 2 Corinthians 2:14-16, Paul makes use of a similar terminology with regard to his own apostolic activity as in Philippians 4:18 pertaining to the Christian charity of the Philippians (ὀσμὴ εὐωδίας). Cf. Balla 2007, 754 in reference to Martin 1986, 45.

law (12:1-2). Paul encourages Christians to offer their bodies as "living sacrifices, holy and pleasing to God" (θυσία ζῶσα ἁγία εὐάρεστος τῷ θεῷ). He characterizes that kind of their daily devotion as their "spiritual (or reasonable) worship" (ἡ λογικὴ λατρεία, v. 1). Once more, his use of language implies a clear conformity to the Jewish temple ceremony or ritual.[17] The Greek words for "holy" (ἁγία) and "pleasing to God" (εὐάρεστος τῷ θεῷ) both recall sacrificial vocabulary (see Philippians 4:18 above).[18] Christians are designated as the priests who offer sacrifices; their bodies are distinguished as the sacrifices that they offer.[19] Briefly, subject and object nicely coincide. Besides, Christians have to undergo a transformation from the inside out in terms of the renewing of their mind (ἀνακαίνωσις τοῦ νοός) and focus their attention on what they do (v. 2). Or else, they are not able to offer themselves to God (cf. 1 Corinthians 13:3). Just as in the Jewish temple liturgy, without the right intention their sacrifices lose the power and they fail to please him.[20] Interestingly, in his Corinthian correspondence Paul speaks of Christians also as "God's temple" (1 Corinthians 3:16) and "the temple of the living God" (2 Corinthians 6:16) or of their bodies as "a temple of the Holy Spirit" (1 Corinthians 6:19). This results in the mind-blowing conclusion that they, on account of his overall theological idea, function as priests who offer their bodies as sacrifices (Romans 12:1-2) in a holy

---

[17] Laato 2021, 83-84.

[18] Thielman 2018, 567-568. Similarly, the verb "offer" (παραστῆσαι) in v. 1 was commonly used of slaughtering animals in religious rituals. For the offerings as "an aroma pleasing to the Lord" in the Old Testament, see, e.g., Lev. 1:9, 13, 17.

[19] Cf. Romans 15:16. There, Paul is the one who offers sacrifices. His offerings are the Gentiles themselves or, alternatively, their ceremonial gifts (such as their obedience, praise, charitable fund raising and collection of money that he is going to bring with himself to Jerusalem). In 1 Cor 9:13-14, the apostolic preachers are compared to the priests "who serve at the altar" and "share in what is offered on the altar," in other words, they "should receive their living from the gospel." As a consequence, subject and object do not coincide. Nevertheless, Romans 15:16 stands in a close relationship with Romans 12:1. Their sacrificial terminology and theology are similar.

[20] See the short summaries of some of the standard works on the Jewish religion in Laato 1991, 16-31 and 1995, 13-25.

place that ultimately is equal to themselves (1 Corinthians 3:16, 6:19, 2 Corinthians 6:16). Sometimes, religious studies are going quite wild!

On the whole, the palpable interrelationship between Romans 1-2 and 12:1-2 has to be accounted for. Gentiles are accused of dishonoring their bodies (ἀτιμάζεσθαι τὰ σώματα αὐτῶν, 1:24). They have worshipped the creature (and created things) instead of the Creator (ἐλάτρευσαν τῇ κτίσει παρὰ τὸν κτίσαντα, 1:25). Since they did not "think it worthwhile" (οὐκ ἐδοκίμασαν) to retain the knowledge of God, he "handed them over to a worthless mind" (εἰς ἀδόκιμον νοῦν, 1:28). Finally, they became entirely depraved (*massa perditionis*). They live an unholy life and are not able to please God (1:24-32). On the other hand, Jews imagine that they truly know God. They open up their minds to his will. They worship him especially in the temple. They are further circumcised with regard to the foreskin of their "body" (male genitalia). Hence, they should be in control of their fleshly lusts. Nonetheless, they still transgress the law and make themselves guilty of heinous sins (cf. 2:17-29, 3:1-3, 9:4-5).[21]

In contrast to both Gentiles and Jews, Christians bring their bodies (τὰ σώματα) as hallowed sacrifices to the one and only God. As his creatures, they continuously render temple service (ἡ λατρεία) to him in their everyday life. They do not display some external ceremonies, but their whole mindset has been transformed (ἀνακαίνωσις τοῦ νοός). It reforms or reshapes their cultic occupation. Therefore, they are able to prove and approve (δοκιμάζειν) what God's will is. They live in harmony with his divine requirements (12:1-2).

Fulfilling the Mosaic law eschatologically in love

Accordingly, the dominion of sin in the pagan world is not broken by the Mosaic law but eschatologically through Christ's salvific death and resurrection in the majestic power of the Spirit. Strictly, the opposite of wrongdoing is not right doing. We all know too well that vices

---

[21] Cf. Thielman 2018, 568-569. He concentrates on the contrasting expressions between Romans 12:1-2 and 1:18-32 but not on the underlying opposition between Romans 12:1-2 and 2:1-29.

cannot simply be replaced by virtues. It never functions like that in practice. Astonishingly, to be "under sin" and to be "under the law" are ultimately synonymous (Romans 6:14). More to the point, the opposite of transgression is the union with Christ and the defeat of all evil's supremacy in him to the max of the subsequent empowering of the Spirit in the new life of Christians. They have died to the law in order to fulfill it in love and charity. Paradoxically, their one step back is their one step forward. Quite clearly, the baptismal parenesis of chapter 6 lies behind the exhortatory composition in 12:1-2. As Christians are advised to offer themselves, respectively, their members to God as weapons of righteousness (6:13, 19), so they are admonished to offer their bodies to God as living sacrifices (12:1). In both texts, the verb is the same (παριστάνω and/or παρίστημι). The object of the verb is similar: in the former case, the persons themselves or their members; in the latter case, their bodies. In other words, the reign of sin in one's life has not been annulled ever since the promulgation of the Mosaic law but on account of the change of rule, commenced in baptism. From then on, Christ exerts total control of Christians and bestows his Spirit in them. Therefore, they are truly transformed.[22]

In everyday life, the fulfillment of the law without a rigorous adherence to every single commandment in the old Sinaitic covenant specifically involves love. It encapsulates the essence of the entire Mosaic legislation. In Romans, a lengthy series of conventional moral exhortations begins with 12:9 and ends with 13:8-10 (leading to some concluding remarks in vv. 11-14). Initially, the common admonishment: "Let love be sincere" functions as the heading for what follows. The resultant lines explain the content of it much more in detail. Finally, the closing phrase: "Love is the fulfilment of the law" summarizes the whole discussion (inclusio).[23] Similarly, Galatians 5:14 avows that "all the law is fulfilled in one command: Love your neighbor as yourself." Equally, the juxtaposition of the three parallel passages of 1 Corinthians 7:19, Galatians 5:6, and 6:15 shows that "keeping

---

[22] See especially Laato 2013, 103, 123-124.

[23] Cf. Moo 2018, 793-795 and 826-834. See especially Wilson who interprets Romans 12:9-21 in depth (1991, 149-199) and draws his conclusion from his exegetical analyses (ebd., 200-212).

God's command" comes to pass only if a new creation has taken place in faith that is active through love.[24] Moreover, Philippians 3:3 asserts the importance of worshipping God by his Spirit instead of promoting the Pharisaic ambition on the law and longing for a faultless righteousness according to the Mosaic standards, consisting of persecuting the church (vv. 5-6). Certainly, it turns out that the difference between the two opposite poles amounts to the contrast between love and hate.[25]

The former more thorough analysis of some basic data in Corinthian correspondence together with a selection of related and relevant passages in other Pauline letters brings forth important and notable insights into the understanding of the Old Testament legislation in the overall context of the apostolic argumentation. In a sense, the several Mosaic commandments are reduced into one single commandment of love. But in actual fact, the rest of the commandments are not simply ignored or disregarded. Rather, they are taken into consideration and transposed into practice with immediate effect. Indeed, the *whole* law is really *fulfilled* in genuine love of neighbor (Romans 13:8-10, Galatians.5:14).[26]

Alternatively, the ambiguous approach to the Old Testament legislation in the context of the apostolic argumentation has been pressed into the diversity between the moral and cultic law. Allegedly, the former remains valid, but the latter has turned out obsolete. The opposite poles of ethics and ritual ceremonies would make the big difference in understanding the contents of permanent and impermanent value. Something of the kind proves prominent and provides much for the traditional differentiation between the two categories in the Christian church. Without doubt, the distinction between the moral and cultic law accounts well for the practical consequences that pertain to the extension of the certain definite parts of the Mosaic legislation into the New Testament period. However, Paul never says that explicitly. Neither does he suggest it. In contrast, he overtly maintains that the prescription of circumcision and the precepts of sacrifices or temple service in

---

[24] See above.

[25] More for Philippians 3:3-9, see Laato 1991, 255-262 and 1995, 202-208.

[26] More for this, see Laato 2004, 357-359.

general are fulfilled by Christians although they do not carry them out exactly to the letter.[27]

The antithesis between the "letter" and the "Spirit"

Taken together, the intention of keeping God's commands (1 Corinthians 7:19) does not result in an overstatement. Paul *does* mean that Christians fulfill the whole law. But he does *not* expect that they fulfill the whole law rigorously or categorically according to the Jewish norms and standards. Jews follow the letter of the Torah. They try to do whatever is prescribed in the Pentateuch merely at the human level. They perform it in their flesh or in terms of outward means but not in the Spirit. Their religious zeal focuses on the literal meaning of the written texts that even call for their unconditional devotion. Therefore, they do not (necessarily) leave out of account inner motives for their good works. They really try to do their very best to do what they should. Nevertheless, their moral efforts largely remain on a position of their own ability and activity. In the final analysis, they absolutely fail to accomplish so much. They do not reach their goal. Paul concludes that Jews absolutely do not comply with the law. He maintains that they transgress it. He denounces them as great sinners like everyone else.[28]

As a consequence, the "letter" seems to denote the literal reading and observing of the law. It does not encompass the characteristics of the new covenant, namely "writing the law on their hearts" (Jeremiah 31:33) and "putting God's Spirit in them" (Ezekiel 36:27). In contrast, it refers back to human capacity and leads to boasting. As a Pharisee, Saul did not "boast in Christ Jesus" but rather about himself. He put his "confidence in the flesh" and did not trust in his Lord (Philippians 3:3-9). In the churches of Galatia, Judaizers likewise boasted about themselves and tried to convince Christians to rely

---

[27] Laato 2009, 216-218 and 2021, 82-84. Cf. also Westerholm 1984, 242-243. In this sense, the cultic and ceremonial aspects have been abrogated for Christians, not in effect but in use.

[28] See especially Laato 1991, 108-119, 212-265 and 1995, 86-95, 169-210. For the common Jewish understanding of human freedom, see Laato 1991, 83-94 and 1995, 67-75. Similarly, e.g., Westerholm 2008.

upon their own flesh in terms of circumcision (Galatians 3:1-5, 5:1-6, 6:12-15). Further, Jews boast about their superiority in comparison with Gentiles and yearn for praise from God. In their vanity, they heavily lean on their obedience to the law even though they transgress his will (Romans 2:17-29). For sure, Saul before his conversion, Judaizers, and Jews in general provide here the warning examples of those who do not fulfill the law.[29]

As already shown, Christians fulfill the whole law in love as they live their life in the Spirit. However, they have not spiritualized their worship into an idealistic sphere of distinct concepts and principles. They offer their *bodies*, instead of sheep or goats, as living sacrifices to God.[30] Likewise, they have circumcised not only a small part of their flesh but, in a sense, their mind and self. They are, so to speak, circumcised in their hearts or in their whole being. They are "a new creation" (2 Corinthians 5:17) and not, for instance, "a new soul" wrapped in or covered by an empty body. Whereas Christ, in Johannine theology, became flesh, it paradoxically seems that the Spirit, in Pauline theology, becomes body. He is embodied in Christians. His in-carnation or, more precisely, in-corporation as his corporeal representation of his divine power in them is their spiritualization or rather their physical Spirit-ualization. Spirit's somatic realization of himself in their existence involves a holistic approach such as their recreation, regeneration, resurrection, or revitalization that presuppose the transformation of their corporate identity. He re-forms them, and they stand firm in his re-formation.[31]

Importantly, the Spirit in contrast to the "letter" (2 Corinthians 3:6) does not solely epitomize questions of ethical values, respectively, virtues. It is about much more. The focus lies on the gospel, the ministry of righteousness (2 Corinthians 3:9). "The letter kills, but the Spirit gives life." The contrast between death and life is as absolute as night and

---

[29] For the Pauline passages, see Laato 1991, 108-119, 216-240, 255-262 and 1995, 86-95, 172-190, 202-208. The Jewish boasting amounts not only to a national pride. It is more about a moral superiority. Cf. Laato 2019.

[30] Laato 2021, 83-84.

[31] Cf. Eastman 2017. She speaks of "corporate identity" or (more often) "participatory identity" (a relational exchange or a close interplay that prevails between social human relations and supra-human realities).

day, dark and light, pitch-black and snow-white. It definitely concerns moral issues but it is not to be reduced to them as such. They simply show *how* to live your life. But they do not amount to the life itself. It stands for the recreation through God's eternal word or for the regeneration by means of faith or for the resurrection together with Christ because of baptism. It is the new mode of existence that the apostolic proclamation of the gospel causes. The Spirit employs—to the exclusion of human merits—the ministry of righteousness to give life. He does not use any other devices to that purpose. "His choice is my chance." For sure, the one who is alive also will live his life in perfect harmony with the Giver of the life. The new life follows from being alive without further ado. Hence, morals or ethics should neither be overlooked nor underestimated. They really need to be accounted for. In any case, they never represent the source of life.[32]

On the whole, the "letter" in 2 Corinthians 3:6 denotes the Mosaic law, especially as a compilation of various legal records that should be read and observed very strictly in punctilious accordance with their literal meaning. It does not call for the pouring out of the Spirit or the divine writing of the Torah on human hearts that will take (or has already taken) place in the new covenant, as written in Jeremiah 31:31-34 and Ezekiel 36:26-27 (see above). More exactly, this comes to pass through the proclamation of the gospel or as a result of "the ministry of righteousness" (2 Corinthians 3:9). The Christian existence does not depend on attempts to work for one's own devout religiosity in severe adherence to the Mosaic law. On the contrary, it harks back to God's stunning and sovereign recreation out of nothing (*ex nihilo*). He makes his light shine on repentant sinners "in the face of Jesus Christ" (2 Corinthians 4:6). He shows his mercy upon them without any merits from their side. Just at that moment, they become alive. Immediately, they also start to live their life and follow the law, not according to the "letter" but explicitly in Spirit. Through his power, they completely fulfill it (including the decree on circumcision and the cultic ordinances). He indeed empowers them. He transforms them. They are "new creatures" (see 2 Corinthians 5:17). Simply put: "The Spirit gives life" (in absolute sense). Therefore, he stands in contrast to the "letter" that kills (2 Corinthians 3:6).

---

[32] More for the new life of Christians, see Laato 2013.

It is worth noticing that the modern distinction between the literal (or verbatim) and non-literal (or metaphorical) meaning has not a lot to offer here. Even less has the differentiation between the conservative and liberal interpretation to bring to the table. No doubt, Paul thinks "outside the box" in a very innovative way. He does believe in the Scriptures. Nowhere does he suggest that they could be annulled (cf. Romans 3:4, 9:6). Quite the opposite, he maintains that *"everything* that was written in the past was written to teach us" (Romans 15:4). That concerns truly everything, for instance the decree on circumcision, the rules for temple service, and the petite principle of "not muzzling the ox while it is threshing the grain" (1 Corinthians 9:9). However, nothing of that should be fulfilled "in flesh" or according to the "letter," but "in Spirit" or through faith that shows itself in love. The two alternatives, the Jewish and the Pauline, exclude each other. Paradoxically, they both represent a word for word reading. We might speak of the "literal-letteral" and "literal-spiritual" study of the Old Testament Scripture.[33] Even if they function on totally different levels, they both are as pragmatic

---

[33] Dunn (2013, 170) holds on to a modern distinction between the literal and non-literal meaning of the biblical texts. He underlines in reference to 1 Corinthians 7:19: "So, Spirit and not letter could mean actually *ignoring and abandoning* the literal meaning of a law." Later, he states (ibid., 171): "The commandments of God are not to be reduced to or confined to the literal meaning, or to doing them at a literal level. And observing God's commandments at the level of heart obedience will mean that the *literal* observance has been relativized and, in some cases, may be *dispensed* with." Further, he underscores: "An understanding of the deeper intention and purpose of scriptural passages could relativize and even set aside the obvious literal meaning and intention of the commandment, of the Scripture." Where, exactly, does Paul assert anything like that? Strictly speaking, he does not "set aside the obvious literal meaning and intention of the commandment" or the Scripture. Quite the reverse, he maintains that through his Christological reading he emphasizes the obvious literal meaning and intention of the commandment or the Scripture. However, he maintains the "literal-spiritual" meaning that is not to be fulfilled "in flesh" but "in Spirit" by faith. Dunn fails to carry conviction since he makes use of a modern and anachronistic distinction between the literal and non-literal interpretation of the Bible. Hence, he does not take the apostolic reading at face value. Cf. also his discussion of "Spirit and Letter Today" (ibid., 175-179). More for 1 Corinthians 7:19, see above.

and realistic. The former exemplifies knowledge that is based on human understanding while the latter epitomizes knowledge that is based on divine understanding. In keeping with his conviction, Paul seems to work on the assumption that since the law is written on the *hearts* in the course of the new covenant it is indeed no longer observed in the *"flesh,"* and since the *Spirit* is poured out in the hearts of Christians their obedience is no more bound to the *"letter"* of the law. As a consequence, it turns out that he succeeds in "Christianizing" his preceding Pharisaic ideal to extend the purity rules of the clergy to pertain to an ordinary person's daily life. His theological persuasion already introduced a sort of universal priesthood in the church.[34]

Romans 7:1-6

In spite of the former comprehensive analysis of the contrast between the "letter" and the "Spirit," it still appears appropriate to prolong the discussion further. In Romans, Paul sheds some more light on their mutual relationship and opposite effect. He underlines the necessity of "being released from the law" (κατηργήθημεν ἀπὸ τοῦ νόμου). Then, he speaks of serving (δουλεύειν) "in newness of the Spirit and not in oldness of the letter" (ἐν καινότητι πνεύματος καὶ οὐ παλαιότητι γράμματος). What does that kind of distinction in 7:6 embrace in the overall context of the chapter?

To begin with, Paul employs an illustration from marriage. He asserts the well-known fact that the law has authority only over living persons. Death severs one's bondage to it. Accordingly, a married woman (literally: "a woman under a husband," ὕπανδρος γυνὴ) "is bound by the law to her husband as long as he lives, but if her husband dies, she is released from the law relating to her husband" and completely free to marry another man with no stigma of becoming an adulteress (vv. 1-3). The illustration leads to an application in v. 4. The first husband designates the law, and the second husband denotes Christ. The woman symbolizes the Christian. However, the question

---

[34] For Paul's understanding of Scripture, cf. Laato 2021, especially 24-25, 29-35, 82-94.

instantly arises: Why does the first husband die in the illustration but the woman in the application "You also died to the law"? To solve the difficult problem, many scholars maintain that the analogy between the illustration and the application should not be pressed too far. In effect, vv. 1-3 make a single point to be drawn upon in v. 4: the death severs relationship to the law.[35] In spite of the wide popularity or recognition of the trivializing interpretation like this, it is hardly true. Paul equally calls attention to the new union that follows death. In addition, he makes use of a similar terminology as he speaks of "becoming joined" to another man (even two times in v. 3: γένηται ἀνδρὶ ἑτέρῳ and γενομένην ἀνδρὶ ἑτέρῳ) or the one who has been raised from the dead (v. 4: γενέσθαι ὑμᾶς ἑτέρῳ, τῷ ἐκ νεκρῶν ἐγερθέντι).[36] Certainly, not all details in the illustration and application necessarily and exactly correspond to each other, but it seems that some prominent proponents of modern exegetics have too easily settled for too little.

As the argumentation moves on, Paul, as already told, affirms that Christians "serve in newness of the Spirit and not in oldness of the letter" (ἐν καινότητι πνεύματος καὶ οὐ παλαιότητι γράμματος). It is preceded by his notion that they have "been released from the law" and died to that in which they "were held captive" (v. 6: κατηργήθημεν ἀπὸ τοῦ νόμου, ἀποθανόντες ἐν ᾧ κατειχόμεθα). Here, he once again repeats that *they* have died to the law. Just for that reason, he emphasizes that they no longer serve in oldness of the letter. As shown, he then suggests that they do not observe the law according to its "literal-letteral" sense, trying to carry out the various rules or instructions in a conventional way "in flesh" as usual in Judaism. Instead, he encourages them to practice their faith in newness of the Spirit. In other words, he maintains that they follow the law according to its "literal-spiritual" sense and fulfill every single commandment "in Spirit" through love. In consequence, the law in its "letteral" form has really been abolished. It has—as it were—died. In Galatians, Paul similarly speaks of the Mosaic law as an edifice that

---

[35] See, e.g., Käsemann 1980, 187. Concisely, he writes: "The only point of comparison is that death dissolves obligations valid throughout life." Similarly, Cranfield 1990, 333-335, Murray 1968, 241-243.

[36] Moo 2018, 439.

has been destroyed and should not be rebuilt. Also there, he immediately writes of himself that *he* has died to the law in order to live to (i.e., for) God (2:18-19).[37] The metaphorical language resembles the illustrative usage in Romans 7:1-6. Both texts show that the law is abrogated. It has died (like a person) or collapsed (like a building). The abolition does not only depend on a salvation-historical change. It assumes a salvation-individual change as well.[38] The law as a "letter" has died when a Christian has died from it! Now, his life as gift does not amount to a correct understanding of the law, even less to doing the works of the law. Rather, it owes its existence to Christ who through his body (i.e., blood and death) has set believers free from the law (Romans 7:4) and to the Spirit who has vivified them through the gospel (7:5-6). From that point on, they fulfill the law not as collectanea of Jewish legislation but as an expression of the new law that has been written on their hearts in accordance with the promises in Jeremiah 31:31-34 and Ezekiel 36:26-27. Hence, it makes sense that the first husband dies in the illustration (Romans 7:1-3) while the wife dies in the application (Romans 7:4) before it becomes clear that the first husband has really passed away. It goes like this in real life. It is not Paul's "fault" that the Christian existence appears exceedingly complicated. He had an impossible task to figure out an illustration that perfectly fits into it. In all probability, he has found the best case in point.

---

[37] Cf., e.g., Martyn 1997, 256. Similarly, Schreiner 2010, 169-171.

[38] *Pace* Moo 2018, 439-448. Currently, the salvation-historical perspective has been often overemphasized. Nonetheless, the salvation-individual perspective should not be underestimated. Both aspects are needed as in Romans 7:1-6. Equally, in Galatians 3:23-25 the coming of Christ and the coming of faith are interrelated. Once, Christ has come in history. But now, he will come through faith. The two approaches do not contradict each other. They are not mutually exclusive options. Additionally, the being under the dominion of sin (v. 22) and under the authority of the law (v. 23) match one to one. Surely, Christ has once and for all atoned the sins of the whole humankind and redeemed them from the curse of the law. Later, he sent his apostles to proclaim the good news: the one who believes is forgiven and free from the law. Cf. further Laato 2004, 358-359.

Romans 7:14

Further forward in Romans 7, Paul develops his argumentation and more indirectly elaborates his understanding of the contrast between the "letter" and the "Spirit." It culminates in his affirmation that "the law is spiritual (πνευματικός)" (v. 14a). The talk about a "spiritual law" sounds quite incredible after the long study of chapters 6 and 7 where the close juxtaposition of the law, sin, flesh, and death prevails. No wonder that it has been discredited as "an irreconcilable contradiction"[39] and "one more blatant self-contradiction."[40] It "is, if anything, even more surprising" than the characterization of the commandment as "holy, righteous and good" (v. 12).[41] Various similar expressions of embarrassment come into sight in academic contexts.[42] In calling the law "spiritual," Paul is often supposed to assert its divine origin and authority.[43] No doubt, he firmly believes all that. The Old Testament abounds in passages where the knowledge and conviction of the holy character of the Torah arise. Nonetheless, the law is never distinguished as "spiritual."[44] Hence, it seems that the distinct meaning of the phrase has not yet been unpacked by simply evoking some self-evident cliches.[45]

---

[39] Räisänen 1983, 45.

[40] Ibid., 153 note 120.

[41] Dunn 1988, 405.

[42] See already, e.g., Nygren 1944, 303-305. Similarly, Longenecker 2016, 661-662.

[43] See, e.g., Moo 2018, 477. A number of commentaries include a similar view.

[44] Ibid.

[45] Cf. Thrall 2004, 235. To begin with, she argues cogently. She maintains that "when the γράμμα-πνεῦμα antithesis occurs in Rom 7.6 it is clear from what follows that it cannot be the law as such that is opposed to the Spirit, since in 7.14 the law itself is described as πνευματικός." She then concludes that "γράμμα is not 'law' pure and simple, but rather the law used in a perverted, i.e., legalistic, way." Here, she (as so many before her) ascribes the killing effect of the law to a *legalistic* misuse of the law. In contrast, Paul speaks of the misuse of the law by sin (Romans 7:11-12). Then, he concludes that through that "sin becomes (not: might become!) utterly sinful" (7:13). Surprisingly, the negative sequence of events has a positive outcome: sin becomes exposed through the law. In a sense, the law has to kill the one who transgresses it, especially if it has been *correctly*

Paul introduces his notion of the spiritual law by saying that "we (Christians) know (οἴδαμεν)" the truth of his statement (v. 14). Already at the outset of the chapter, he asks them if they do "not know (ἀγνοεῖτε)." Next, he addresses them as those who "know (γινώσκουσιν) the law" (v. 1).[46] His whole argumentation aims at the conclusion that the law in its "literal-letteral" form does not concern them any longer. On purpose, he speaks of their new service in the Spirit, in other words, their fulfillment of the law in its "literal-spiritual" sense (v. 6). Persuasively, the law is "spiritual" as to its intent and content. In v. 14a, Paul easily draws his inferences from his theological analysis of the law as he has developed his views not only in vv. 7-13 but also in vv. 1-6. Once again, his line of thought is luminous and brilliant.

The reason why the plain meaning of the "spiritual law" has been ignored and overlooked in mainstream exegetics goes back to the widespread misunderstanding that Romans 7:14-25 describe the non-Christian. What does he know about the Christian reading of the Torah? Why should he care and be concerned about it? Obviously, he does not have what it takes to interrelate and -act with the spiritual law. In another place, I have already shown that "there is nothing in 7:14-25 that does not fit Paul (or any Christian), and everything fits him alone." He is the "I" of the monologue telling his story in very personal terms.[47] Here, the discussion cannot be prolonged. The previous studies should suffice. However, one misapprehension has to be

---

understood. Thrall overlooks the fact that the law (or sin through the law) kills by any reading. In addition, she tries to convince her readers that "γράμμα is not 'law' pure and simple." I think her suggestion fails to carry conviction. To be sure, νόμος and γράμμα are not synonymous. Yet, they both represent the law "pure and simple" but with a nuance of difference. See the analysis below. *Pace* Provence 1982, 64-65 as well. Cf. Kamlah 1954, 277. He underscores: "Es [γράμμα] wird aber nicht völlig mit νόμος synonym, sodass man beide Begriffe miteinander vertauschen könnte. Denn während sich bei dem Apostel mit νόμος zwei gegensätzliche Beurteilungen verbinden, ist γράμμα eindeutig negativt bestimmt." Later on, he asserts: "Soll die *bleibende* Bedeutung der Schrift hervorgehoben werden, so wird sie γραφή genannt" (ibid.). Similarly, Schneider 1953, 190.

[46] Also, in Romans 6, Paul often refers to the common knowledge of Christians even if he had not yet visited their congregation in Rome and taught them (vv. 3: ἀγνοεῖτε, 6: γινώσκοντες, and 9: εἰδότες). See Laato 2013, 99.

[47] See Laato 1991; 1995; 2003; 2018a.

cleared up. Constantly, the big difference between the two chapters, Romans 6 and 7, is found in the common suggestion that the former describes the Christian as not being under the law whereas the latter defines the "I" as being under the law. Plainly put, it does not hold true and rather comes close to a stereotype. The tendentious construction needs some precision. Certainly, the Christian does not stand under the law. He is not obliged to do the law to the letter or according to the "literal-letteral" meaning. He is redeemed from the curse of the law. He is indeed free from all the accusations of the law. Neither does the "I" say that he really stands under the law. Instead, he overtly speaks of the complete impossibility to obey the spiritual law[48] as long as the carnal corruption causes wear and tear on him. He is an appropriate example of the service "in newness of the Spirit and not in oldness of the letter" which does not initiate flawless uprightness or sinlessness (7:6). He explicitly suffers from "not understanding what he does" (v. 15) or what ultimately sin does in him (vv. 17, 20). The object of the verb "to do" (κατεργάζομαι) is "every kind of covetous desire" (v. 8) and "death" (v. 13) that sin as an active actor or doer produces. Accordingly, the "I" does not understand that sin has brought him lethal death by calling forth every kind of covetous desire. He lives in tension with himself and his divine service "in newness of the Spirit" who creates life and all good efforts to fulfill the divine will. In vv. 14-25, he delineates the inward struggles and torments he confronts in his new mode of existence. Since "we know" in v. 14 indicates that "Christians know" and since the "I" is—logically thinking—counted among "we" ("one of us"), it follows that the "I" is a Christian who knows the spiritual law but perceives in himself contrasting depravity and infirmity. The startling discrepancy between the two opposite powers explains the exceptionally harsh formulation in his monologue.[49]

---

[48] Strictly, Paul distinguishes between "doing (ποιεῖν) the entire law (ὅλος ὁ νόμος)" and "fulfilling (πληροῦν) the whole law (ὁ πᾶς νόμος)" through love. He insists on the impossibility of the former alternative and, hence, speaks for the possibility of the latter option. See below. Romans 7:14-25 shows that Christians cannot "do" the law while Romans 8:3-14 shows that they can "fulfill" it. Cf. further Galatians 3:10, 12, 5:3, 14, 6:13.

[49] More for the dichotomy of the "I" in Romans 7, see Laato 1991, 143-163; 1995, 113-129; 2003, 218-226; 2018a, 742-755.

The "letter" kills but the "Spirit" gives life

Taken as a whole, it should not escape notice that the law *per se* causes curse, death, and condemnation. It is not actually the misreading of the Torah that makes the reading of the Torah precarious. As if the impending doomsday were only a fatal error! No, it is not about a distortion of the law. On the contrary, the question concerns the essence of the Sinaitic legislation. It is indeed a matter of life and death or, strictly speaking, of death alone. The commandment came and the "I" died (Romans 7:9). The "letter" kills (2 Corinthians 3:6). It brings death. It does that by any reading. In the main, it functions as it does. Hence, the severity of the issue should not get out of sight. The killing effects of the Mosaic law cannot be avoided by the "correct" understanding of it or the "right" use of it. Not even the gospel alters the divine purpose of condemning sinners. Rather, it assumes their total defeat and absolute judgment. First then, it delivers them release from their transgressions and results in justification as well as eternal life. After their conversion and inner transformation, they do not obey the law as before, ostensibly with an "appropriate" attitude instead of an "inappropriate" insight. Re-creation or regeneration does not amount to an intellectual training or manipulative brainwashing or rigorous mind control. More accurately, Christians are "new creatures" (2 Corinthians 5:17). They serve "in newness of the Spirit" who engenders love that is the fulfillment of the law. Still, they agonize over their corruption. Although sin no longer *reigns* in them, they have to push back evil desires in their mortal body (Romans 6:12). Alternatively, even if evil desires abide in their heart and soul, they are able to pull and put down the bad *deeds* of their mortal body (Romans 8:13). As shown and known, Romans 7:14-25 between chapters 6 and 8 tells us the story behind the scenes. The law is spiritual whereas the "I" is carnal. The service "in newness of the Spirit" takes place in this tension of "already—not yet" until "the imperfect disappears" (1 Corinthians 13:10).[50]

To the point, the new covenant does not restrictively end up as a new knowledge or understanding but as a totally new reality through

---

[50] More for the tension of "already—not yet" in Christian life, see Laato 1991, 143-182; 1995, 113-145; 2003, 218-229; 2018a, 738-763.

Christ in the Spirit or through the Spirit in Christ. Christians live a new life as they have died from the law. They have obtained a new law, written on their hearts and minds. They fulfill the whole law "in Spirit" or according to the new "literal-spiritual" meaning, not "in flesh" or according to the "literal-letteral" meaning. Thus, the old law does not turn into the new one by any mental hocus-pocus or abracadabra. It does not change at all. It remains the condemning "letter" that kills. It functions like that. Ultimately, death is the only way to get rid of it. In the death of Christ, the new life is hidden. Participation in him necessarily results in resurrection, already now on earth and once there in heaven. Only in him has the law that kills then passed away.

Romans 3:27 and 8:2

The clear-cut clarification of the contravening contrast between the "letter" and the "Spirit" sparks off an analytical evaluation of some growing tendencies in modern exegetics. In regard to Romans 3:27 and 8:2, the increasing thrust moves toward the interpretation that the right understanding of the Torah alters "the law of works" to "the law of faith" (3:27) or "the law of sin and death" to "the law of the Spirit of life" (8:2). In consequence, the condemning and killing law is once again merely a misunderstanding. It looks like a fleeting nightmare that rapidly disappears in the morning. Alternatively, it resembles a raging bull that finally has been tamed and poses no risk to the safety of the orthodox group.[51] Yet, "the law of works" continuously presses for works; "the law of sin and death" continually leads to sin and death. No one can stop that. Not believers through their innovative and progressive rethinking. Not Christ who succeeded where the others failed. Not even God who disclosed his everlasting will at Sinai. (Only in heaven will the condition completely change when human corruption is brought to an end.) Thus, "the letter kills." It can do nothing else and, in reverse, nothing else can be done to

---

[51] The new trend in interpretation of Romans 3:27 and 8:2 started especially with Friedrich 1954, 401-417. Since then, it has increased and spread widely. In short, see my own discussion in Laato 1991, 238 n 2 and 1995, 189 n 88 with numerous references. Cf. further, e.g., Jewett 2007, 297-298, 480-482 or Middendorf 2013, 294-296, 604-609. For another option, see below.

it. Astonishingly, the gospel proclaims that the salvation is found in Christ alone and carried out in the Spirit alone. It makes the big difference! A new existence of a wholly different kind opens up.

Such being the case, "the law of faith" (3:27) and "the law of the Spirit of life" (8:2) are, in general, understood as polemical expressions. They speak of divine benevolence as if it were dependent on a certain kind of law. In fact, they assert that it is not at all dependent on the law but only based on the "order, principle or rule" (the wide meaning of νόμος) of the new covenant. Paul obviously plays on words. He depicts his gospel in legal terms for nonlegal (or anti-legal) purposes. His verbal gimmick makes good sense. Salvation stays intact from a detrimental mixture of meritorious works and gracious compassion.[52]

In more specific terms, it opens up another alternative option of explanation that leads to much the same conclusion. Strictly, the difference or contrast between the law of the old covenant and the law of the new covenant does not first and foremost hark back to a change in human attitude. An anthropocentric approach lies far away from Paul's mind. Instead, his theology focuses on Christocentric thinking. It is primarily about a salvation-historical shift in Christ that then secondarily, for sure, includes a change in human attitude. Notably, the latter always follows from the former but never *vice versa*. Consequently, the transparent polarity between the law of the old covenant and the law of the new covenant does not vanish like mist in the heat through the correct *understanding* of the Torah. Quite the opposite, the *correct* understanding of the Torah demonstrates and substantiates the incongruity that continually prevails between the two. In Romans, the "law of works" (3:27) and the "law of sin and death" (8:2) stand for the "literal-letteral" reading and observing of the law. It dooms and kills everyone who does not do everything that has been inscribed and prescribed there. That verdict is still in force in 1:18-3:20 and wherever the gospel is missed or dismissed. Conversely, "the law of faith" (3:27) and "the law of the Spirit of life" (8:2) might characterize the "literal-spiritual" reading and fulfilling of the law. It denotes what the Spirit engenders as he gives life to Christians and

---

[52] More for the academic discussion and references, see Laato 1991, 238 n 2; 1995, 189 n 88. Cf. commentaries.

helps them to sustain in faith that shows itself through love. The prophecies of the outpouring of the Spirit who vivifies their stony hearts and dry bones (Ezekiel 36-37) come to pass. Simultaneously, the law is written on their hearts (Jeremiah 31). Evidently, the phrase "the law of the Spirit of life" directly relates to those scriptural texts. Thus, it does not have anything to do with human attempts or efforts in verification of the truth that "the law of sin and death" no longer pertains to Christians. They are now free from condemnation because they have been justified by grace in Christ (Romans 8:1). They need not observe the commandments according to the "literal-letteral" meaning since it leads to sins and calls forth death. Rather, they live a new life according to the "literal-spiritual" meaning and in the power of the Spirit (v. 2). In the new covenant, the conditions are indeed different. The salvation-historical shift in Christ marks the turning point. As expected, all sorts of human co-operation (fleshly means) are in vain (v. 3). The new life of the Christians takes place in passive forms. God's action comes to the fore through them. The righteous requirement of the law (τὸ δικαίωμα τοῦ νόμου) focuses on their loving care for their neighbors and foreigners. It is explicitly fulfilled (*passivum divinum*: πληρωθῇ) in them (v. 4).[53] Paradoxically, they act most actively insofar as they recognize that they are "*created* in Christ Jesus to do good works, which God *prepared* in advance for them to do" (see Ephesians 2:10) with the intention that "no one can boast" (Ephesians 2:8). Boasting is excluded once and for all "by the law of faith" (Romans 3:27) at the same time as faith establishes the (literal-spiritual) law (Romans 3:31).[54]

Remarkably, the former analysis of the subtle differentiation between "the law of works" and "the law of faith" or "the law of sin and death" and "the law of the Spirit of life" does not ascribe the distinction to human intelligence or sophistication but the salvation-historical shift due to the inauguration of the new covenant. In addition, it does not render void the intention of the Mosaic law to

---

[53] More for Romans 8:1-4, see Laato 1991, 163-167 and 1995, 129-132. It is worth asserting that 8:2 explicitly speaks of the liberation from "the *law* of sin and death." Hence, it does not relate to the question of the "I" in 7:24 where he speaks of "this *body* of death." See Laato 1991, 149-150 and 1995, 118-119.

[54] More for Romans 3:27-31, see Laato 1991, 229-240 and 1995, 182-190.

condemn and kill sinners but rather assumes and affirms it as a necessary pre-stage of the reviving and resuscitating power of the Spirit through the gospel. This antagonism in permanent tension should not be set down in modern efforts to reinterpretations.[55]

Romans 10:5-8 and the quotation of Deuteronomy 30:12-14

It is not possible to dwell much longer on Romans here. The discussion has to be carried on in another place. However, some initial reflections on chapter 10 are still needed. There, Paul quotes Leviticus 18:5 as well as Deuteronomy 30:12-14, two different parts of the *same* Torah, and put them in sharp contrast to each other in vv. 5-8. Does he understand what he is doing? Alternatively, does he simply disrupt the context of his citations and read into them whatever he likes?

Already in the Old Testament, Leviticus 18:5 is quoted many times to confirm the judgment over Israel as a result of their religious decay (see, e.g., Nehemiah 9:29, Ezekiel 20:11, 20:13, 20:21). Since they did not do "these things," they could not "live by them" in the promised land of "milk and honey" (or along with an extended sense: in the heavenly kingdom). The judicial scene of the day of reckoning works well with the intention in Romans 10.[56]

As expected, also Deuteronomy 30:12-14 speaks of the obedience to the Mosaic law (see v. 11: "what I am commanding you today") in the historical context of Israel's failure to do so. In truth, their Lord has not given them "a heart to understand or eyes to see or ears to hear" (29:4). They are still uncircumcised in their hearts (10:16). At long last, they have to bear the curse that will fall on them (28:15ff., 31:16-18). Apparently, the Israelites are not able to keep the Mosaic law. It does not have any effect on them. Nevertheless, Moses announces that he sets before them life and death (30:15). He encourages them to "choose life, so that you and your children may live" (30:19). After all, they should acknowledge that "the Lord is your

---

[55] Cf. Räisänen 1980, 101-117.
[56] More for Romans 10:5, see Laato 2021, 56-57.

life" (30:20). Thus, it appears that the line of thought in Deuteronomy is strongly reminiscent of Leviticus 18:5 (see above).[57]

To begin with, Paul likewise reproaches the Jews of his time for having uncircumcised hearts (see above, Romans 2:28-29). Then, his view of them and the whole of mankind culminates in the judgment of them (3:9-18). Here, he very closely follows the reasoning in Deuteronomy.[58] Later on, he instead quite astoundingly reads his Christological faith into Deuteronomy 30:12-14. He promptly maintains that the "word" that "is near you" or "in your mouth and in your heart" explicitly depicts "the word of faith" he proclaims (10:8) even if he knows (or should know) that it in the Hebrew original for sure relates to the Mosaic law. Indeed, it looks a bit odd. However, Paul seems to understand his quotation from the perspective of "realized history." He assumes that the Israelites never complied with Deuteronomy 30:12-14. Very badly, they fell short of their expectations. The one and only who truly kept the whole law was Christ. He fulfilled everything that was written. Reasonably, Deuteronomy 30:12-14 in the long run points to him and concerns the preaching of the gospel.[59]

On further reflection, the Pauline reading of Deuteronomy goes far beyond the retrospective interpretation of historical data. Along with the Christological use of Scripture, it also seems to apply the text to the Christian way of living. The preaching of the gospel brings about a radical change among them who in faith assent to the message. God forgives their sins. He justifies them freely in his great grace. They receive a new life as a result of recreation, respectively, regeneration. The Spirit has resuscitated them. They are what they are by his mighty power. As new living creatures, they then naturally start to live this new life in faith that becomes apparent in love. It amounts to "the fulfillment of the law" (Romans 13:10) and the completion of a true circumcision (Romans 2:28-29). Therefore, the gospel surely confirms Deuteronomy 30:12-14 since it soundly conforms to the demands of the passage. Besides, the Lord in the context of the chapter guarantees that he will gather his own people

---

[57] More for the context of Deuteronomy 30:12-14, see Laato 2021, 58-59.

[58] For some other details and similarities, see Laato 2021, 59-61.

[59] Laato 2021, 59-61.

"from all the nations" and circumcise their hearts and make them love him (vv. 4-6). For understandable reasons, Paul adheres to his Old Testament quotation and firmly maintains that it designates "the word of faith we are proclaiming" (Romans 10:8). He finds there the core of his theological teaching: Christ who loves first and has fulfilled the law vis-à-vis Christians who love in imitation of him and now fulfill the law by following in his footsteps. No doubt, the emphasis lies on the former but the latter at least indirectly relates to the contrast with Leviticus 18:5 as an impending judgment of every sort of disobedience.[60]

Taken as a whole, Paul does not misread Deuteronomy 30:12-14. On the contrary, he interprets the passage in concert with the eschatological context that surrounds it. Here, the messianic or Christological interpretation dominates. In chorus, the underlying idea of the Christian existence as the fulfillment of the law and the expression of true circumcision does not disappear into oblivion. Romans 10:6-8 shows how the literal-spiritual (alternatively, scriptural-spiritual) understanding of the Torah or the Mosaic legislation permeates the Pauline exposition of the Old Testament. Without giving regard to it, some quotations might seem completely detached or somewhat removed from the original meaning. Thus, the importance of the perspective is attested by the fact that many things will fall into place easily or naturally because of it.

Being "under Christ's law" and fulfilling "the law of Christ"

As a result, the Christological interpretation of Deuteronomy 30:12-14 reveals that the true circumcision of the heart and the real fulfillment of the law at long last come to pass according to the original eschatological context of the passage. This aspect and the common Christian conviction of keeping God's commands in their "literal-spiritual" meaning (see above) have a direct impact on how to clarify the difficult idioms of being "under Christ's law" (ἔννομος Χριστοῦ,

---

[60] Here, the very close connection between the love of Christ and the love of Christians is once again worth noticing.

1 Corinthians 9:21) and fulfilling "the law of Christ" (ὁ νόμος τοῦ Χριστοῦ, Galatians 6:2). Surely, it is initially about the "new commandment" that Jesus has given his disciples: "Love one another" (see John 13:34-35, 15:12, 17). His teaching spread everywhere in Christianity. In 1 Corinthians 9:1-23, Paul speaks of his apostolic right of receiving his living from the gospel. But he has not made any use of it. He has shown love without charge, not asking or requesting any payment for it.[61] In Galatians 6:1-10, Paul equally urges to "do good to all people, especially to those who belong to the family of believers" (v. 10). He encourages to "carry each other's burdens" (v. 2). That is how love, "the fulfillment of the whole law" (5:14), functions in practice.[62] Still, "the law of Christ" is not to be reduced to one single commandment to the absolute exclusion of the more precise and specific commandments. An oversimplification should be avoided to the very end. Nothing is gained by it. Therefore, "the law of Christ" indicates the Old Testament law as a total (*in toto*), however not according to the strict "literal-letteral" meaning that entails an implementation of the commandments "in flesh" but according to the free "literal-spiritual" meaning that encompasses an implementation of the commandments "in Spirit" (for certain, by faith that engenders love). Also now, it seems that the analysis of the contrast between the "letter" and the "Spirit" facilitates a more profound comprehension of the Pauline terminology elsewhere. Different pieces are coming together.

Either to do or to fulfill the whole law

Further, Paul differentiates between two verbs ποιεῖν and πληροῦν as well as between two expressions ὅλος ὁ νόμος and ὁ πᾶς νόμος in his polemic discussion on the righteousness of the law versus the righteousness of faith. In Galatians, he evidently avoids saying that Christians should do (ποιεῖν) the entire law (ὅλος ὁ νόμος). Instead, he underlines that they are capable of fulfilling (πληροῦν) the whole law (ὁ πᾶς νόμος) through love (cf. 3:10, 12, 5:3, 14, 6:13).

---

[61] See, e.g., the discussion in Garland 2003, 431-432.
[62] See, e.g., Bruce 1990, 260-261 and Fung 1953, 286-289.

Once again, there are two "totalities" that are set against each other. Quantitatively, they match one to one. Qualitatively, they differ. The former is the law according to the "literal-letteral" meaning and is accomplished on the level of the flesh and leads to small-minded boasting. The latter is the law according to the "literal-spiritual" meaning and is completed on the level of the Spirit and leads to broad-minded thanksgiving. Surely, it does not make sense to "begin in the Spirit" and "finish in the flesh" (3:3). The obsolete old covenant would in that case become valid once again. The extensive discussion of the Christian freedom in chapters 5-6 does not suggest that a kind of libertinism prevails among Galatians along with legalism as two unrelated forms of heresy. No, it rather shows the necessity of explaining more in depth the liberty from the Mosaic law that paradoxically ushers in the conformity to the Mosaic law but in another sense (to reiterate: not in the flesh but in the Spirit). On the other hand, the severe adherence to the Mosaic law perplexingly initiates a never-ending quest to do the commandments and allegedly "live by them" (3:12). So far, the promise of life in reference to Leviticus 18:5 has never come true (cf. the Old Testament times as defined in brief above) since "cursed is everyone who does not abide by all the things written in the book of the law, to do them" (3:10). That condition will not change until the new covenant shall enter into force and take effect.[63]

As already made known, the same distinction between "doing" and "fulfilling" comes into view in Romans 7-8. On the one hand, 7:14-25 affirms that Christians cannot "do" the law whereas, on the other, 8:3-14 asserts that they can "fulfill" it. The law is "spiritual" (7:14). It exactly assumes a "literal-spiritual" reading. Doing it "in

---

[63] For the difference between the two verbs ποιεῖν and πληροῦν as well as between the two expressions ὅλος ὁ νόμος and ὁ πᾶς νόμος, see Laato 2004, 357-358. For certain, the verb ποιεῖν is also used in Galatians with reference to Christians. In 6:9-10, they are explicitly exhorted to do good. Similar paraenetic passages can be found in Romans 13:3, 1 Corinthians 10:31, 2 Corinthians 13:7, Philippians 3:14, etc. Strictly speaking, the difference concerns the *polemic* discussion on the righteousness of the law versus the righteousness of faith. More for the qualitative aspects of Christian obedience in opposition to Jewish disobedience, see ibid., 353-359. For the severe and bitter conflict between Paul and Judaizers in Galatia, see Laato 1991, 216-228 and 1995, 172-181.

flesh" is not going to work. The "I" knows that. Besides, he is one of "us" who know (7:14). It is then about the common Christian comprehension. As long as Christians live in their "mortal body" that covets (6:12) or because "sin dwells" in them (7:17 and 20) and produces in them every kind of coveting (7:8), they cannot "do" the law that interdicts "coveting" (7:7). Hence, they do not "do" the law from absolutely pure motives. Still, they can "fulfill" it if and since they follow the "literal-spiritual" meaning of it.[64]

Christ's fulfillment of the law

Without doubt, the current discussion could be extended still more, though it would scarcely add much to the ensuing outcomes. Suffice it to say that some parts of the Mosaic law exclusively relate to Christ and the Christological creed of the early church. He alone is the offering for the sins of the world (for instance, see Romans 8:3, 2 Corinthians 5:21). He alone is the bloody sacrifice on the Day of Atonement that is sprinkled on the atonement cover (or "mercy seat") in the Most Holy Place (Romans 3:25). He alone is the Passover Lamb who has been slaughtered on the cross (1 Corinthians 5:7) even if Christians are exhorted to "get rid of the old yeast" and become "a new batch without yeast" and keep the Jewish ritual and feast, "not with the old yeast, the yeast of malice and wickedness, but with bread without yeast, the bread of sincerity and truth" (1 Corinthians 5:7-8). Adding this and that—it would not alter or change the undeniable fact that the new covenant does not abolish "the law or the prophets" but fulfills them. Truly, nothing will "disappear from the law" until "everything is accomplished" (cf. Matthew 5:17-18). In Pauline theology, the goal is not reached in the sphere of the flesh according to the "literal-letteral" meaning of the law. Instead, it will come to reality only through Christ in the sphere of the Spirit according to the "literal-spiritual" meaning of the law. The Christians really fulfill the law because they no longer stand under it. Since they once died from it, they always live in harmony with it. Paradoxically, continuity

---

[64] Laato 2018a, 738-763 (especially 742-745, 751-752). See also Laato 1991, 143-144, 156-160 and 1995, 114, 124-127.

takes full effect as a result of discontinuity. The contrast between the "letter" and the "Spirit" gains importance just here.

The Christian freedom in Spirit

Still, one open question should be accounted for. As already made known, the structure in 2 Corinthians 3 is rounded off with references to the special activity of the Spirit (*inclusio* in vv. 3, 6, 8, 17-18). The argumentation culminates in the simple but the more puzzling phrase: "Where the Spirit of the Lord is, there is freedom" (v. 17).[65] It absorbs a mixture of meanings because of the context. Since the Old Testament setting revolves around the book of Exodus, the rescue from the slavery in Egypt naturally shimmers in the background. The removal of the veil points to another kind of freedom. At the same time, it suggests an upheaval of blockades to spiritual understanding. Besides, it also implies release from sin, death, and condemnation (vv. 7-11). Even the free entrance into the celestial bliss gains attention for the very reason that those who are saved will then behold the glory of the Lord "with unveiled faces" (v. 18).[66] So far, so good. But the loop is not yet closed. The link to the Spirit as the opposite pole of the "letter" (v. 6 that stands in connection with v. 3) is missing. As a consequence, the crucial question arises how the two ends of the *inclusio* go together.

In the context of v. 17, Paul twice writes that "the old covenant is read" (v. 14) or "Moses is read" (v. 15). In both cases, he underscores that the reading yields nonsense since the veil has not been removed (v. 14), and it still covers the hearts of his opponents (v. 15). Definitely, Jews read and understand the plain meaning of Holy Scripture. Their interpretations are, in general, ingenious. Their conceptions often brim with brilliance and brightness. Their theological conclusions abound in intensity and interest. But alas, they fully fail even so![67] They read and apprehend their holy Scripture

---

[65] See above, chapter 3. Dunn (2013, 174) writes on v. 17: "This is entirely in keeping with Paul's emphasis on the Spirit in this passage [. . .]."

[66] See above, chapter 6.

[67] Cf. Schechter 1965, 18. He writes with biting irony that exegesis of the Pauline letters leaves room for a weird alternative: "Either the theology of the

according to the "literal-letteral" meaning. They think it has to be observed "in flesh" (not overlooking nor forsaking pure motives if possible). They have no insight to recognize that God in the new covenant has put his law in the minds of his people and written it on their hearts (Jeremiah 31:33). He has done it in and through his Spirit (Ezekiel 36:26-27). Therefore, the Torah should be read and understood according to the "literal-spiritual" meaning. Referring back to v. 6 and taking into consideration vv. 14-15, Paul emphasizes in v. 17 that the Spirit is freedom and liberates Christians from the "literal-letteral" meaning of the law that illustrates the total failure of the Jewish approach.[68] Succinctly, he maintains the profound reason for the breakthrough of the gospel. The dawn has risen, and the night has waned away. Accordingly, the Spirit will not allow himself to be shackled by any external principles of the law. He preserves his liberty. He does not become "flesh" but "body" as Christians in faith

---

Rabbis must be wrong, its conception of God debasing, its leading motives materialistic and coarse, and its teachers lacking in enthusiasm and spirituality, or the Apostle to the Gentiles is quite unintelligible." *Tertium non datur.* However, I would be glad to offer a third alternative: the Apostle to the Gentiles is quite intelligible and his criticism of the Jewish beliefs very comprehensible even if the theology of the rabbis and their leading motives are not coarse. The discrepancy between both parties goes much deeper than the famous Moldavian-born American rabbi Schechter was able to imagine. His urgent voice should be heard but not recited by rote.

[68] In Galatians, the main content is about "freedom" (2:4, 5:1, 13), not compelling anyone to be circumcised or "Judaize" (2:3, 13; 6:12). On the other hand, those who pursue the righteousness of the law are obliged to do the entire law (for instance, see 3:10 and 5:3). The hard pressure and coercion lie on them (see Laato 2004, 353-359). Further, the contrast of Hagar, the slave woman, and Sarah, the free woman, stands for two completely opposite covenants (the old and the new one) as they bear their children to slavery, respectively, freedom (4:21-31). The passage speaks especially to those who "want to be under the law" (v. 21) and let themselves be circumcised. For sure, it shares close similarities with 2 Corinthians 3:12-18 (cf. Grindheim 2001, 103 and Thrall 2004, 275). As a consequence, one essential aspect of "freedom" in Galatians relates to the Christian independence from the Jewish reading and understanding of the Sinaitic law. It is based on the redemption acquired by Christ alone (5:1) and brought to fruition by the Spirit (3:1-5, 4:1-6, 5:16-6:10). Indeed, "where the Spirit of the Lord is, there is freedom" (2 Corinthians 3:17).

through love fulfill in their corporal reality what he accomplishes among them. It follows that v. 17 accurately harks back to vv. 14-15 and further to v. 6 and finally to v. 3. Largely, it is about the instructions for reading the Old Testament. Here, the *inclusio* has been set up. The loop in chapter 3 is closed.

8
The "Lutheran" Paul—
a modern version

Preliminary remarks

Undeniably, Luther ranks as one of the foremost exponents among New Testament scholars in the history of Pauline research. His interpretation of justification by faith in Romans launched the entire Reformation at the beginning of the 16th century. Ever since, he has pinpointed future guidelines for the reading, understanding, and preaching of the gospel for centuries to come.

Yet, the previous balance and the weighing up of doctrinal arguments in order of Protestant precedence begins to turn. At present, Luther suddenly and surprisingly appears as the villain of the story rather than the hero. He has put forward his controversial inquiries and taken them to an extreme. In brief, he contends that the final salvation is not based on human works. In contrast, it rests on divine mercy alone. The former attitude exemplifies the Jewish soteriology whereas the latter aspect epitomizes the Pauline soteriology. They completely rule each other out. That kind of serious oversimplification encounters strong headwinds in recent research.[1]

Luther and the new perspective on Paul

Currently, the so-called new perspective on Paul is on the rise. It gains rather wide acceptance and stands out as the prevailing trend today.

---

[1] See my overview of research, Laato 1991, 6-37 and 1995, 5-30.

To a large extent, it is an anti-Lutheran approach. New perspective advocates fault Luther for initiating a very serious misreading of Pauline theology. Frankly speaking, he seems to have projected his fervent debate with the pope onto the time of the New Testament, whereby Judaism takes the role of Medieval Roman Catholicism and Christianity the part of Lutheranism.[2] Hence, correctives need to be applied to his understanding. Now, the time has arrived to "deluther-anize" Paul and to discredit the anachronistic interpretation of him. The process of readjustment or revisionist reorientation is already underway. Yet so far—no end is in sight.

The ongoing discussion cannot be extended here as much as it should, but I have made my contributions elsewhere. To conclude: covenantal nomism, the Jewish interrelationship between gracious election and required obedience, involves the thought of coopera-tion that draws on an optimistic anthropology (the notion of free will). Therefore, it does not promote anything like God's grace alone. But saying this does not uphold different, distorted pictures of Judaism(s) or search to defend them. Paul has reason to criticize the self-righteousness and boasting arising from covenantal nomism. His serious criticism hits the target accurately. To "be righteous" in Judaism means staying within the covenant through obeying the law. As a result, the final salvation indeed depends on human efforts.[3]

In consequence, the new perspective portrayal of Luther occa-sionally approaches a cheesy parody as it tries to correct his putatively imbalanced interpretation of Pauline letters. The revisionists seem to have gone to extremes in their harsh disapproval of Reformation. They dig a hole for another and fall into it themselves. The alleged "Lutheran captivity" of Pauline letters amounts to a deception. It blurs the lines between illusion and reality. For that reason, a much more well-adjusted evaluation is needed as the following quotation makes clear:

> "That Luther, to this extent at least, gets Paul 'right' is part of what I intended when I once suggested, somewhat epigrammatically, that Pauline scholars can learn from the Reformer. [. . .] Still, one has only

---

[2] See, e.g., Sanders 1977, 57. Cf. Laato 1991, 26-27 and 1995, 21-22.
[3] Laato 2019, 302. Further, see Laato 1991, 1995, 2004, 2008, 2018a.

to read a few passages of his writings (most any will do) to realize that, in crucial respects, he inhabits the same world, and breathes the same air, as the apostle [. . .]. Such kindredness of spirit gives Luther an inestimable advantage over many readers of Paul in 'capturing' the essence of the apostle's writings. On numerous points of detail, Luther may be the last to illumine. For those, however, who would see forest as well as trees, I am still inclined to propose a trip to the dustbins of recent Pauline scholarship—to retrieve and try out, on a reading of the epistles, the disregarded spectacles of the Reformer."[4]

It still remains to determine what harmony there is between the corollaries of the preceding analysis of 2 Corinthians 3:1-18 and the overall theology of Luther. Do they thoroughly square with each other, or do they only overlap in part?

The Lutheran emphasis on anthropology

Without a doubt, the Lutheran emphasis on the absolute corruption of the whole humankind holds true. People are unable to keep the Mosaic commandments. They fail with regard to the quantitative and qualitative aspects of the law. As a result, they are dead in their sins and in need of the vivifying power of God's Spirit in accordance with Ezekiel 36-37. He will restore them to life again. He will resuscitate and transform them. Through his recreative action, they indeed become "new creatures" (2 Corinthians 5:17). In accordance with Jeremiah 31, God all at once writes the law on their hearts. They now know him. They fulfill his demands. Hence, he is their God. They are his people. The Old Testament concepts of recreation, regeneration, resuscitation, resurrection, and revitalization bear upon the monergistic content and intent of the expressions. Synergistic tendencies disappear. Human cooperation is missing. God alone ensures and guarantees the new life. He acts and operates through the proclamation of the gospel, respectively, the ministry of the Spirit. That is how he begets faith and trust in him (2 Corinthians 3:7-11, 4:6). It is also worth noticing the difference between the life itself and the living of the new life that follows, in other words, being God's newborn child

---

[4] Westerholm 2004, 37-38.

and growing as his amenable child. Surely, they belong together. Yet, the latter does not in the least engender the former. The proper distinction between justification (salvation in faith) and sanctification (good works in love) stands firm as ever. Thus far, the crucial truths in Lutheran dogmatics are corroborated abundantly and overwhelmingly. Here, one scarcely necessitates any further confirmation for the basics of Reformation.[5]

The Lutheran notion of simul iustus et peccator

Further, the Lutheran thought of *simul iustus et peccator* genuinely renders the core of the Pauline anthropology and soteriology especially in Romans 7:14-25 (though the conclusion is, to be sure, highly controversial in modern exegetics). Christians do not stand under the law. They have died from it to be released from it. The "literal-letteral" meaning of the Torah no longer concerns them. Yet, the law is "spiritual" (v. 14). It conforms to the scriptural standards and teachings that are in force in the new covenant. Then and there, it will be written on human hearts. Accordingly, Christians freely consent to it. They start to fulfill it at the deepest level of reality in faith through love, not according to the external extent and extension of the Jewish legislation. In spite of their new life, Romans 7:14-25 authenticates and substantiates their internal wrestling with their fleshly and deadly body that is still coveting and producing evil desires to be oppressed by the divine control (6:12).[6]

The Lutheran understanding
of the killing effect of the Mosaic law

In addition, Luther has really made a strong case for himself as he (maybe more persuasively than anyone else) has drawn attention to the killing effect of the Mosaic law. He has not put himself on a temptation to temper or tone down the negative force it exerts

---

[5] In need of evidence, see, e.g., Laato 2008.

[6] More for the Lutheran concept of *simul iustus et peccator*, see especially Laato 2018a.

on those under it. Truly, he never stooped to that kind of teaching. Rather, he pressed on his apostolic preaching that only the one who has been brought to death can be restored to life. Obviously, "the letter kills." Rightly understood, it indeed kills. It does not kill because of a possible *mis*understanding. No, the law has its divine commission to mortify so that the gospel will have its divine mission to vivify. Seldom do the same clarity and precision prevail in modern exegetics. Here, Luther stands vindicated as the master of theology. He gains himself a reputation of being *primus inter pares* (first among equals) or *princeps doctrinae Christianae apud omnes* (the very best of all in Christian Doctrine). There is no comparison.[7] *Dixi.*

Luther's interpretation of some commandments

From another angle, each great man casts a big shadow over his own footsteps—a real tragedy that always befalls he who makes his story history. I assume it is not to be changed. Rather, it amounts to the salt of life that just for that reason brings tears to the eyes of those who hoped for something even better. Luther is no exception. He has put emphasis on Sola Scriptura and encouraged all his readers to read the

---

[7] In Lutheran theology, there is sometimes too much talk about the proper distinction between the law and the gospel ad nauseam. It has been misunderstood as a kind of hocus-pocus that turns every biblical statement into a weird jargon of a reformative prevalence. (*Sit venia verbo.*) Luther did not make use of that specific expression as a magic formula. Rather, he was more interested in the dialectical theology behind it. For instance, see his superb explanation of Psalm 51: "This is the twofold theological knowledge which David teaches in this psalm, so that the content of the psalm is the theological knowledge of man and also the theological knowledge of God. [. . .] The proper subject of theology is man guilty of sin and condemned, and God the Justifier and Savior of man the sinner. Whatever is asked or discussed in theology outside this subject, is error and poison. All Scripture points to this, that God commends His kindness to us and in His Son restores to righteousness and life the nature that has fallen into sin and condemnation. [. . .] Whoever follows this aim in reading the Holy Scriptures will read holy things fruitfully." In short: "The issue here is not this physical life—what we should eat, what work we should undertake, how we should rule our family, how we should till the soil." See Luther 1955, 311.

holy writings more than his own writings. A good piece of advice that I have tried to heed even though I have also studied the texts of the prominent Reformer to a great extent. Therefore, Luther is to be set straight, if needed, on the basis of the divine authority of the Bible or, in this case, on account of the teaching of the Pauline letters. This was his last will and testament. The next lines serve to respect and honor his memory. They grant him his own wish.

In his Large Catechism, Luther starts to explain the Ten Commandments. As he comes to his explanation of the third commandment, he recognizes that it "was given to the Jews alone" as regards the "external observance" of it. Later on, he asserts that it "does not concern us Christians" according to "its gross sense." To quote him:

> "(80) Now, in the Old Testament, God separated the seventh day, and appointed it for rest, and commanded that it should be regarded as holy above all others. As regards this external observance, this commandment was given to the Jews alone, that they should abstain from toilsome work, and rest [. . .]. (82) This commandment, therefore, according to its gross sense, does not concern us Christians; for it is altogether an external matter, like other ordinances of the Old Testament, which were attached to particular customs, persons, times, and places, and now have been made free through Christ."[8]

No doubt, Christians need not keep the Jewish sabbath day instead of their own Sunday as the day of Christ's resurrection. The "gross sense" of the third commandment does not really concern them. As a matter of fact, Paul acknowledges and affirms with similar import that "one man considers one day more sacred than another"

---

[8] Quoted according to Concordia Triglotta 1921, 603. In German: "(80) Nun hat Gott im Alten Testament den siebenten Tag ausgesondert und aufgesetzt [eingesetzt, angeordnet] zu feiern, und geboten, denselben vor allen andern heilig zu halten, und dieser äusserlichen Feier nach ist dies Gebot allein den Juden gestellt, daß sie sollten von groben Werken stillstehen und ruhen [. . .]. (82) Darum geht nun dies Gebot nach dem groben Verstand uns Christen nichts an, denn es ein ganz äusserlich Ding ist, wie andere Satzungen des Alten Testaments an sonderliche Weise, Person, Zeit und Stätte gebunden, welche nun durch Christum alle freigelassen sind."

and "another man considers every day alike" (see Romans 14:5). On the surface, he certainly consents to the tantamount conclusion that observing "special days and months and seasons and years" does not make any difference (Galatians 4:10). Still, a fine distinction prevails between the two related cases. Paul underlines his adherence to the Torah. He explicitly maintains that Christians fulfill the whole law. But they do not keep it in flesh, respectively, in accordance with the "literal-letteral" meaning of it but in Spirit, respectively, in accordance with the "literal-spiritual" meaning of it. Decisively, Paul thinks in a Jewish manner from start to finish. He puts his emphasis on the Old Testament roots of his gospel as it now has been accredited and authenticated in the new covenant.

In his joint explanation of the ninth and tenth commandments, Luther expresses himself in a rather similar manner. He succinctly writes as follows:

> "(293) These two commandments are given quite exclusively to the Jews; nevertheless, in part they also concern us."[9]

Once again, Luther seems to emphasize that the adherence to the Jewish Torah does not fully concern Christians. In a sense, he is right. He knows that the old covenant has already gone, and the new covenant has now come. Truly, that makes a big difference. Paul agrees. Notwithstanding, he avows that the ninth and tenth commandments "do not covet" or "whatever other commandment there may be" (Romans 13:9) are fulfilled in sincere love. He does not say a single word about the "partial" futility of them in a Christian context.[10]

The problem of "the third use of the law" by Luther

Further, Luther speaks much of the "proper use" of the law (as indicated already in 1 Timothy 1:8). He concentrates on the double use

---

[9] Quoted according to Concordia Triglotta 1921, 663. In German: "(293) Diese zwei Gebote sind fast den Juden sonderlich gegeben, wiewohl sie uns dennoch auch zum Teil betreffen."

[10] For the relationship between the Old and New Testament in Lutheran theology, cf. Wenz 1996, especially 44-48.

of the law (*duplex usus legis*). He distinguishes between "the civil or political use" (*usus civilis sive usus politicus*) of the law and "the elenctic or pedagogical use" (*usus elenchticus sive usus paedagogicus*) of the law. The former (so-called preparative) use restrains evil and secures civil order in community while the latter (so-called preservative) use confronts and condemns sinners in order to point them to Christ. In his antinomian disputations with Johann Agricola, Luther strongly rejects the conclusion that "the law belongs in the town hall and not in the pulpit" as it was propagated by his opponents. He knows better. He grasps that Christians need to hear the law to the exclusion of their self-satisfaction and self-righteousness that still seriously bother them. Only then do they remain humble and turn for comfort in their Savior. Else, they will be finally damned and doomed.

In his dealing with the Antinomists, it is startling that Luther does not focus on "the third use of the law" (*tertius usus legis*), "the didactic or normative use" (*usus didacticus sive normativus*) of the law. Indeed, he does not underscore "the use of the law among the born again" (*usus in renatis*) as a rule of conduct. Rather, he explains that Christians freely or spontaneously do good works, but never under the compulsion of the law. His refraining from the third (so-called restorative) use of the law relates to his resistance against the impending danger of work-righteousness.[11] Definitely, Luther has a right intention, but he fails to carry full conviction. He does not adequately take into consideration the distinction between doing (ποιεῖν) the entire law (ὅλος ὁ νόμος) and fulfilling (πληροῦν) the whole law (ὁ πᾶς νόμος) in Galatians. In other words, he does not

---

[11] See above all Elert 1948, 168-170 and Ebeling 1963, 62-73. For a corrective of their interpretation and for the ongoing discussion, cf. Engelbrecht 2011, 135-150. In the final analysis, the thorough argumentation shows that Luther seems to be familiar with the former medieval concept of "the third use of the law" (announcing the coming of Christ) as he reinterpreted it in his *Weihnachtspostille* of 1522. However, he does not *focus* on "the third use of the law" (as a rule of conduct) but *concentrates* on the double use of the law (see above). His formulation principally differs from that of his successors. On purpose, he makes use of a distinctive language (see below). Later on, the so-called Gnesio-Lutherans stood firm in their speaking of the double use of the law (*duplex usus legis*) against the so-called Philippists and their interpretation of the threefold use of the law (*triplex usus legis*).

account for the particular difference between the "literal-letteral" and "literal-spiritual" meaning of the Mosaic law.[12] It would more easily sort out the problem of legalistic tendencies without losing sight of the obvious fact that Christians truly follow the Mosaic law as it is written on their hearts through the Holy Spirit. Since they do not observe the Torah "in flesh" and according to their innate power, they do not pursue their own righteousness as a result of their good works. Thus, the Pauline line of thought does more justice to the core of the new covenant in continuity with the old covenant. In consequence, it sets out the Jewish contours of the gospel in their place. They are part and parcel of the original apostolic message. In that case, the later systematic or dogmatic jargon of "the threefold use of the law" (*triplex usus legis*) similarly remains a torso. It was formulated by Melanchthon in the second edition of his *Loci communes* (1535) and defended by the authors of the Formula of Concord (1577) in their contribution to "the third use of the law" (Article VI). Besides, it has been adopted and strongly supported by Calvin and in many Calvinist circles.[13] However, the same underlying problem in another form persists here. "The threefold use of the law" ushers in a simplistic link between Christian obedience and the Mosaic law. Alternatively, it reads a truncated content into the Mosaic law and reduces the Torah into "a moral law with ethical dimensions" (and the equivalent). The fresh Pauline perspective is missing. It should be recognized and no longer overlooked.

---

[12] See above, especially chapter 7.

[13] For a short summary of the theological development, see Vogel 2005, 192-203. He notices that Melanchthon has introduced the concept of *tertium usus legis* already in the third edition of his *Scholia* (1534). He asserts (in reference to T. J. Wengert): "By 1534, when Melanchthon published the third edition of his *Scholia*, he formalized his view on the necessity of good works by adding a Third Use to his (and Luther's) previously two-fold categorization of the Law's function. The Third Use then arose as part of a whole clarification of the relationship of justification and good works." (Quotation from his article, page 193.) The whole issue of *CTQ* 69:3-4 (July/October 2005, 187-308) with many stimulating and interesting contributions is dedicated to the third use of the law. The discussion cannot be prolonged here. For Calvin's insights into the three uses of the law, see, e.g., Horton 1995, 10-43 (especially 24-32).

The distortion of the Epistle of James by Luther

Moreover, Luther draws far-reaching conclusions from his inter-pretation of the Pauline letters and the apostolic reluctance against work-righteousness. They concern his view of the canon of the New Testament and have an immense impression on his reformative prin-ciple of *Sola Scriptura*. As well-known, he displays a considerable distrust of the teaching on justification in the Epistle of James. In his estimation, it "is a right strawy epistle," since it has "no evangel-ical" content. On the other hand, Luther praises the letter given that "it sets no human doctrine and drives hard the law of God." Still, he regards it "as no apostolic writing," not proclaiming or driving at Christ ("Christum predigen und treyben"). In consequence, he shifted its place from the beginning to the end of the catholic epistles. But he did not directly exclude it from the canon.[14]

It does not fall within the purview of the present study to delve into the exegetical problems in the Epistle of James. They have been more thoroughly dealt with elsewhere.[15] Here, some short, pointed remarks will suffice.

Obviously, it is an oversimplification to argue that James "drives hard the law of God." Indeed, he does insist on good works, but he does *not* push for "the works of the law." Surprisingly, he does not even once mention the expression in his whole letter. Both Abraham and Rahab, two models for the right righteousness (2:21-25), lived before the law, or respectively, without the law. Hence, they did not do a single work of the law. In the same way, James always makes the law more precise through some kind of narrow designation. He does not speak of the law as such. Rather, he puts emphasis on "the perfect law of freedom" (1:25), "the royal law" (2:8), and "the law of freedom" (2:12). It seems that he wittingly avoids the identification with the Sinaitic law.[16] In addition, he connects the content of the law with the loving turn toward the neighbor (2:8) and assumes the eschatological freedom of Jeremiah 31:31-34 as the basis of Christian

---

[14] More for Luther's view of the letter of James with references, see Laato 1997, 43-45 (cf. 82-84).

[15] See Laato 1997.

[16] Ibid., 65-66.

obedience (1:25, 2:12) ever since "the word of truth" (1:18) or the gospel that saves has been implanted in the human hearts (1:21).[17] Strikingly, James and Paul are in full harmony with each other in their respective approach to their Jewish heritage. They both read the Old Testament from the perspective of the New Testament. In consequence, they regard the new life in faith and love as the fulfillment of Jeremiah 31:31-34. It is also the fulfillment of the law but not on the level of ordinary nomistic activity. Instead, it harks back to the divine recreation or regeneration. That creates or generates the conditions of the true obedience consistent with the intent of the Torah (2 Corinthians 4:6 and James 1:18).[18]

To say the least, Luther misinterprets the Epistle of James. Apparently, he does not understand the theological nuances in it. The one who on good grounds reforms the medieval church, paradoxically at the next moment, on bad grounds deforms the early church as far as he distorts the Holy Writ of a leading figure during the apostolic era. Shame on him! In his reading of the Epistle of James, Luther amplifies and magnifies his mistake as he does not regard the fact that New Testament authors (like Jewish sages) do not abolish the law though they affirm (unlike Jewish sages) that the law has been abrogated. He does perfectly recognize the latter point. That's why he became the Reformer. But he does not fully realize the former point. That's why the Reformer has to be reformed according to his own main principle of *Sola Scriptura*.

Concluding remarks

It might have meant a lot to Luther and his later extreme views on Jews if he had obtained a better perception of the overall Jewish setting of the theology of Paul and James. Ultimately, he seems not to grasp the full scope and scale of their fervent intention to underline the real fulfillment of the Old Testament law in Christian love and, at the same time, to underscore the completely different fulfillment

---

[17] More for the eschatological line of thought in the Epistle of James, see Laato 1997, 47-61.

[18] Laato 1997, 71-78.

of the Old Testament law through Christian faith. In conclusion: A more "Lutheran" Paul assumes a more "Jewish" Luther. That is the cornerstone in the new quest for both of them.[19]

---

[19] Here, I decline from dealing with the deep-rooted causes or far-reaching effects of Luther's views on Jews. At least, he has not presented any theories of racial differences that produce an inherent superiority or inferiority of a particular race or ethnic group. Cf. Alfsvåg 2019, 237-244. In general, Luther's theology is largely based on his semitic reading and interpretation of the biblical texts. For instance, he discarded scholastic logomachy and Aristoteles' philosophy as the real foundation of his thinking. In consequence, he is a case in point given that his successors "test everything" and "hold on to the good" (1 Thessalonians 5:21).

9

The state of research
after this research

Overview

The Pauline line of thought in 2 Corinthians 3:1-18 has proven exceptionally challenging. Its notorious reputation of "a tortuous passage"[1] hits the
nail right on the head. Therefore, it has also caused a gamut of different
explanations. In one way or another, they commonly revolve around the
specific antithesis between the "letter" and the "Spirit" in v. 6. In the main,
four chief alternatives stand out in research history. They have already
been outlined as they were partially exposed to opposing and supporting
arguments.[2] That former discussion should now be taken forward here.

1. The "letter" as the literal sense
of the Old Testament

First, the "letter" has traditionally been seen as the literal sense of the
Old Testament in contrast to the "Spirit" as the spiritual sense of it.
Yet, nowhere in Pauline letters does the "Spirit" stand for the deeper
meaning of the text. In 2 Corinthians 3, πνεῦμα represents "the Spirit
of the living God" (apparently, v. 6 harks back to v. 3). Therefore, the
chapter does not, as expected, call for an allegorical interpretation.[3]

---

[1] Martin 1986, 72. See also above, chapter 1.
[2] See above, chapter 2.
[3] See above, chapter 2: point 1.

In defense of the traditional approach, it seems to have an element of truth. For sure, Paul does not read the Old Testament law according to the "literal-letteral" meaning. He underlines that Christians should not let themselves be circumcised and obey all the commandments "in flesh" or in a conventional Jewish fashion. Instead, he underscores that they should fulfill all the commandments "in Spirit" or in sincere love that faith generates. He *does* read the Old Testament law according to the "literal-spiritual" meaning. In one particular respect, he indeed speaks for the spiritual sense of the text. However, he does not call for the allegorical-spiritual interpretation. It is much more about fulfilling the law on another level ("in Spirit" versus "in flesh") in tangible, practical, and even material terms. The special line of reasoning in Pauline letters might explain why some Church Fathers hold on to *two* concurrent clarifications of 2 Corinthians 3:6 in their writings. On the one hand, they affirm that the "letter" relates to the superficial literal sense of Scripture in contrast to the profound spiritual sense of it. On the other hand, they simply assert that the "letter" refers to the written law that kills the guilty sinner in contrast to the Spirit who gives life through the apostolic proclamation of the church.[4] In the light of the original meaning of 2 Corinthians 3:6, their ambiguity becomes more understandable. However, I am not an expert in patristics. I have to leave the issue here.

2. The "letter" as the legalistic misunderstanding and misuse of the Mosaic law

Second, the "letter" has been recognized as the legalistic misunderstanding and misuse of the Mosaic law. However, Paul for sure speaks of the initial law-giving in 2 Corinthians 3:7. He would hardly have attributed a degree of glory to a distortion of the divine revelation in vv. 7-11. Neither would he presume that Moses functions as a minister of a badly maltreated Torah. It is the "letter" (read: the law) *per se* that kills. The "letter" does not kill only when it has been *mis*understood.[5]

---

[4] Schneider 1953, 163-187, especially 184-187. See further above, chapter 2: point 1.

[5] See above, chapter 2: point 2. Here, we should keep in mind that the glory of the Mosaic ministry in Exodus 33-34 refers to God's gracious presence in the midst of the rebellious Israel. It anticipates the apostolic ministry in

Nonetheless, the utmost caution of hardening in vv. 14-15 relates to the misreading and misunderstanding of the old covenant document (v. 14) and the books of Moses (v. 15). It is very hard for the Jews to see what is right in front of their eyes. Thus, their failure *does* involve an intellectual dimension of religious rebellion. More precisely, they believe that they should observe the Mosaic law "in flesh" and according to the "literal-letteral" meaning, instead of fulfilling the Mosaic law "in Spirit" and according to the "literal-spiritual" meaning. They do not realize that simple truth that "the more they win, the more they lose" since the "letter" kills and does not give life (v. 6). Their very best endeavors run into the sand. Maybe then, they try even harder, but without much or any success at all. Their condition will not change whatever changes they make in their thoughts and behaviors as long as they stay inside the boundaries of the "letter" and on the level of their "flesh" (as demonstrated in the preceding inquiry). A real change will take place only when they consent to their own death and their new life that starts as soon as the Spirit brings forth faith. Next, he brings forth also the fruit of the Spirit in them. That's the way they fulfill the whole law. In other words, the legalistic and incorrect use of the Mosaic law does not, in a strict sense, stop by means of the non-legalistic and correct use of the Mosaic law. No, the route from the former to the latter goes via a transcendental transformation and not through an immanent instruction (or indoctrination). In traditional biblical terms, recreation or regeneration is required.

3. The "letter" only as an outward conformity to the Mosaic law and devoid of any inward obedience

Third, the "letter" has been acknowledged as an outward adherence to the Mosaic law but with no inward assent to it. The real conversion and the true alteration of the mind come about by the Spirit. Hence, the antithesis in 2 Corinthians 3:6 is rather understood in continuum and not in contrast. Deep down, it turns into a complementary relationship.

---

correspondence with the preaching of the gospel in the new covenant (see above, chapters 5 and 6).

There is no change in the Mosaic law but in the ability of believers to obey the Mosaic law. By dint of the Spirit, they are enabled and empowered to fulfill it. Yet, despite the right emphasis on the continuity between the old and the new covenant, the specific focus on the killing effect of the "letter" in 2 Corinthians 3 principally remains out of sight. The Mosaic law amounts to a fiasco. It becomes a mere problem to be overcome. It simply appears deficient. But definitely, the very opposite is the case. The "letter" delivers death. It executes those under its authority. That aspect should not fall into obscurity or oblivion.[6]

In plain terms, it follows that the antithesis between the "letter" and the "Spirit" as a mere contrast between an outward and inward obedience compares to a case where the negative turns into the positive if or when the Spirit functions as an intermediary link between the two. The former disappears. The latter remains. As a result, the killing "letter" has been rendered harmless with the Spirit's help. In Pauline theology, it is not that easy. The ministry of death cannot somehow be subsumed into the ministry of life. They both have to do their devoir. The former mortifies. The latter vivifies. Yet, the continuity between the old and the new covenant prevails. The "letter" stands for the law as it has to be kept "in flesh" and according to the "literal-letteral" meaning. Instead, the Spirit causes faith that produces love. Simply put, he brings forth the new life in faith (justification) that is lived out in love (sanctification). In consequence, Christians fulfill the law. They keep the commandments "in Spirit" and according to the "literal-spiritual" meaning. There is the sum and substance of the matter.

4. The "letter" as the Mosaic law that condemns and kills the sinner

Fourth, the "letter" has been connected with the Mosaic law that condemns and kills those who do not obey it. It certainly epitomizes

---

[6] See above, chapter 2: point 3. Cf. Westerholm 1984, 239. He writes with reference to Romans 7:6 as follows: "It must be emphasized that serving God 'in the new way of the spirit' replaces service 'in the old way of the letter'; it is not added to it." He then avows that Christians who have died to the law are no longer "under obligation to fulfil its concrete commands" (ibid.). Here, I disagree. For my own view, see below.

the Sinaitic legislation that "was engraved in letters on stone" (v. 7) at the inauguration of the old covenant. The use of language further-more harks back to "tablets of stone" (v. 3). Besides, the text points forward to the metonymy of "the old covenant or Moses being read" (vv. 14-15). As a consequence, the "letter" and the "Spirit" stand in contrast to each other and not in continuum (as in the third alternative above). They represent the antagonism of the traditional Reformation (Lutheranism) between the law and the gospel. The former refers to "Moses in action." The latter relates to "Christ in action."[7]

As sound and solid as the conventional dichotomy between the law and the gospel proves itself also in modern exegetics, the fact remains that it does not do full justice to 2 Corinthians 3. The chapter strictly speaks about the opposition between the "letter" and the "Spirit" (v. 6). The "letter" indeed designates the Sinaitic legislation that requires a perfect scrupulous observance of all the commandments. They should really be done from the smallest to the biggest ones "in flesh" and according to the "literal-letteral" meaning. However, Paul does *not* use the word "law" (νόμος) in 2 Corinthians 3. Astonishingly, he does not use it *anywhere* in the whole Epistle.[8] Instead, he draws attention to his own notion of the Jewish Torah as the "letter" that depicts the reading he disqualifies. As an alternative, he prefers the studying of the Old Testament from the perspective of the Spirit. Here, he certainly denotes the outcome of his apostolic ministry or the goal of his proclaiming of the gospel. His preaching causes re-creation resp. regeneration. He emphasizes that the Spirit "gives life." It obviously equates with justification since "the ministry of the Spirit" (v. 8) and "the ministry of righteousness" (v. 9) precisely match each other.[9] Nonetheless, the thought runs further. The new life is to be lived out as well. The justification leads to sanctification: Christians are brought to life from the death in

---

[7] See above, chapter 2: point 4.

[8] Dunn 2013, 165. See also above, chapter 2: point 4.

[9] See, e.g., already Kamlah 1954, 280. *Contra* the quite speculative character of Provence's interpretation (see 1982, 72-73). He states: "Nowhere in this section does Paul emphasize the life-giving character of the New Covenant" (ibid., 72). Further, he maintains that Paul "does not here have in mind the life-producing function of his ministry" (ibid., 73).

their sins (justification) and now they live their new life in obedience (sanctification). They fulfill the law but not "in flesh" but "in Spirit" and not according to the "literal-letteral" meaning but according to the "literal-spiritual" meaning. Hence, the whole span of Christian existence comes into view. It does not fit into a framework of any tight circumlocution.[10]

Evaluation

As to the third and fourth alternatives, they are largely mirror images of each other. The one denies what the other admits. Either the antithesis between the "letter" and the "Spirit" is to be read in continuum and not in contrast or, vice versa, in contrast and not in continuum. Attention focuses either on continuity/similarity or discontinuity/ dissimilarity. Both extremes absolutely go much too far. As made known, the third alternative principally overlooks the killing effect of the Mosaic law whereas the fourth alternative primarily overleaps the apparent intention of fulfilling the Mosaic law. Hence, I play the middle and use the best from the two options in order to strike the right balance and find a happy medium.

In addition, there are some modifications or combinations of the former main four alternatives, but they are not to be dealt here. What has been written above, can quite easily *mutatis mutandis* ("once the necessary changes have been made") be applied to them as well.[11]

Along with the different approaches to the antithesis between the "letter" and the "Spirit," the perplexity of New Testament scholars increases all the more as a result of the fact that they seem not to know

---

[10] In his valuable article, Grindheim takes a good notice of the large context of Pauline theology (2001, 114). He writes: "In a number of other passages, Paul makes statements about the continuing value of the Mosaic law. His expectations regarding the ethical standard of the believers are modeled upon the Mosaic law." Then, he maintains that the question of "continuity and discontinuity with the Mosaic law for Pauline ethics" and the problem of "consistency and inconsis-tency" in Pauline thought fall outside the scope of his article. In fact, they are included in the antithesis between the "letter" and the "Spirit" (see above).

[11] However, for my short discussion with Dunn 2013, see above chapter 2.

with certainty what to search in 2 Corinthians 3 and, accurately, from which angle to read and analyze the whole chapter. E. Käsemann lays emphasis on the hermeneutical questions while S. Westerholm puts stress on the ethical terms. Both fully endorse their own positions and firmly exclude other perceptions. This is not the place to go at length into their lines of reasoning and range of arguments.[12] In light of the overall theology in the Pauline letters, they both are right in their convictions. No doubt, the antithesis between the "letter" and the "Spirit" leads to strong ethical obligations. Christians fulfill the whole law in faith that brings forth love. Their transformation has taken place and continually takes place in various situations. They live the new life they have received as a gift. Since they do not fulfill the whole law "in flesh" and according to the "literal-letteral" meaning but "in Spirit" and according to the "literal-spiritual" meaning, their ethical reorientation draws upon an overwhelming reassessment of the Jewish hermeneutics and understanding of the Old Testament. It leaves only the Christological reading of Holy Scripture. At that moment, the hardening stops. The veil finally drops off. Very simply, Paul's ethics has its theoretical basis in his hermeneutics, and his hermeneutics has its practical consequences in his ethics. In his thinking, they both belong together.[13]

Quite surprisingly, the state of research shows that all the main alternative interpretations of 2 Corinthians 3 have at least something going for them. None of them totally distorts the refined argumentation of the chapter. Ultimately, it seems that the well-balanced and wide-ranging reading by Paul of the Old Testament generally and Exodus 33-34 particularly allows for many different aspects and approaches. At any rate, a part of him or some central components of his theology are always left out of the picture. The pieces that do not appear to fit are telling signs of the inadequacy of the modern

---

[12] More for their views, see above chapter 1.

[13] Cf. Hays 1989, 131. First, he quotes Westerholm who underlines that the contrast between the "letter" and the "Spirit" has nothing to do with Pauline hermeneutics but rather with Pauline ethics. Then, he concludes that "Westerholm is certainly correct in what he affirms," but "his denial is not equally justified" because "a transformation occurs that is fundamentally hermeneutical in character" (see above).

methods or analyses. Then, other elements in Pauline letters are stretched and overloaded. It follows that the overall theoretical construction or exegetical explanation is thrown off equilibrium. At the end of my research, I now dare to hope that everything has finally fallen into place perfectly.

10

Summary and conclusions

Summary

2 Corinthians 3 has a reputation of being a very complex and per-
plexing passage. It presents a huge challenge for the interpreters. No
wonder if they hesitate to enter the arena. Some of them have invested
time and energy trying to make sense of the entire argumentation
in the chapter. It seems: "So many scholars, so many minds." That
reminds the reader of the ancient, unpromising dictum: "Abandon
all hope, ye who enter here."[1]

Hence, this book deals with an analysis and evaluation of the
line of thought in 2 Corinthians 3, especially from the perspective
of the antithesis between the "letter" and the "Spirit." Other related
texts are examined to shed more light on the main issue. Among
them the Epistle to the Romans, written not so long after Corinthian
correspondence and in Corinth itself, draws the most attention. The
same antithesis between the "letter" and the "Spirit" prevails there
(2:29, 7:6).

Given the considerable obscurity and uncertainty of 2 Corinthians 3, it appears next to impossible to write a history of interpretation.
The core question revolves around the antithesis between the "letter"
and the "Spirit" (v. 6). On the whole, there are four main alternatives
for the reading of the text. They all contribute important aspects to
the right understanding. Nevertheless, they do not solve every single
feature of the exegetical problems. Neither do they cover the entire

---

[1] See chapter 1.

field of distinct scriptural issues. Therefore, the search for a better overall view continues.[2]

On closer examination, 2 Corinthians 3 shows a rather coherent structure. It appears as a consistent whole. The different parts are clearly and distinctively marked. In terms of their content, they integrally fall into vv. 1-3, 4-6, 7-11, 12-17, and 18. The last verse brings the line of reasoning to a close and functions as a summary of the chapter.[3]

Further, 2 Corinthians 3 displays a recurring catchword bonding, in which one sense of a term implies another or several other ideas leading to a textual multiplicity and polyphonic diversity. The argumentation does not proceed in a strictly Aristotelian manner where syllogism, enthymeme, or any kind of rational scheme is applied. Rather, a free association of interrelated thoughts runs through the text. They tumble one upon the other and occasionally call for other associations. That is the way the line of reasoning proceeds. The same goes for the interplay of scriptural allusions in chapter 3. Their extensive concatenation and wide-ranging juxtaposition work in tandem on the metaphorical and nonmetaphorical levels. Paul piles up and pulls them together. He releases them into the semantic agenda of the new covenant where they speak for and from the perspectives of the fulfillment as obvious evidence for his readers' competence.[4]

As shown, the most relevant scriptural passages in and behind 2 Corinthians 3 are Exodus 34:29-35, Jeremiah 31:31-34, and Ezekiel 36:26-27. The three Old Testament texts closely belong together as a result of a verbal and non-verbal linking. The notion of glory in Exodus 32-34 stands for the god-ness and goodness of the Lord and his gracious presence in the midst of the idolatrous Israel (see especially 34:5-9). As such, it anticipates the future visions of the new covenant in Jeremiah 31:31-34 and Ezekiel 36:26-27. They do not forecast any kind of renewal of the old covenant (like king Josiah's reform was). Instead, they comprise a thoroughly fresh start, a complete shift and change in God's dealing with his own people, although his will, as once attested in the Mosaic law, remains unchangeable.

---

[2] See chapter 2.
[3] See chapter 3.
[4] See chapter 4.

Moreover, they both emphasize total human depravity and the need for divine intervention in providing release from corruption. Hence, they speak of the necessity of the spiritual heart transplantation.[5]

In his analysis of Exodus 32-34, Paul follows the Old Testament guidelines and explicates the chapters in light of Jeremiah 31:31-34 and Ezekiel 36:26-27. He does exactly what can be expected from the one who knows the Sacred Scripture inside out. All the three scriptural passages underline the divine benevolence and compassion in the face of heinous sins. Moreover, the juxtaposition of the glory of Moses and that of Paul in 2 Corinthians 3:7-11 suggests that there must be some element common between them or else the argument falls to the ground. They do agree on the glorious presence of the Lord in his mercy and grace. This is shown up there on the mount of Sinai in his theophany and down here on earth in his Christophany. They thus synchronize with each other. In other words, the glorious appearance of God to Moses in Exodus 33-34 lies on the side of the gospel, but the *ministry* of Moses yet amounts to that of death and condemnation in Exodus 19-32 as the entire discourse in 2 Corinthians 3 makes clear. In particular, the particle δέ with an adversative force in v. 7 underlines the paradoxical fact that the ministry of death and condemnation, nevertheless, came with the glory, splendent with clemency and leniency. In the mainstream exegesis, the motive of the shining face of Moses has as a rule been misinterpreted. It mostly represents the reproving factor in his role of mediator.[6]

Evidently, Exodus 34:29-35 does not spell out any explanation for Moses' placement of a veil over his face. However, his practical decision has widely been understood as an act of judgment that cuts off the access to the divine presence. As a consequence, 2 Corinthians 3 has been read along those lines. It ushers in a total distortion of the interpretation. Rather, Moses veiled himself to obviate the Israelites to see the end of his glory as a sign of divine presence among them. He persisted in his care for them, consistent with his intercessions for them. He did not relent from his role of mediator. The setting up of the Tabernacle (and the later erection of the temple) has then substantiated the manifestation of God and his gracious

---

[5] See chapter 5.
[6] See chapter 6.

glory (Exodus 35-40) just as the departure of his present glory from the sanctuary in Jerusalem symbolized the cessation of his covenantal compassion and tolerance (Ezekiel 10-11).[7]

The accurate and adequate analysis of the Old Testament setting helps in understanding the adversative force of the introductory conjunction "but" (ἀλλά) in v. 14: "But their minds were hardened." Certainly, it has neither an intensive sense ("indeed") nor an ascensive sense ("still more") as if Moses in v. 13 veiled himself with the purpose of condemning the Israelites. No, he did everything in his power not to call their free amnesty into question. He sought to prevent them from assuming that God's gracious glory does not stand firm. "But their minds were hardened." Indeed, they did not recognize their constant need for mercy. Later, they did not believe in the gospel either. Even to this day the veil remains over their reading of the old covenant (v. 14). Also, it covers their hearts as well (v. 15). Only if they turn to the Lord, will it be taken away (v. 16).[8]

Despite the principal coherence of divine glory in the old and new covenants, some weighty differences stand out between them (see especially 2 Corinthians 3:7-11):

1) As already the Mosaic ministry came with glory so also and with even more convincing *certainty* the Pauline ministry is attended with glory.
2) Since there was glory in the Mosaic ministry, then the Pauline ministry possesses an incomparably *greater* glory.
3) The glory of the Mosaic ministry was done away with, but the glory of the Pauline ministry remains or *endures forever*.
4) In the Old Testament, the divine glory relates to Moses alone. In the New Testament, it even pertains to Paul and *each believer* (v. 18).[9]

In addition, the figure of Moses and his intercessions for the benefit of the Israelites do not change the undeniable fact that the Mosaic

---

[7] See chapter 6.
[8] See chapter 6.
[9] See chapter 6.

law amounts to the ministry of death and condemnation (vv. 7, 9). It represents "the letter" that kills (v. 6). That is simply what it continuously does. Thus, it is not about any misreading. The law as a "letter" does kill by any reading. That is exactly its divine commission always. In contrast, the Spirit "gives life" (v. 6). He does his work through the apostolic ministry by the proclamation of the gospel. In terms of the Old Testament visions, he instigates re-creation, regeneration, resuscitation, resurrection, and revitalization. He alone ensures and guarantees the new life in faith. In the realm of his sovereign dominance, only that which has been brought to naught (death or non-existence) can be made alive or called into being. Human cooperation is missing here. Hence, synergistic currents disappear. All are bound in their own sins. The true freedom is found in the Spirit. He holds it (v. 17). Outside, there is nothing but more slavery.[10]

As a result, the "letter" denotes the literal reading and observing of the law. It does not encompass the characteristics of the new covenant, namely "writing the law on their hearts" (Jeremiah 31:33) or "putting God's Spirit in them" (Ezekiel 36:27). On the contrary, it refers back to human capacity and leads to boasting. Accurately, the "letter" comprises the whole compilation of legal records that should be read and observed very strictly in punctilious accordance with their literal meaning. For sure, it does not allow for a freedom of choice or variation of love. On the other hand, the "Spirit" brings about a new life through faith that shows itself in the deeds of charity. Evidently, he does not only represent some moral or ethical values but a totally different mode of existence that takes place because of the proclamation of the gospel. In his power, the Christians really fulfill the law in its entirety including the command of circumcision, the ceremonial or cultic ordinances of the temple, kosher regulations, and all other scrupulous decrees. However, they always follow them in love that is the fulfillment of the law (Romans 13:10). They do not practice them "in their flesh" in an outward manner. Simply, they do not Judaize.[11]

The antithesis between the "letter" and the "Spirit" does not mean that Christians might have spiritualized their fulfillment of the

---

[10] See chapter 6.
[11] See chapter 7.

law into an idealistic sphere of some distinctive principles. No, their moral life consists of offering their *bodies* and *themselves* as living sacrifices to God (Romans 12:1). In their conversion, the transformation concerns their *whole* being. Neither does the modern distinction between the literal and non-literal meaning make any difference here. Even less does the out-of-date contrast between the conservative and liberal interpretation carry weight. Obviously, Paul thinks, so to speak, "outside the box" in a very innovative manner. He understands the "letter" and the "Spirit" as two opposite ways of a word for word reading. It is about a "literal-letteral" and "literal-spiritual" study of Scripture. They exclude each other. Moreover, they function on totally separate levels. The former Jewish alternative relates to life "in flesh," while the latter Pauline alternative pertains to life "in Spirit." Ultimately, the pivotal issue turns on the question whether to read the Old Testament according to the "literal-letteral" or "literal-spiritual" sense. In both options, firm trust and strong confidence in Scripture prevails.[12]

Remarkably, Paul nowhere affirms that the several Mosaic commandments are reduced to one single commandment of love. He does not simply ignore or disregard them as redundant. Rather, he transposes them all into practice with immediate effect. He maintains that the whole law is truly fulfilled in genuine love of neighbor (Romans 13:8-10, Galatians 5:14). Neither does Paul affirm anywhere that the cultic aspects have turned out passé whereas the moral precepts still remain valid. Instead, he insists that Christians are circumcised, and they offer themselves as living sacrifices and undertake the temple service though they do not carry out any of it exactly to the letter but in Spirit. Definitely, Paul as a Jew does rely on Scriptures. Hence, he does not suggest that some parts of them should be left out of account. Quite the opposite, he announces that "everything that was written in the past was written to teach us" (Romans 15:4). However, everything should be read, understood, and lived out "in Spirit" and not "in flesh."[13]

The fresh insight into the antithesis between the "letter" and the "Spirit" in Pauline theology helps in identifying and evaluating the

---

[12] See chapter 7.

[13] See chapter 7.

characteristic facets of the "Lutheran" Paul who has ruined his previous good name and lost his highest reputation in modern exegetics
(and especially among the prominent proponents of the so-called new
perspective). At the moment, he appears as the villain of the story.
However, Luther has made a strong case for himself as he (maybe
more than anyone else) has drawn attention to the killing effect of
the law. He has not put himself before a temptation to temper the
negative force it exerts on those under it. For certain, he is one of the
very few scholars to grasp that crucial aspect in 2 Corinthians 3. The
letter indeed kills (v. 6). It does not kill by reason of any probable *mis*-
understanding. Instead, the law has its divine commission to mortify
so that the gospel will have its divine mission to vivify. Seldom does
similar clarity and precision prevail in modern exegetics. Besides,
Luther has rightly underscored the total human depravity and the
Christian life as *simul iustus et peccator*.[14]

Yet, Luther has not entirely accounted for the Jewish origins
of the apostolic proclamation. He has not in full measure perceived
that the whole Old Testament concerns all Christians. It really pertains to *"everything* that was written in the past" (Romans 15:4) and
applies—righty understood—to the Mosaic legislation as well without
exception. In his anxiety for a new form of legalism, Luther does not
insist on "the third use of the law" (*tertius usus legis*). Ultimately,
he has a right intention, but he fails to carry conviction. He does
not do enough justice to the continuity between the Old and the
New Testament. As told, Paul emphasizes that Christians fulfill the
whole Mosaic law including every single commandment, even those
instructions relating to circumcision, meals or foods, festivals, sacrifices, and temple service. However, he argues that they do not fulfill
the numerous orders of the Torah "in flesh" and according to their
"literal-letteral" meaning but "in Spirit" and according to their "literal-spiritual meaning." His conception makes more sense than the
later attempts to rewrite his thinking. Simply put, a more "Lutheran"
Paul assumes a more "Jewish" Luther.[15]

Finally, the outcomes of this research are related to the history
of research. The four main alternatives of the previous interpretations

---

[14] See chapter 7.
[15] See chapter 7.

of 2 Corinthians 3 have at least something going for them. Still, none of them puts all the pieces together and in their right places. Those parts that do not fit are telling signs of the inadequacy of modern analysis. It follows that the common exegetical assessment in that case is thrown off balance. This research is intended to add all the pieces to the puzzle and at last finish it and show the full picture. 2 Corinthians 3 is a good and balanced mixture of Paul's hermeneutics and ethics. Deep down, his ethics has its theoretical basis in his hermeneutics. Vice versa, his hermeneutics has its practical consequences in his ethics. In his thinking, they blend into each other.[16]

Conclusions

The fresh insights into the antithesis between the "letter" and the "Spirit" as well as its various important implications to Pauline theology throw light on the parting of the ways between Christianity and Judaism. The process of separation of the two religions from each other looks much more complicated than generally assumed. For certain, a brief exegetical study like this does not stand to track and trace the whole historical development. Nevertheless, the pulling apart of Paul from his Pharisaic past did not grow out of the naïve and very simplistic notion that his previous beliefs were not his present faith. Allegedly, he rejected Judaism precisely because it was not Christianity.[17] Neither did he depreciate "the works of the law" supposedly as the "Jewish identity markers" (circumcision, Sabbath, kosher food or food regulations in general).[18] Nor did he pretend that the main failure of Israel amounts to an imaginary state of their ongoing exile.[19] All those speculative made-up interpretations (including some others) of the New Perspective fail to explain the core of the religious conflict or the bone of the scriptural contention between Paul and Judaism. They are not radical enough. In a sense, they err on the side of caution. Evidently, the New Perspective has run its course. It should be laid to rest and rather leave the space for the New Quest that

---

[16] See chapter 8.
[17] Sanders 1977, 552. For criticism, see Laato 2019, 296-302.
[18] Dunn 2005, 22-26. For criticism, see Laato 2019, 302-306.
[19] Wright 2013, 139-162. For criticism, see Laato 2019, 306-318.

comprises the outcomes of the research at hand. As a consequence, Paul definitely breaks up with Judaism and pulls down "the works of the law" since he strongly competes against the illusion of observing the Torah "in flesh" and according to the "literal-letteral" meaning of the text. He considers that kind of religious interest and pursuit as the worst form of human self-righteousness and self-praise (notwithstanding the efforts to true piety and absolute dedication). In terms of innate capacity and capability, there is no way out of the quandary and dilemma. The shortage of remedies promising any solution depends on the fact that the actuality and reality of the new covenant, namely the writing of the Torah on hearts (Jeremiah 31:31-34) and the pouring out of the Spirit (Ezekiel 36:26-27), are missing. Thus, every hope for something better including even the last, desperate chance for change is doomed. It is all gone. The "letter" kills. Death remains and reigns.

Hence, Paul's rejection of the works of the law does not aim at a limitation of the works as Jewish identity markers or signs of national priority. He does not say anything about that kind of definition. It has been disastrously (mis)read into his writings. In his theology, the works of the law *are* simply the works of the law, namely whatever is done out of obedience to the Torah. In a Christian context, they are excluded. For sure, Christians do fulfill the whole Mosaic law. Yet, they fulfill it "in Spirit" and not "in flesh," in other words, according to the "literal-spiritual" and not "literal-letteral" meaning of Scripture. For that reason, they do not boost or bolster their self-righteousness and self-praise. Their good works show that they live a new life that has taken place in their inner being through the apostolic proclamation of the gospel. They live in a new covenant where the Torah has been written in their hearts (Jeremiah 31:31-34) and the Spirit poured out in their souls (Ezekiel 36:26-27). It makes a big difference. Christians have undergone a transformation in terms of re-creation, regeneration, resuscitation, resurrection, or revitalization. The Spirit gives them life. He remains and reigns in them.

Taken as a whole, Paul puts himself at odds with any kind of Judaism. On purpose, he drifts into a frontal collision with it in his reading of the Old Testament. He speaks for a new mode of existence. That's why there is no room for the old manner of living as Jews truthfully try to do what is written in the Torah. All the same, they still do it "in flesh" and only according to the "literal-letteral" sense of Scripture. In consequence, they are without exception bound to fail. It is indeed about a total failure. To say this is not to say that old-fashioned and outdated distortions (or conscious falsifications) of the Jewish religion in exegetical research in the end prove right. Absolutely not, they should never come back to the agenda of modern scholarship.[20] They are dead and buried. If they reappear, they are zombie-like monsters, and a time of horror will restart. Then, the future seems very much less attractive.

Notwithstanding, Paul's full-scale break with Judaism needs to be clarified. Strictly speaking, he also represents Judaism and reads the same Old Testament as Jews do. Similarly, he solidly insists on "everything that was written in the past" (Romans 15:4). Accordingly, he underlines that Christians fulfill the whole Mosaic law but not, as already shown, "in flesh" and according to the "literal-letteral" meaning of the Torah but "in Spirit" and according to the "literal-spiritual" sense of Holy Scripture. The radical and innovative shift in his thinking carries weight and makes his break with Judaism unreconcilable. He really thinks "outside the box." Over the past many years, the New Perspective has failed to explain the actual difference in his line of reasoning. Hence, the utter necessity for the New Quest becomes apparent.

Rightly, a serious word of caution: a new beginning should not cause a return to the outmoded positions. One of the very last and most prominent proponents of the old-line school is surely E. Käsemann. In a sense, he stood at a clear watershed between the past and the future. He learned his lessons while others never did. Ideologically, he sturdily confronted his teacher, R. Bultmann, and got many things right with the one-sided existential interpretation in exegetics at that time. However, the New Quest that just goes forward beyond the New Perspective should not fall back into the main concept of Käsemann but leave it and not reiterate more of the same. Accordingly, an assessment of some of his theological suppositions appears necessary to stay out of his false overall framework.[21]

---

[20] See Laato 1991, 6-37 and 1995, 5-30.

[21] For my critical confrontation with Bultmann and Käsemann, see especially Laato 2004, 343-353 and 2008, 59-62 (and some minor remarks in my other publications).

In his analysis of the antithesis between the "letter" and the "Spirit," Käsemann applies it to "a dividing line even through Scripture" in Pauline theology.[22] As his clear-cut criterion and condition for separating the scriptural data and determining "a canon within the canon,"[23] he strongly recommends "the difference between promise and law or—to put it in even stronger terms—the message of justification."[24] He then goes on and asserts that his "point must be carried even further." Because of "the dialectical handling of the Old Testament," he presumes that "large parts of the Old Testament have become meaningless for Paul." Logically, "a critical interpretation of scripture and of all tradition in general" follows. In consequence, the apostle "was forced to set scripture against scripture, tradition against tradition, the law as promise against the Torah as a demand for works." Yet, "he did not discuss this theoretically."[25]

Käsemann's theological reconstruction of the apostolic hermeneutics cannot stay up. He has built it on loose arguments as if on sand. The evidence for his fabrication falls down for two main causes.

First, Käsemann in his Lutheran ardor for a proper distinction between the law and the gospel errs in claiming that the demanding and condemning aspects of the Torah drop out of canon as "useless" or "meaningless" parts of Scripture. For that reason, he has totally misunderstood the "usefulness" or "meaningfulness" of the killing effect of the "letter" as the necessary presupposition of the vivifying power of the gospel. His overall viewpoint shows a precarious misconception of Pauline theology in its entirety.

---

[22] Käsemann 1971, 159.

[23] Ibid., 165: It "would hardly be going too far to talk in epigrammatic terms about a canon within the canon."

[24] Ibid., 159.

[25] Ibid., 159-160. See further ibid., 164-165. Käsemann speaks of Paul's "hermeneutical approach" and affirms that "it consistently determined his interpretation of Scripture and, from the perspective of the antithesis between law and gospel, gave it a critical determination." Paul "arrived at a curious dialectic" and "finally permits him to play off scripture against scripture." Käsemann refers to Romans 10:5-13 as "a test case." He thinks the passage confirms his main point. It shows Paul's freedom of dealing with the Old Testament as he will on the basis of his Christian beliefs or convictions (ibid., 155-166). For another interpretation of Romans 10:5-8, see above, chapter 7.

Second, Käsemann does not perceive that there are no "useless" or "meaningless" parts in the Old Testament canon at least as far as the apostolic reading of Scripture is concerned. As shown, the Torah does not lose any of its relevance and significance in the new covenant. Christians do not nullify it on account of their conversion. Neither do they downgrade it to a source of a reduced "mini-law." In contrast, they now fulfill the whole of it in faith since they follow all the commandments "in Spirit" and according to the "literal-spiritual" sense but no longer "in flesh" and according to the "literal-letteral" meaning.

Finally, it is not only the theological hermeneutics of Käsemann in terms of the antithesis between the "letter" and the "Spirit" that ultimately collapses. Almost all of his academic analysis of Pauline theology alters in content and emphasis as well. He illuminates that his reading of Romans 7:14-25 as a description of a non-Christian underpins his overall study of Romans. A different kind of reading of the passage undermines his whole exegesis, not just his interpretation of the context, but also all that "Paul says about baptism, law, and the justification of the ungodly, namely all that he says about the break between the aeons." The wide-ranging debate culminates in the question of the authenticity of Romans 7:25b. If it is original, vv. 14-25 turn into a description of a Christian.[26] In that case, a thorough shift of thinking follows. So, there is a lot at stake here.

---

[26] Käsemann 1980, 211: "[. . .] the price which has to be paid for assuming authenticity [of Rom 7:25b] should not be underestimated. For in this case, it is not just our interpretation of the context that falls. All that Paul says about baptism, law, and the justification of the ungodly, namely all that he says about the break between the aeons, will have to be interpreted differently." In a similar way, Dunn 1975, 257: "Rom 7 is one of those key passages in Paul's writings which offers us an insight into a whole dimension of Paul's thought and faith. Even more important, it is one of the few really pivotal passages in Paul's theology; by which I mean that *our* understanding of it will in large measure determine our understanding of Paul's theology as a whole, particularly his anthropology and soteriology. As interpretations of Rom 7 differ, so interpretations of Paul's anthropology and soteriology markedly alter in content and emphasis. Dispute about a tense, a phrase, a half-verse in Rom 7 means in fact dispute about the whole character of Paul's gospel." Further, see Garlington 1990, 197-198 and Wilder 2011, 1-2.

In contrast to Käsemann's mainstream or common-sense exegesis of Romans 7, the fresh insights into the antithesis between the "letter" and the "Spirit" call into question the outlines of his interpretation of the chapter. It follows that almost all of his analysis of Pauline theology should indeed be altered in content and emphasis. The law is "spiritual" (7:14). It therefore assumes a "literal-spiritual" reading. Paul or any Christian (the "I" of chapter 7) cannot "do" it especially on account of the constant evil desires in their hearts, but they still can "fulfill" it "in Spirit" (as presented in chapter 8). In consequence, a shift in thinking results concerning "baptism, law, and the justification of the ungodly," namely whatever relates to "the break between the aeons."

On the whole, the New Quest goes beyond the New Perspective. All the more, it leaves behind the old school of Käsemann, Bultmann, and other prominent proponents of existential theology. Thus, it has wide-ranging effects on the understanding of Pauline thinking. There is a need for and necessity of much revision in the future.

Selected Literature

Alfsvåg, K.	"Hur kunde du, Luther? Om Martin Luther, islam och judarna." In: *Den mångfacetterade reformationen. Red. R. Imberg och T. Johansson.* (Göteborg: Församlingsförlaget, 2019)
Allen, L. C.	*Ezekiel 20-48.* WBC 29. (Dallas: Word Books 1990).
Allen, L. C.	*Jeremiah: A Commentary.* OTL. (Louisville, London: Westminster John Knox Press. 2008).
Baker, W. R.	"Did the Glory of Moses' Face Fade? A Reexamination of καταργέω in 2 Corinthians 3:7–18," *Bulletin for Biblical Research* 10, 1–15 (2000).
Balla, P.	"2 Corinthians." In: *Commentary on the New Testament Use of the Old Testament.* (ed.) G. K. Beale and D. A. Carson. 753-765, (Grand Rapids, Nottingham: Baker Academic – Apollos, 2007)
Bauckham, R.	*Jesus and the God of Israel: God Crucified and Other Studies on the New Testament's Christology of Divine Identity.* Milton Keynes, (Colorado Springs: Paternoster, 2008).
Bauer, W.	*A Greek-English Lexicon of the New Testament and Other Early Christian Literature.* (Rev. and ed.), F. W. Danker. (Chicago and London, The University of Chicago Press, 2000).

Beale, G. K.   *We Become What We Worship: A Biblical Theology of Idolatry.*
(Downers Grove: IVP Academic, 2008).

Belleville, L.   Reflections of Glory: Paul's Polemical Use of the Moses-Doxa Tradition in *2 Corinthians 3.1-18.* JSNTS 52. (Sheffield: Sheffield Academic, 1992).

Blass, F., and   *A Greek Grammar of the New Testament*
Debrunner, A.   *and Other Early Christian.*
Literature. transl., Rev. R. W. Funk. (Chicago and London: The University of Chicago Press 1961).

Block, D. I.   *The Book of Ezekiel: Chapters 1-24.* (Grand Rapids, Cambridge: Eerdmans, 1997).

Block, D. I.   *The Book of Ezekiel: Chapters 25-48.* (Grand Rapids, Cambridge: Eerdmans, 1998).

Blunck, J.   "Freedom" in *The New International Dictionary of New Testament Theology*, ed. Colin Brown. (Carlisle, Grand Rapids: The Paternoster Press, 715-721, 1986).

Brown, R.   *The Message of Numbers: Journey to the Promised Land.* BST. (Leicester: Inter-Varsity Press, 2002).

Bruce, F. F.   *The Epistle to the Galatians: A Commentary on the Greek Text.* NIGTC. (Exeter. Grand Rapids: The Paternoster Press: Eerdmans, 1990).

Brueggemann, W.   *A Commentary on Jeremiah: Exile and Homecoming,* (Grand Rapids, Cambridge: Eerdmans, 1998).

Buttmann, Philip   *Buttmann's Larger Greek Grammar: A Greek Grammar for the Use of High Schools and Universities.* transl. from German, additions, E. Robinson (New York: Gould, Newman and Saxton, [2]1839).

Childs, B. S.   *The Book of Exodus: A Critical, Theological Commentary.* OTL. (Louisville, London: Westminster, John Knox Press, 2004).

Concordia	*The Lutheran Confessions. A Reader's Edition of the Book of Concord*, general ed. P. T. McCain, (Saint Louis: Concordia Publishing House, ²2007).
Concordia Triglotta	*The Symbolical Books of the Evangelical Lutheran Church, German-Latin-English* (St. Louis: Concordia Publishing House, 1921).
Cover, M.	*Lifting the Veil: 2 Corinthians 3:7-18 in Light of Jewish Homiletic and Commentary Traditions*. Beihefte zur Zeitschrift für die neutestamentliche Wissenschaft 210. (Berlin: De Gruyter, 2015).
Cranfield, C. E. B.	*A Critical and Exegetical Commentary on the Epistle to the Romans: Introduction and Commentary on Romans I-VIII.* (Edinburgh: T & T Clark, 1990).
Dillard, R. B.	2 Chronicles WBC 15. (Waco: Word Books, 1987).
Dunn, J. D. G.	2 Corinthians III 17 in *the Lord Is the Spirit*, NTS XXI, 309-320, (1970).
Dunn, J. D. G.	Romans 7:14-25 in *the Theology of Paul*, ThZ 31, 264-273, (1975).
Dunn, J. D. G.	Romans 1-8 in *World Biblical Commentary*, (Dallas: Word Books, 1988).
Dunn, J. D. G.	"The New Perspective: Whence, What, Whither?" in: *The New Perspective on Paul: Collected Essays*, 1-88, (Tübingen: Mohr Siebeck, 2005).
Dunn, J. D. G.	"'*The Letter Kills, but the* Spirit Gives Life,' 2 Corinthians 3:6," *Pneuma* 35, 163-179, (2013).
Durham, J. I.	*Exodus*. WBC 3. (Waco: Word Books, 1987).
Eastman, S. G.	*Paul and the Person: Reframing Paul's Anthropology*. (Grand Rapids: Eerdmans, 2017).
Ebeling, G.	"On the Doctrine of the Triplex Usus Legis in the Theology of the Reformation" in *Word and Faith*, 62-73 (London: SCM Press, 1963).

Elert, W.	"Eine theologische Fälschung zur Lehre vom tertius usus legis," *ZRGG* 1, 168-170, (1948).
Engelbrecht, E. A.	"Luther's Threefold Use of the Law," *CTQ* 75, 135-150 (2011).
Enns, P.	*Exodus*. The NIV Application Commentary. (Grand Rapids: Zondervan, 2000).
Fitzmyer, J. A.	"*Glory Reflected* on the Face of Christ, 2 Corinthians 3:7–4:6 and a Palestinian Jewish Motif," (*TS* 42, 630—44, 1981).
Friedrich, G.	"*Das Gesetz des Glaubens Römans 3, 27,*" *ThZ* 10, 401-417, (1954).
Friesen, I. I.	*The Glory of the Ministry of Jesus Christ: Illustrated by a Study of 2 Corinthians 2:14-3:18* (Basel: Friedrich Reinhardt Kommissionsverlag, 1971).
Fung, R. Y. K.	*The Epistle to the Galatians*, NICN, (Grand Rapids: Eerdmans, 1953).
Gardner, P.	*I Corinthians: Exegetical Commentary on the New Testament* (Grand Rapids: Zondervan, 2018).
Garland, D. E.	*1 Corinthians* BECNT, (Grand Rapids: Baker Academic, 2003).
Garlington, D. B.	*Romans 7:14-25 and the Creation Theology of Paul TrinJ* 11, 197-235, (1990).
Georgi, D.	*The Opponents of Paul in Second Corinthians. (Philadelphia: Fortress Press, 1986).*
Gleason, R. C.	"Paul's Covenantal Contrasts in 2 Corinthians 3:1–11," *BSac* 154, 61–79, (1997).
Greenberg, M.	*Ezekiel 21-37: A New Translation with Introduction and Commentary* The Anchor Bible 22A (New York: Doubleday, 2004).
Grindheim, S.	"The Law Kills but the Gospel Gives Life: The Letter-Spirit Dualism in Corinthians 3.5-18," *JSNT* 84, 97-115, (2001).
Guthrie, G. H.	*2 Corinthians* BECNT, (Grand Rapids: Baker Academic, 2015).

Hafemann, S. J.   *Paul, Moses, and the History of Israel: The Letter/Spirit Contrast and the Argument from Scripture in 2 Corinthians 3* (Tübingen: Mohr Siebeck/Paternoster, 2005).

Hafemann, S. J.   "The Covenant Relationship" in *Central Themes in Biblical Theology: Mapping Unity in Diversity* ed. S. J. Hafemann and P. R. House, 20-65, (Nottingham: Inter-Varsity Press, 2007).

Hagelia, H.   *Hvordan lese Det gamle testamentet: Innføring i Det gamle testamentets historie og litteratur.* (Oslo: Cappelen Damm, 2017).

Hamilton, V. P.   *Exodus: An Exegetical Commentary.* (Grand Rapids: Baker Academic, 2011).

Hanson, A. T.   "The Midrash in II Corinthians 3: A Reconsideration," *JSNT* 9, 2-28, (1980).

Harris, M. J.   *The Second Epistle to the Corinthians: A Commentary on the Greek* Text. NIGTC. (Grand Rapids: Eerdmans, 2005).

Hartenstein, F.   *Das Angesicht JHWHs: Studien zu seinem höfischen und kultischen Bedeutungshintegrund in den Psalmen und in Exodus 32-34.* Forschungen zum Alten Testament 55. (Tübingen: Mohr Siebeck, 2008).

Hays, R. B.   *Echoes of Scripture in the Letters of Paul.* (New Haven & London: Yale University Press, 1989).

Hermann, I.   *Kyrios und Pneuma: Studien zur Christologie der Paulinischen Hauptbriefe.* Studien zum Alten und Neuen Testament 2. (München: Kösel-Verlag, 1961).

Hickling, C. J. A. "The Sequence of Thought in II Corinthians, Chapter Three." *NTS* 21, 380–395, (1975).

Hofius, O.   "Gesetz und Evangelium nach 2. Korinther 3" in O. Hofius: *Paulusstudien.* WUNT 51, (Tübingen: Mohr Siebeck, 75-120, 1989).

Horton, M. S.   "Calvin and the Law-Gospel Hermeneutic" in *The Beauty and the Bands.* Papers presented

at Congress on the Lutheran Confessions
April 20-22, 1995. ed. J. R. Fehrmann,
D. Preus, B. Lukas. (Crestwood, MO, Minne-
apolis, MN: Luther Academy, 1995).

Hughes, P. E.   *Paul's Second Epistle to the Corinthians: The*
                     English Text with Introduction, Exposition
                     and Notes. Grand Rapids: Eerdmans, 1962).

Hulmi, S.   *Paulus und Mose: Argumentation und*
                     Polemik in 2 Kor 3. (Göttingen:Vanden-
                     hoeck-Ruprecht, 1999).

Hummel, H. D.   *Ezekiel 1-20,* Concordia Commentary. (Saint
                     Louis: Concordia Publishing House, 2005).

Hummel, H. D.   *Ezekiel 21-48,* Concordia Commentary. (Saint
                     Louis: Concordia Publishing House, 2005).

Japhet, S.   *I & II Chronicles: A Commentary* The Old
                     Testament Library (Louisville-London:
                     Westminster John Knox Press, 1993).

Jewett, R.   *Romans: A Commentary.* Hermeneia (Min-
                     neapolis: Fortress Press, 2007).

Johansson, H.   *Andra Korinthierbrevet 1-7.* KNT 8a.
                     (Uppsala: EFS-förlaget, 1990).

Kamlah, E.   "Buchstabe und Geist. Die Bedeutung dieser
                     Antithese für die alttestamentliche Exegese des
                     Apostels Paulus," *EvTh* 14, 276-282, (1954).

Käsemann, E.   "The Spirit and the Letter" in *Perspectives on*
                     Paul, tr. by M. Kohl 138-166, (Philadelphia:
                     Fortress Press, 1971).

Käsemann, E.   *Commentary on Romans,* tr. and ed. by G. W.
                     Bromiley (Grand Rapids: Eerdmans, 1980).

Kim, S.   *The Origin of Paul's Gospel.* WUNT 4.
                     (Tübingen: Mohr Siebeck, 1981).

Klein, R. W.   "Back to the Future: The Tabernacle in the
                     Book of Exodus," *Interpretation: A Journal*
                     of Bible and Theology, Vol. 50, 264-276, (NY:
                     Union Theological Seminary, 1996).

Klein, R. W.	*2 Chronicles: A Commentary.* Hermeneia. (Minneapolis: Fortress Press, 2012).
Laato, T.	*Paulus und das Judentum. Anthropologische Erwägungen.* (Åbo: Åbo Academy Press, 1991).
Laato, T.	*Paul and Judaism. An Anthropological Approach.* South Florida Studies in the History of Judaism 115, (Atlanta: Scholars Press, 1991).
Laato, T.	"Justification According to James: A Comparison with Paul," (*TrinJ* 18NS, 43–84, 1997).
Laato, T.	"Römer 7 und das lutherische simul iustus et peccator." (*Lutherische Beiträge* 8, 212–234, 2003).
Laato, T.	"Paul's Anthropological Considerations: Two Problems" in *Justification and Variegated Nomism.* Vol. 2: The Paradoxes of Paul ed. D. A. Carson, P. T. O'Brien, and M. A. Seifrid WUNT 2:181, (Tübingen: Mohr Siebeck, 343-359, 2004).
Laato, T.	"'God's Righteousness' - Once again" in *The Nordic Paul. Finnish Approaches to Pauline Theology.* Library of New Testament Studies 374, ed. L. Aejmelaeus and A. Mustakallio. ESCO 374. (London and New York: T & T Clark, 40–73, 2008).
Laato, T.	Paulus och lagen, in *Troen, teksten og konteksten.* Festskrift til Torben Kjær. (Hillerød: LogosMedia, 212-221, 2009).
Laato, T.	"Crucified with Christ and the new life of Christians, Romans 6:1–14 (and 15-23) revisited." in *Fri och bunden. En bok om teologisk antropologi.* Red. av J. Hellberg, R. Imberg, T. Johansson. Församlingsfakultetens skriftserie nr 13. (Göteborg: Församlingsförlaget, 95–127, 2013).
Laato, T.	"Salvation by God's Grace, Judgment According to Our Works: Taking a Look at Matthew and Paul," *CTQ* 82, 163-178, (2018).

Laato, T.   "*Simul Iustus et Peccator* through the Lenses
                             of Paul." *JETS* 61:4, 735-766, (2018a).

Laato, T.   "The New Quest for Paul. A Critique of the
                             New Perspective on Paul," in *The Doctrine
                             on Which the Church stands or Falls: Justifi-
                             cation in Biblical, Theological, Historical, and
                             Pastoral Perspective,* ed. M. Barrett. (Whea-
                             ton: Crossway, 291-321, 2019).

Laato, T.   *Hermeneutics in Romans: Paul's Approach to
                             Reading the Bible,* (Irvine: 1517 Publishing,
                             2021).

Lambrecht, J.   "Structure and Line of Thought in 2 Corin-
                             thians 2,14–4,6," (*Biblica* 64, 344–80, 1983).

Larsson, G.   *Uppbrottet: Bibelteologisk kommentar till
                             Andra Moseboken,* (Stockholm: Verbum,
                             ²1997).

Legarth, P. V.   *Jesus er Herren: Studier i nogle aspekter af
                             Kyrios-kristologien hos Paulus.* Menigheds-
                             fakultetets Videnskabelige Serie 9. (Århus:
                             Forlaget Kolon, 2004).

Lenski, R. C. H.   *The Interpretation of St. Paul's First and Sec-
                             ond Epistles to the Corinthians.* (Minneapolis:
                             Augsburg Publishing House, 1963).

Lindqvist, P.   *Sin at Sinai: Early Judaism Encounters
                             Exodus 32,* Studies in Rewritten Bible 2.
                             (Turku—Winona Lake: Åbo Akademi Uni-
                             versity, Eisenbrauns, 2008).   .

Longenecker, R. N.   *The Epistle to the Romans: A Commentary
                             on the Greek Text.* NIGTC. (Grand Rapids:
                             Eerdmans, 2016).

Longman III, T.,   *An Introduction to the Old Testament.* (Grand
and Dillard, R. B.   Rapids: Zondervan, ²2006).

Lundbom, J. R.   *Jeremiah 1-20: A New Translation with
                             Introduction and Commentary,* The Anchor
                             Bible 21B, (New York: Doubleday, 1999).

Lundbom, J. R.   *Jeremiah 21-36: A New Translation with Introduction and Commentary,* The Anchor Bible 21A, (New York: Doubleday, 2004).

Luther, M.   "Psalm 51" in *Luther's Works 12: Selected Psalms,* ed. J. Pelikan. (St. Louis: Concordia Publishing House, 301-410, 1955).

Martin, R. P.   *2 Corinthians,* WBC 40, (Waco: Word Books, 1986).

Martyn, J. L.   *Galatians: A New Translation with Introduction and Commentary,* The Anchor Yale Bible (New Haven & London: Yale University Press, 1997).

Meyer, J.   "Justification, the Law, and the New Covenant" in *The Doctrine on Which the Church Stands or Falls: Justification in Biblical, Theological, and Pastoral Perspective,* ed. M. Barrett. (Wheaton: Crossway, 533-560, 2019).

Middendorf, M. P.   *Romans 1-8,* Concordia Commentary, (Saint Louis: Concordia Publishing House, 2013).

Moo, D.   *The Epistle to the Romans.* NICNT, (Grand Rapids: Eerdmans, ^{2}2018).

Murray, J.   *The Epistle to the Romans: The English Text with Introduction, Exposition and Notes (Chapters 1 to 8).* NICNT, (Grand Rapids: Eerdmans, 1968).

Nathan E.   *Re-Membering the New Covenant at Corinth: A Different Perspective on Corinthians 3.* WUNT 514, (Tübingen, Mohr Siebeck, 2020).

Newman, C. C.   *Paul's Glory-Christology: Tradition and Rhetoric.* Library of Early Christology. (Waco, Baylor University Press, 2017).

Nygren, A.   *Pauli brev till romarna.* Tolkning av Nya Testamentet VI. (Stockholm, Svenska kyrkans diakonistyrelses bokförlag, 1944).

Olson, D. T.	"Numbers," *Interpretation: A Bible Commentary for Teaching and Preaching.* (Louisville, John Knox Press, 1996).
Philpot, J. M.	"Exodus 34:29–35 and Moses' Shining Face," (*BBR* 23.1, 1-12, 2013a).
Philpot, J. M.	*The Shining Face of Moses: The Interpretation of Exodus 34:29-35 and its Use in the Old and New Testaments.* A Dissertation Presented to the Faculty of The Southern Baptist Theological Seminary, 2013b.
Provence, T. E.	"'Who Is Sufficient for These Things?' An Exegesis of 2 Corinthians ii 15 - iii 18." (*NovT* 24, 54–81, 1982).
von Rad, G.	*Theologie des Alten Testaments II: Die Theologie der prophetischen Überlieferung Israels.* (München: Chr. Kaiser Verlag, 1987).
Räisänen, H.	"Das 'Gesetz des Glaubens' (Römans 3:27) und das 'Gesetz des Geistes' (Römans 8:2)," (*NTS* XXVI, 101–117, 1980).
Räisänen, H.	*Paul and the Law.* WUNT 29, (Tübingen, Mohr Siebeck, 1983).
Richard, E. J.	"Polemics, Old Testament, and Theology: A Study of 2 Corinthians 3:1–4:6," *RB* 88, 340-367, (1981).
Richardson, P.	"Spirit and Letter: A Foundation for Hermeneutics," *The Evangelical Quarterly* 45, 208–18, (1973).
Saleska, T.	"The Clarity of Paradox: A Meditation on Exodus 34:6-7." In *Simul:Inquiries into Luther's Experience of the Christian Life.* ed. R. Kolb, T. Johansson, and D. Johansson. (Göttingen, Vandenhoeck & Ruprecht, 2021).
Sanders, E. P.	*Paul and Palestinian Judaism: A Comparison of Patterns of Religion,* (London, Fortress Press, 1977).

Sanders, E. P. *Paul, the Law, and the Jewish People*, (Phila-delphia, Fortress Press, 1983).

Savage, T. B. *Power through Weakness: Paul's Understand-ing of the Christian Ministry in 2 Corinthians.* SNTS 86. (Cambridge, Cambridge University Press, 2004).

Schechter, S. *Aspects of Rabbinic Theology.* (New York: Schocken Books, 1965 (= 1909).

Schneider, B. "The meaning of St Paul's antithesis 'the letter and the spirit'," *The Catholic Biblical Quarterly* 15.2: 163-207, (1953).

Schreiner, T. R. *Romans.* BECNT 6. (Grand Rapids, Baker Academic, 1998).

Schreiner, T. R. *Galatians: Exegetical Commentary on the New Testament.* (Grand Rapids, Zondervan, 2010).

Seifrid, M. *The Second Letter to the Corinthians.* PNTC. (Grand Rapids, Cambridge: Eerdmans, 2014).

Stockhausen, C. K. *Moses' Veil and the Glory of the New Cove-nant: The Exegetical Substructure of II Corin-thians 3,1-4,6.* Analecta Biblica 116. (Roma: Editrice Pontificio Instituto Biblico, 1989).

Thielman, F. *Romans.* Zondervan Exegetical Commen-tary on the New Testament. (Grand Rapids: Zondervan, 2018).

Thrall, M. E. *The Second Epistle to the Corinthians I: Introduction and Commentary on II Corin-thians I—VII.* (Edinburgh: Clark, 2004).

Thurén, J. *Korinttilaiskirjeet, Tessalonikalaiskirjeet, Pai-menkirjeet.* (Helsinki: Aurinko Kustannus, 2008).

Ulonska, H. "Die Doxa des Mose," *EvT* 26, 378-388, (1966).

van Unnik, W. C. "'With Unveiled Face,' an Exegesis of 2 Cor-inthians iii 12-18. *NovT* 6, 153-169, (1963).

Vegge, I. *2 Corinthians—a Letter about Reconcilia-tion: A Psychagogical, Epistolographical and*

	Rhetorical Analysis. WUNT 239. (Tübingen: Mohr Siebeck, 2008).
Vogel, L. M.	"A Third Use of the Law: Is the Phrase Necessary?" *CTQ* 69, 191-220, (2005).
Watson, F.	*Paul and the Hermeneutics of Faith.* (London, New York: T & T Clark, 2004).
Watts, J. W.	"Aaron and the Golden Calf in the Rhetoric of the Pentateuch," *JBL* 130, 417-430, (2011).
Wenz, A.	*Das Wort Gottes—Gericht und Rettung: Untersuchungen zur Autorität der Heiligen Schrift in Bekenntnis und Lehre der Kirche.* (Göttingen: Vandenhoeck & Ruprecht, 1996).
Westerholm, S.	"*Letter and Spirit: The* Foundation of Pauline *Ethics*," *NTS* 30, 229-248, (1984).
Westerholm, S.	"The 'New Perspective' at Twenty-Five," in *Justification and Variegated Nomism.* Vol. 2: The Paradoxes of Paul. ed. D. A. Carson, P. T. O'Brien, and M. A. Seifrid. WUNT 2:181. (Tübingen: Mohr Siebeck, 1-38, 2004*).*
Westerholm, S.	"Paul's Anthropological 'Pessimism' in its Jewish Context." In *Divine and Human Agency in Paul and His Cultural Environment.* ed. John M. G. Barclay and Simon J. Gathercole. (London: T & T Clark, 71-98, 2008).
Wilder, T. L.	"Introduction." in *Perspectives on Our Struggle with Sin. 3 Views of Romans 7.* ed. T. L. Wilder. (Nashville: B&H Publishing Group, 2011).
Wilson, W. T.	*Love without Pretense: Romans 12.9-21 and Hellenistic-Jewish Wisdom Literature.* WUNT 46. (Tübingen: Mohr Siebeck, 1991).
Wright, N. T.	*Paul and the Faithfulness of God.* (London: SPCK, 2013).

Appendix

A Critique of the
New Perspective on Paul[1]

In New Testament scholarship, Pauline research continues to triumph.[2] The debate about the New Perspective on Paul broadens and gains depth, yet it also becomes more difficult and complicated with time. Interpretations diverge strongly. For the moment, they mostly exhibit diversity.[3]

The present debate was launched in 1977 with the publishing of E. P. Sanders' broad work *Paul and Palestinian Judaism*.[4] Since then, we

---

[1] The following chapter was originally published in *The Doctrine on Which the Church Stands or Falls*, ed. Matthew Barrett (Wheaton, IL: Crossway, 2019): 295-325. Republished here with permission of Crossway.

[2] This essay is dedicated to Professor Mark A. Seifrid on his sixty-fifth birthday, in appreciation of his scholarship and friendship.

[3] The New Perspective advocates are a large number of scholars who do not often find any consensus in their interpretations. Still, they do have something in common; otherwise, it would not make sense to speak of a fresh wave of research. Writing an overall research history seems next to impossible. In a brief article it is necessary to limit not only one's subject but also the number of scholars to include in one's notes. Who could demand more? No need to settle for less. On the research history, see Stephen Westerholm, "The 'New Perspective' at Twenty-Five," in *Justification and Variegated Nomism*, vol. 2, *The Paradoxes of Paul*, ed. D. A. Carson, Peter T. O'Brien, and Mark A. Seifrid, WUNT, 2nd ser., vol. 181 (Grand Rapids, MI: Baker Academic, 2004), 1–38.

[4] E. P. Sanders, *Paul and Palestinian Judaism: A Comparison of Patterns of Religion* (Philadelphia: Fortress, 1977).

have been overwhelmed with thousands of articles and essays, studies and investigations, volumes, monographs, and dissertations. Among the large number of scholars, two especially stand out: James D. G. Dunn and N. T. Wright.[5] They stand—so to speak—"a head taller than any of the others" (1 Sam 9:2).[6] Additionally, in recent times J. M. G. Barclay has made his mark on the state of research and distinguished himself from his equals. He has presented fresh insights into some stagnating problems and imparted a very welcome disturbance in the current debate.[7]

My task is to critically analyze the turning point in Pauline research that took place through Sanders and was later developed by Dunn and Wright. Last, but not least, the recent progress, initiated by Barclay, deserves attention. It goes without saying that not every detail in their overall views can be scrutinized. One must be selective, while at the same time recognizing that all involved, the present author included, attempt to contribute through their own unique work. Therefore, certain crucial themes are picked up and reflected on in more depth. Clearly, they are distinct from case to case: Those prominent scholars have their marked centers of gravity. To be sure, I hope that my selective use of their writings adequately embodies what they really want to say. The discussion, if needed, has to be continued on a wider scale in the future. Self-evidently, the view of Sanders is first in line, then those of Dunn, Wright, and Barclay.

E. P. Sanders
Covenantal Nomism in Judaism

Interestingly, the New Perspective on Paul basically arises from the new perspective on Judaism. If the old perspective on Judaism as a

---

[5] Cf. Douglas J. Moo: "Israel and the Law in Romans 5–11: Interaction with the New Perspective," in Carson, O'Brien, and Seifrid, *Justification and Variegated Nomism*, 2:185: "These two scholars [J. Dunn and N. T. Wright] are the best representatives of the 'new perspective.' [. . .] They will serve therefore as my major 'sparring partners.'"

[6] Unless otherwise noted, Scripture quotations in this chapter are my own translations (often in reliance on the NIV).

[7] See his major work: John M. G. Barclay, *Paul and the Gift* (Grand Rapids, MI: Eerdmans, 2015).

religion of gaining merits and earning salvation is no longer valid, it is no more possible to stand up for the old perspective on Paul as preaching against the legalistic understanding of God's grace. As a result, we have to reconsider the reasons for his break with his former beliefs.

Sanders dubbed the common Jewish "pattern of religion" *covenantal nomism*. He helpfully summarizes the position as follows:

> God has (1) chosen Israel and (2) given the law, which implies both (3) God's promise to maintain the covenant and (4) the requirement of obedience. (5) God rewards obedience and punishes disobedience. (6) The law ordains means of expiation and (7) the expiation restores the broken covenant. (8) All who through obedience, expiation and God's grace remain in the covenant will be saved.[8]

In other words, one gets in the covenant through acceptance of the law and remains in it through fulfillment of the law. Both the election (point 1) and the salvation of Israel (point 8) depend on God's grace, not on human merit. Succinctly, obedience as such earns neither election nor salvation. It effects the remaining within the covenant.[9]

Over the years, the sketch of covenantal nomism as the common denominator of the Jewish religion has caused much debate. It has been defended; it has been rejected; it has been modified; it has been amplified.[10] Still, Sanders has absolutely shown that Judaism should not be identified with a religion of complete self-salvation ("eine Religion völliger Selbsterlösung").[11] He rightly affirms God's

---

[8] Sanders, *Paul and Palestinian Judaism*, 422. Surprisingly, the depiction of covenantal nomism includes no answer to the question of how one gets into the covenant. See Timo Laato, *Paulus und das Judentum: Anthropologische Erwägungen* (Åbo: Åbo Academy Press, 1991), 73–74. Also available in English: Timo Laato, *Paul and Judaism: An Anthropological Approach*, trans. T. McElwain, SFSHJ 115 (Atlanta: Scholars Press, 1995), 58–59.

[9] Sanders, *Paul and Palestinian Judaism*, 419–22.

[10] Cf., e.g., the discussion in James D. G. Dunn, "The New Perspective: Whence, What, Whither?," in *The New Perspective on Paul: Collected Essays* (Tübingen: Mohr Siebeck, 2005), 55–63. See previously Laato, *Paulus und das Judentum*, 38–82; Laato, *Paul and Judaism*, 31–66.

[11] Contra Paul Billerbeck in Hermann L. Strack und Paul Billerbeck, *Exkurse zu einzelnen Stellen des Neuen Testaments: Abhandlungen zur neutestamentlichen*

grace as the basis of fulfilling the law. In other words, covenant is the origin of nomism. Therefore, the concept of covenantal nomism as an interrelationship between gracious election and required obedience clarifies the main lines well enough.[12]

To say this, however, is not to say that the concept of covenantal nomism achieves precision and clarity. It leaves, indeed, a great deal to be desired.

First, Sanders never explains in the most fundamental way why Jewish *texts* frequently fall short of such constitutive elements as covenant and election. He asserts, for example, that "rabbinic discussions are often at the third remove from central questions of religious importance."[13] However, he immediately rushes forward paying no attention whatsoever to his observation. Further, how does Sanders know that the rabbinic discussions about different halakic matters are merely "at the third remove from central questions"? If they are unimportant for him and his academic research, they still may be crucial for the original authors who wrote about them. No one would produce thousands of large sheets (e.g., Mishnah and Talmud) if he did not greatly appreciate his literary work.[14]

Second, the concept of covenantal nomism implies the question of human action and capacity in salvation. Sanders, however, mostly ignores anthropological emphases or premises. Only in

---

Theologie und Archäologie, KNTTM 4 (München: C. H. Beck, 1928), 6. See Laato, *Paulus und das Judentum*, 11–12, 32–37; Laato, *Paul and Judaism*, 9–10, 26–30.

[12] Dunn, "New Perspective," 62. Evidently, his conclusion reiterates the outcome of the fiery academic debate between Sanders and Jacob Neusner already in the 1980s. The latter asserts what the former, based on his (confusing) definition of the task, should have compared. On the other hand, the former affirms what he in fact did compare. Still, they both concede the existence of covenantal nomism in the rabbinical texts. For the whole discussion, see Laato, *Paulus und das Judentum*, 67–72; Laato, *Paul and Judaism*, 54–58.

[13] Sanders, *Paul and Palestinian Judaism*, 71.

[14] Laato, *Paulus und das Judentum*, 71–72; Laato, *Paul and Judaism*, 56–58. Sanders admits that he has not sufficiently taken into account the special features of the various forms of Judaism. Rather, he has focused on one common thread (i.e., covenantal nomism) running through his main sources. See Laato, *Paulus und das Judentum*, 68–69; Laato, *Paul and Judaism*, 54–55.

passing does he acknowledge that the Jews should obey the law in their own strength.[15] In this respect his line of reasoning needs to be completed. As Sanders specifically investigates how a religion functions, the definition of his task begs the question of what an adherent of that religion can and cannot do on behalf of his or her salvation. Where does one receive the power to move step-by-step to the final goal?[16] Even though the notion of God's grace permeates covenantal nomism, the whole process of redemption from beginning to end is not necessarily by God's grace alone.[17]

I have pointed out elsewhere that the idea of human free will amounts to *opinio communis* in Judaism. (One exception confirms the rule: the Qumran community seems to represent an absolute fatalism.[18]) Consequently, in covenantal nomism the Jews are supposed to contribute to their attaining of eternal life by doing their very best. They can and should do their best in their own strength but not to the exclusion of divine grace altogether. The issue at stake is cooperation. Covenantal nomism is a synergistic soteriology.[19]

Third, as Sanders delineates the main lines in covenantal nomism, he frequently causes confusion by using the word *salvation* in a narrow sense. It denotes either (1) the salvation-historical action of God (the establishing of the covenant at Sinai) or (2) the present state of salvation (belonging to the covenant) but not (3) the final salvation (eternal life). Thus, it remains unclear who in the end will be saved. The Jews must, after salvation is gained, carry on and exert themselves to achieve the future salvation, or else they might forfeit it. In other words, all's well that ends well (but not before the end arrives).[20]

---

[15] Sanders, *Paul and Palestinian Judaism*, 114–15, 261–70.

[16] Laato, *Paulus und das Judentum*, 58–63; Laato, *Paul and Judaism*, 47–50.

[17] Laato, *Paulus und das Judentum*, 73–78; Laato, *Paul and Judaism*, 58–62; these sections also include a similar discussion of Pauline soteriology.

[18] Laato, *Paulus und das Judentum*, 83–94; Laato, *Paul and Judaism*, 67–75. Later, Stephen Westerholm, "Paul's Anthropological 'Pessimism' in Its Jewish Context," in *Divine and Human Agency in Paul and His Cultural Environment*, ed. John M. G. Barclay and Simon J. Gathercole, LNTS 335 (London: T&T Clark, 2008), 71–98.

[19] Laato, *Paulus und das Judentum*, 185–211; Laato, *Paul and Judaism*, 147–68.

[20] Laato, *Paulus und das Judentum*, 196–98; Laato, *Paul and Judaism*, 156–57.

From that point of view, fulfilling the Mosaic law is the *conditio sine qua non* for final salvation in covenantal nomism. The Jews have to be obedient and carry out their good deeds in order to ensure their entrance into the world to come. Their contributions through human free will make the difference. Covenantal nomism is not a "pure" religion of grace without synergistic tendencies.[21]

Barclay has summed up the shortcomings in Sanders's overall portrayal of Judaism cogently:

> Sanders's analysis of the structure and content of Judaism emphasized primarily the *priority* of grace, the divine initiative that founded the people of Israel and contextualizes their observance of the Torah. He succeeded in demonstrating that, understood in these terms, grace is everywhere in Second Temple Judaism.[22]

Later he states,

> Sanders leaves unclear to what extent Jewish texts from this period do, or do not, *also* perfect the incongruity of grace. . . . Finding grace everywhere, he gave the impression that grace is everywhere the same, and that one perfection (priority) necessarily entails another (incongruity).[23]

Therefore, a comprehensive anthropological analysis bears heavily on the new perspective on Judaism. A reading along those lines has come to stay (without the prospect of any backtracking). By now, it has largely been acknowledged as an indispensable outcome and a turning point in the present state of research.[24]

---

[21] Laato, *Paulus und das Judentum*, 195–99; Laato, *Paul and Judaism*, 155–58.

[22] Barclay, *Paul and the Gift*, 152; italics original.

[23] Barclay, *Paul and the Gift*, 158; italics original; see also 191–92.

[24] Stephen Westerholm, "Finnish Contributions to the Debate on Paul and the Law," in *The Nordic Paul: Finnish Approaches to Pauline Theology*, ed. Lars Aejmelaeus and Antti Mustakallio, LNTS 374 (London: T&T Clark, 2008), 14. For other references to secondary literature, see Timo Laato, "'God's Righteousness'—Once Again," in Aejmelaeus and Mustakallio, *Nordic Paul*, 41–44. See also Preston M. Sprinkle, *Paul and Judaism Revisited: A Study of Divine and Human Agency in Salvation* (Downers Grove, IL: IVP Academic,

Participatory Eschatology in Pauline Theology

Following Albert Schweitzer, Sanders brings to the fore "participatory" categories in place of "juristic" ones. In other words, he promotes the idea of Christians being in Christ (in the Spirit) or participating in Christ (in the Spirit) rather than the message of justification through faith. Salvation is to be incorporated into Christ, to be united with his death and resurrection. The new life begins, persists, and reaches its completion in him.[25] The doctrine of justification is seen as one attempt to argue why Gentiles are admitted into the people of God without fulfilling the Mosaic law.[26]

Consequently, Paul thinks "backward." He proceeds "from solution to plight." Insofar as Christ exercises his lordship over those who

---

2013). Sprinkle writes that "a full-scale treatment of the anthropology was lacking until Timo Laato published his dissertation, *Paul and Judaism: An Anthropological Approach*." Then, he insists that many opponents of the New Perspective "have taken Laato's conclusion at face value." As a result, they have "assumed that Laato's study ended the discussion, hammering the proverbial nail in the coffin" and that "Laato's study is proof enough" (126–27). Next, Sprinkle asks if my work is "the final word on anthropology" and concludes rightly that "there is much more to be said" (127). He refers to Stephen Westerholm's important studies. To be sure, "Westerholm arrives at a conclusion similar to Laato's" (127). Therefore, Sprinkle sets before himself the laudable task of examining "the soteriological structure of Paul and Judaism" more closely. However, in the end he examines the soteriological structure of Paul and the Dead Sea Scrolls (28). He concludes that the anthropological view is more pessimistic in Qumran than in Judaism in general (125–44). All in all, his conclusion is in full agreement with the outcomes of Westerholm's studies and mine. They simply give expression to well-known facts that are generally recognized—now also by Sprinkle himself. Cf. Laato, *Paul and Judaism*, 72; Laato, *Paulus und das Judentum*, 91: "In summary: it appears that free will in the domain of soteriology among the Jews from Sirach until the Babylonian Talmud was *opinio communis*. A single (important) exception confirms the rule: the Qumran community seems to represent an absolute fatalism." (A question of much more weight concerns the consequences of anthropology in the soteriological context, discussed further below.)

[25] Sanders, *Paul and Palestinian Judaism*, esp. 463–68; see also 434–41, 491–95, 502–3.

[26] Sanders, *Paul and Palestinian Judaism*, 497. See also E. P. Sanders, *Paul, the Law, and the Jewish People* (Philadelphia: Fortress, 1983), 47–48 and passim.

believe in him, it follows inevitably that sin exercises its lordship over those who do not believe in him. As evidence Paul refers to the irrefutable experience that we all sin. Thus, he deduces from his soteriology his anthropology. He starts from the axiom *Christ is the Savior* and then derives his anthropological premise: *everyone needs a Savior.*[27]

On the whole, Sanders calls the Pauline way of reasoning "participatory eschatology." He describes it as follows:

> 1. God sent Christ in order that all (Jews and Gentiles) might be saved. 2. One is saved when he is united to Christ, that is, dies and is resurrected with him. 3. Only on the Day of Judgment will the Christian be fully incorporated into Christ. 4. Already in this time the behavior of Christians should be an expression of their new existence in Christ. 5. Since Christ died for all, all must have been under the dominion of sin. They have lived "in the flesh" and not "in the spirit."[28]

In the wake of the initial contribution of Sanders, the discussion has advanced to a great extent in close connection with his innovative arguments. It has been shown that a sharp polarization of participatory and juristic categories is in fact more or less artificial. They rather support and explain each other. Often, they even appear side by side in the same verse. To illustrate this, I have presented participatory expressions in bold and juristic expressions in italic as follows:[29]

> Of him you are **in Christ Jesus**, who has become for us wisdom, *righteousness*, holiness, and redemption from God. (1 Cor. 1:30)

> God made him who had no sin to be sin for us, so that **in him** we might become the *righteousness* of God. (2 Cor. 5:21)

> If, while we seek to be *justified* **in Christ**, it becomes evident that we ourselves are sinners, does that mean that Christ promotes sin? Absolutely not! (Gal. 2:17)

---

[27] Sanders, *Paul and Palestinian Judaism*, 442–47, 474–75, 499.

[28] Sanders, *Paul and Palestinian Judaism*, 549.

[29] Laato, "'God's Righteousness,'" 63. See also Timo Laato, "Paul's Anthropological Considerations: Two Problems," in Carson, O'Brien, and Seifrid, *Justification and Variegated Nomism*, 2:348–49.

... and be found **in him**, not having a *righteousness* of my own that comes from the law, but that which is through faith in Christ—the *righteousness* that comes from God and is by faith. (Phil. 3:9)

Compare further these similar passages:

... and are *justified* by his grace as a gift, through the redemption that is **in Christ Jesus**, whom God put forward as a propitiation by his blood [Gk. **in his blood**], to be received by faith. This was to show God's *righteousness*. (Rom. 3:24–25)

Therefore, there is now no *condemnation* for those who are **in Christ Jesus**. (Rom. 8:1)

But you were washed, you were sanctified, you were *justified* **in the name of the Lord Jesus Christ and by the Spirit of our God**. (1 Cor. 6:11) [God's name (as known) is frequently identified with God himself in the Old Testament.]

So the law was put in charge [παιδαγωγός] to lead us to Christ that we might be *justified* by faith. . . . You are all sons of God through faith **in Christ Jesus**. (Gal. 3:24, 26).

Under such circumstances, it is no longer worth inquiring whether participatory or juristic terminology expresses the center of Paul's theology better or more accurately. He makes no (theological) distinction between them. Rather, he integrates them together. From different perspectives they both illustrate his soteriology. They are like two sides of one coin. One does not exist without the other.[30]

---

[30] Peter Stuhlmacher states, "Führende Vertreter der New Perspective propagieren aufs neue die uralte Zweiteilung der paulinischen Soteriologie in einen juridischen und einen partizipatorischen Teil. . . . Diese Aufteilung wird überflüssig, wenn man den von Paulus selbst klar herausgestellten Zusammenhang von Rechtfertigung, Sühne und Versöhnung beachtet und bedenkt, dass der Christus Jesus für den Judenchristen Paulus immer auch eine korporative Repräsentationsfigur ist." "Zum Thema Rechtfertigung," in *Biblische Theologie und Evangelium: Gesammelte Aufsätze*, WUNT 146 (Tübingen: Mohr Siebeck, 2002), 54. Dunn also states, "It is important at this

Still, in connection with his soteriology, Paul emphasizes the Christian's being in Christ but not, strictly speaking, Christ's being in the Christian. Accordingly, he always preserves the objectivity of the salvific event. It does not fade into a merely subjective experience. Justification happens outside the believer. He is counted righteous in Christ.[31]

Linked to the previous point, there is a kind of "instrumentalism" or "sacramentalism" to justification. The participation in Christ and in his righteousness is completed explicitly in the proclaimed and written gospel, in baptism (see Rom. 6:1–11; 1 Cor. 6:11; Gal. 3:24–27), and in Holy Communion (1 Cor. 10:16–17; 11:23–29). It does not depend on internal persuasion, though it surely has a connection to it.[32]

Although Sanders lays great weight on the participatory categories, he does not sufficiently take them into consideration in his further appraisal of Pauline theology or soteriology. Granted that anyone not incorporated into or united with Christ stands under the dominion of sin, it definitely follows that he is not free and not even able to free himself from his bondage. Surely, he needs help. More than that: he needs to become "a new creature" (2 Cor. 5:17) through God's creative word (4:6). He cannot rely on his own strength at some stage in his conversion. Neither at some stage after his conversion can he trust in his own power. On the contrary, he lives if and since Christ lives in him (Gal. 2:20). Alternatively, he fulfills the law if and since the Spirit produces fruit in him (5:22).[33]

---

point to avoid the polarisation of 'justification' and 'participation' encouraged by the well known assertion of A. Schweitzer." "New Perspective," 83–84n354. Yet in the same context, Dunn does not recognize the need to distinguish between soteriological and ethical aspects. According to him, justification and sanctification blend together, and thus salvation is reduced to "*a process of transformation* of the believer." "New Perspective," 84.

[31] Paul applies participatory and juristic categories also in the area of ethics. They are then not to be mixed up with his teaching of justification (cf., e.g., Romans 1–4; 6). This is where Dunn makes a cardinal error! See "New Perspective," 80–86.

[32] Laato, "'God's Righteousness,'" 63–65. See also Laato, "Paul's Anthropological Considerations," 348–49.

[33] Laato, *Paulus und das Judentum*, 190–94, 199–204, 207–9; Laato, *Paul and Judaism*, 150–54, 158–62, 164–66.

Thus, in contrast to synergistic tendencies in covenantal nomism, Paul unambiguously represents a monergistic soteriology.[34] He maintains that salvation depends only on God's grace. As a consequence, he asserts that justification by the same token is by faith, not by any other means. On the whole, an obvious correlation exists between anthropology and soteriology. The idea of the total depravity of the human race implies the notion of the absolute superiority of divine mercy.[35]

Finally, the theory of Paul's thinking "from solution to plight" (and not vice versa) holds true as a *historical* description of his conversion: the shocking encounter with Christ on the road to Damascus started a far-reaching process in him and led him to rethink his theology, including anthropological premises. Yet the *theological* reflection runs the other way around, "from plight to solution" (and not vice versa): the anthropological analysis of human existence under the lordship of sin in Romans 1–3 points to the necessity of Christ's salvific death on the cross. Precisely in this respect Paul does not think "backward" but "forward" (as Rudolf Bultmann has stated).[36]

Paul's Break with Judaism

Since Sanders insists that covenantal nomism is not at all based on self-righteousness, merit, and boasting, he concludes that Paul did not discard Jewish religion because of its assumed legalistic soteriology. No, not in the slightest! The main reason was first and foremost Christological. Paul stands for a very exclusive Christology. He affirms that no other can save but Christ. Sanders argues that Paul did not consent to the Jewish soteriology simply (and this is somewhat simplified) because it was not *Christ*ianity: "In short, *this is what Paul finds wrong in Judaism: it is not Christianity.*"[37]

Later Sanders clarifies his position as follows: "What is wrong with the law, and thus with Judaism, is that it does not provide for

---

[34] See Matthew Barrett, *Salvation by Grace: The Case for Effectual Calling and Regeneration* (Phillipsburg, NJ: P&R, 2013).

[35] Laato, *Paulus und das Judentum*, 210–11; Laato, *Paul and Judaism*, 167–68.

[36] See Laato, "Paul's Anthropological Considerations," 343–53.

[37] Sanders, *Paul and Palestinian Judaism*, 552.

God's ultimate purpose, that of saving the entire world through faith in Christ, and without the privilege accorded to Jews through the promises, the covenants, and the law."[38]

Thus, the Christological argument is accompanied by emphasizing that salvation is meant for all and everyone, Gentiles as well as Jews. Accordingly, as the apostle to the Gentiles, Paul could no longer stay inside the narrow boundaries of the Mosaic law. In his thinking, particularism had to give way to universalism. The old covenant was replaced by the new.

However, neither a Christocentric nor an ethnocentric reading of Pauline theology—important as they are in themselves—should replace an anthropocentric perspective. Without a doubt, covenantal nomism amounts to a synergistic soteriology. Sanders himself admits that "to be righteous" in Judaism means staying within the covenant through fulfilling the law.[39] As a result, the final salvation depends on human efforts. Covenantal nomism involves the thought of cooperation that is based on an optimistic anthropology (the notion of free will). Indeed, it does not promote anything like God's grace alone.[40] Saying this does not mean that we should return to different, distorted pictures of Judaism(s).[41]

On the whole, it follows that Paul has reason to criticize the self-righteousness and boasting arising from covenantal nomism. His critical remarks go back to his highly pessimistic (or realistic) anthropology.[42]

James D. G. Dunn
The Question of Synergism

Initially, the New Perspective on Paul was so dubbed by James D. G. Dunn. He also emphasizes that it in fact flows from the new

---

[38] Sanders, *Paul, the Law, and the Jewish People*, 47.

[39] Sanders, *Paul and Palestinian Judaism*, 544–45 and passim. See also above.

[40] Laato, *Paulus und das Judentum*, esp. 263–65; Laato, *Paul and Judaism*, esp. 209–10. See also above.

[41] Laato, *Paulus und das Judentum*, 32–37; Laato, *Paul and Judaism*, 26–30.

[42] Laato, *Paulus und das Judentum*, 263–65 and passim; Laato, *Paul and Judaism*, 209–10 and passim.

perspective on Judaism (as has already been pointed out above).[43] Thus, he principally shares the overall delineation of covenantal nomism.[44]

Yet Dunn argues that "it may well be the case, no doubt is the case, that some of Sanders' statements are imbalanced in that they overstate the covenant side of the inter-relationship."[45] Despite this, "there was an inter-relationship between given election and required obedience in the soteriology of Second Temple Judaism," an inner linkage "which prior to Sanders was not sufficiently recognized, and which can now be fairly and effectively characterized in the phrase 'covenantal nomism.'"[46] Accordingly, Dunn also nicely consents to the outcome of the previous analysis.

In addition, Dunn even acknowledges a clear-cut synergism in Judaism.[47] Therefore, he actually admits that Judaism does teach salvation by human cooperation but based on God's amazing grace (covenant). Once again, his conclusion seems obvious (for the very reasons stated earlier).

Then, Dunn goes one step further and suggests that Paul himself allows for synergistic tendencies to permeate his soteriology. Dunn specifically refers to judgment according to works.[48] He makes his readers wonder whether they have to face the theological dispute from the past relating to Pelagius and his heretical teachings. Was it that we discuss the *New* Perspective on Paul? Frankly speaking, one must wonder whether we are here involved in *Pauline* theology at all.

At long last, Dunn fervently denies that "Paul's understanding of salvation was synergistic." Rather, his concern was "to question whether the charge of synergism should be laid so confidently at

---

[43] Dunn states that the New Perspective on Paul "builds on Sanders' new perspective on Second Temple Judaism, and Sanders' reassertion of the basic graciousness expressed in Judaism's understanding and practice of covenantal nomism." "New Perspective," 15.

[44] Dunn, "New Perspective," 55–63.

[45] Dunn, "New Perspective," 56.

[46] Dunn, "New Perspective," 62.

[47] Dunn, "New Perspective," 54–80, esp. 69–72, 80.

[48] Dunn, "New Perspective," 72–79.

the door of Judaism when some of Paul's language seems vulnerable to the same charge" and "to take more seriously and with due seriousness the other Pauline teaching" (predominantly on judgment according to works).[49] By and large, Dunn's back-and-forth rhetoric is aimed at downplaying the notion of human cooperation. Ultimately, he would be willing to drop the verdict against legalism in Pauline soteriology, provided that the charge of synergism in Judaism is not taken at face value!

Dunn's overall thinking becomes even more bewildering as he on another occasion writes as follows: "In all these cases [i.e., Rom. 4:4–5; 10:2–4; Phil. 3:7–9], therefore, it is difficult to sustain the claim that Paul was polemicizing against 'self-achieved righteousness.' *Of course, the texts just reviewed can be read that way.*"[50] In reality, Dunn admits here that his own reading of the Pauline texts is *not* the only one. Indeed, it is possible to understand Paul polemicizing against self-achieved righteousness (which goes back to the synergistic trends in Judaism).[51] That is exactly what "the later Paul"

---

[49] Dunn, "New Perspective," 80.

[50] James D. G. Dunn, *The Theology of Paul the Apostle* (Grand Rapids, MI: Eerdmans, 1998), 370; italics added. Cf. Dunn, "New Perspective," 41: "Here again I do not question the fundamental statement of principle which Paul enunciates in these passages [Rom. 3:20; 4:4–5; 9:11–12]. But again I wonder if the conclusion that Paul is attacking a works-righteousness attitude, an attitude embraced by Jews of his time, is *quite so soundly* based as most think, and whether Paul's attack is again *somewhat broader*" (italics added). Contra Dunn, cf. further Robert W. Yarbrough, "Paul and Salvation History," in Carson, O'Brien, and Seifrid, *Justification and Variegated Nomism*, 2:308.

[51] Cf. some remarkable passages in James D. G. Dunn, *Romans 1–8* (Dallas: Word Books, 1988): "What is attacked, therefore, is the self-confidence of the synagogue attender who faithfully hears the law being read Sabbath by Sabbath and who in consequence counts himself as one of the righteous, one of the chosen people (an equation encouraged not least once again by the Wisdom of Solomon and *Psalms of Solomon*), that is, one who is already assured of a favorable final verdict because as a member of the covenant people he has remained within the covenant, loyal to the covenant" (104–5). Or later: "In any case we must assume that Paul, in looking back on his life as a Pharisee, had long ago concluded that the law, far from binding individuals closer to God in truthful obedience, actually separated them from God and prevented them from accepting God's grace in its complete gratuitousness" (352). Or

(the one who wrote Ephesians)[52] does. Dunn suggests, "That [the disapproval of self-achieved righteousness] may have happened already in Eph. 2:8–9, where the issue does seem to have moved from one of works of law to one of human effort."[53]

Later, in another context, he writes,

> Here [in Eph. 2:8–9] the thought seems to have broadened out to refer to human effort in general as inadequate to the demands of salvation; salvation could be accomplished only by grace alone through faith alone. At the very least that implies that the Reformation understanding of Paul's theology of justification was already shared by the first Christian commentator on that theology.[54]

All in all, Dunn seems to saw off the branch on which he is sitting. He acknowledges that

1. Judaism was synergistic,
2. some crucial Pauline texts can be read as polemicizing against self-achieved righteousness, and
3. "the later Paul" does exactly that as he disapproves every kind of legalism.

So, the question naturally arises: Why not interpret the theology of Paul and his break with Judaism along these lines? Is there any compelling or convincing need for the New Perspective? Truly, it looks as if there is none. Rather, one should simply say that the

---

later: "With insight born of his conversion Paul sees that attitude to have been motivated (subconsciously) in large part by fear—a fear of failing to match up to a standard of exact obedience, a fear in other words not so much of God as of what his fellow Pharisees might think or say of his failure to conform. Paul thus, in all probability, extrapolates his own experience to that of his readers, confident that his Jewish and God-worshipping audiences have found in Christianity the same liberation as he had himself (v 2)" (460).

[52] Dunn, "New Perspective," 51. The later Paul is the one who also wrote the Pastorals. "New Perspective," 53–54.

[53] Dunn, *Theology of Paul*, 371.

[54] Dunn, "New Perspective," 52. That kind of reasoning continues also in Dunn's treatment of the Pastorals. "New Perspective," 53–54.

Judaism of what Sanders christened as covenantal nomism was synergistic. As a result, Paul has every reason for criticism.

"Works of the Law" as Jewish Identity Markers

In his concise summary of the New Perspective on Paul, Dunn does not simply build on Sanders's new perspective on Second Temple Judaism. He also observes and emphasizes "a social function of the law" as an integral feature of covenantal nomism. To put it in a well-defined dictum, the Mosaic law serves to mark off Israel from all the other nations.[55] Accordingly, Dunn argues as follows:

> When Paul said in effect, "All are justified by faith and not by works," he meant *not* "Every individual must cease from his own efforts and simply trust in God's acceptance," however legitimate and important an interpretation of his words that is. What he meant was, "Justification is not confined to Jews as marked out by their distinctive works; it is open to all, to Gentile as well as Jew, through faith."[56]

Consequently, Dunn contends that "works of the law" in the Pauline Epistles serve as "Jewish identity markers." They especially indicate circumcision, food, and Sabbath laws, even if they should not be narrowed to boundary issues only. By focusing particularly on those regulations, the Judaizers in Galatia put to the test the willingness of the Gentiles to enter into covenant membership and their readiness to remain faithful to the whole of Old Testament traditions and customs.[57]

The explicit emphasis on national separation or division by Dunn has caused much turbulence in the ongoing discussion. In the first place, Mark Seifrid raises objections. He regards it as "highly questionable" that Jewish identity markers symbolize "*mere* national identity."[58]

---

[55] Dunn, "New Perspective," 15.

[56] James D. G. Dunn, "The Justice of God: A Renewed Perspective on Justification by Faith," in Dunn, *New Perspective on Paul*, 199.

[57] Dunn, "New Perspective," 22–26.

[58] Mark A. Seifrid, "Blind Alleys in the Controversy over the Paul of History," *TynBul* 45, no. 1 (1994): 77.

Rather, he contends that circumcision (for instance, in Josephus's account of the circumcision of King Izates) symbolizes "not merely separation from other nations, but an ethically superior monotheism."[59]

On balance, Dunn seems not to have turned a deaf ear to a call to revise his position. Later he writes as follows:

> I have no doubt that "works of the law" refer to what the law requires, the conduct prescribed by the Torah; whatever the law requires to be done can be described as "doing" the law, as a work of the law.... The phrase "works of the law" is a way of describing the law observance required of all covenant members, and could be regarded as an appropriate way of filling out the second half of the Sanders' formula—"covenantal *nomism*."[60]

Taken at face value, the quotation shows undeniably that "works of the law" point not simply to distinctive *ethnic* features but also to diverse *ethical* features.[61] In that case, Paul renouncing "works of the law" excludes not merely Jewish national priority but arrogant, human superiority as well. I am in full agreement with Seifrid: "All these observations give us reasons for thinking that in ἔργα νόμου as a guarantee rejecting of salvation, Paul rejects a moral superiority gained by obedience, notwithstanding that Jews who adopted such a stance would have attributed their progress to God's gracious covenant with Israel."[62]

Astoundingly, Dunn himself applauds these words as "a basis for a richer synthesis,"[63] even though they actually overturn his New

---

[59] Seifrid, "Blind Alleys," 79. Later Seifrid adds that it is "impossible to sustain the claim that Jewish 'boundary markers' signalled exclusivism or national identity alone. I must confess considerable puzzlement that both Dunn and Wright, who recognise that some Jews could regard other Jews as outside the community of the elect on the basis of halakhah, regard distinctive practices as simply 'exclusivistic,' borders without interior meaning." "Blind Alleys," 80–81.

[60] Dunn, "New Perspective," 22–23.

[61] Cf. R. Barry Matlock, "Sins of the Flesh and Suspicious Minds: Dunn's New Theology of Paul," *JSNT* 21, no. 72 (1999): 78–80.

[62] Seifrid, "Blind Alleys," 85.

[63] Dunn, "New Perspective," 26n107. In addition, Dunn affirms that Seifrid "is much more nuanced than the others."

Perspective on Paul! Rejecting "a moral superiority gained by obedience," the apostle to the Gentiles at the same time abrogates every
kind of synergism in Jewish soteriology. In the end, this is what he
finds wrong with covenantal nomism.

The Request for Consistency

By and large, reading Dunn (and above all, his copious commentary
on Romans) is puzzling. He indicates that he has reconsidered his
position. Despite his apparent reassessment, it seems that he still
tries to hold on to his original understanding of works of the law
as "Jewish identity markers." To quote him, "I confess to being a
little surprised by the difficulty apparently experienced by some
respondents in recognizing how ἔργα νόμου can denote what the
law requires, but with special reference to such crucial issues [as
Jewish identity markers]."[64]

Without doubt, Dunn was obliged to reassess his previous position to avoid the morbid criticism that it caused. However, the extension of "works of the law" to "what the law requires" with special
reference to Jewish identity markers is not the same as the notion of
"works of the law" as solely Jewish identity markers. All that the law
requires (notwithstanding the special reference to the Jewish identity
markers) comprises not only *ethnic* but also *ethical* dimensions. This
is completely at odds with what Dunn suggests. In this case, we are
talking not just about Jewish national priority; at stake is arrogant
human superiority combined with strong synergistic tendencies.

Elsewhere, I have emphasized that Dunn has modified his
former stance considerably.[65] It is not surprising at all that he fervently denies such a conclusion.[66] He maintains to have adjusted
his "initial formulation" only,[67] a claim of which I am strongly

---

[64] See James D. G. Dunn, "Yet Once More—'The Works of the Law':
A Response," in Dunn, *New Perspective on Paul*, 208. *Pace* Dunn, see Francis
Watson, *Paul and the Hermeneutics of Faith* (London: T&T Clark, 2004), 334–
35n41; Matlock, "Sins of the Flesh," 78–80.

[65] Laato, "Paul's Anthropological Considerations," 356n71.

[66] Dunn, "New Perspective," 22n94.

[67] Dunn, "New Perspective," 22.

suspicious. The discussion above runs completely counter to any denial. The fact remains that Dunn has fundamentally altered the content of "works of the law." Besides, he admits that Judaism is pervaded by human cooperation (synergism). As a result, what will be left of his New Perspective? On the whole, it seems to me that his overall interpretation has really collapsed under its own weight.

N. T. Wright
Preliminary Remarks

By and large, N. T. Wright (like Dunn) makes his case for the new perspective on Judaism. He wholeheartedly hails Sanders for bringing to light that "Judaism, so far from being a religion of works, is based on a clear understanding of grace, the grace that chose Israel in the first place to be a special people. Good works are simply gratitude, and demonstrate that one is faithful to the covenant."[68] In addition, Wright also (like Dunn) especially understands circumcision "as a badge of national identity"[69] and acknowledges it as defining boundaries between Jews and Gentiles.[70] Therefore, there is no need to prolong the discussion on those aspects beyond what has been confirmed so far.

Yet it might be added that even Wright (like Dunn) ultimately shows the necessity for an extension of "works of the law" from "Jewish boundary markers" to all that the law requires. He maintains that Israel still lives in exile. Though she came back from Babylon, the divine promise of a glorious future remained unfulfilled. Thus, Wright asks what Israel should be doing in the present to hasten the time when God would act on her behalf.[71] Accordingly, he indicates that she,

---

[68] N. T. Wright, "The Paul of History and the Apostle of Faith," *TynBul* 29 (1978): 80 and later passim.

[69] Wright, "Paul of History," 65.

[70] N. T. Wright, *The Climax of the Covenant: Christ and the Law in Pauline Theology* (Minneapolis: Fortress, 1993), 240–44. See also Dunn, "New Perspective," 25n106.

[71] N. T. Wright, *The New Testament and the People of God* (Minneapolis: Fortress, 1992), 268–69.

"sheltered behind the religious boundary-markers," should do her very best to "keep the covenant" with all her might.[72] In that case, the Jews (as expected) are indeed to obey the *whole* law, possibly concentrating on those aspects that isolate themselves from the Gentiles but not to the exclusion of other aspects in their Torah. For that reason, Jewish badges of covenant membership imply a wider reference to covenantal nomism, the entire body of Israel's sacred traditions.

Saying this is not tantamount to approving the thought of ongoing exile. Wright suggests that Israel (despite her strong emphasis on nomism in reliance on human freedom as a vital feature of covenant membership) is guilty not of any legalistic works righteousness but of "national righteousness." The law functions "as a charter of national privilege."[73] The future return from exile would amount to the fulfillment of distinct *Jewish* longing. Then God will rescue his own people and do this by his grace. At that moment he brings the good old times (or even better times) back again. What is more, Gentiles were also supposed to be flocking into Zion to acknowledge him as their Lord. Their imminent coming occurs according to the Old Testament expectations.[74]

On the other hand, Wright suggests that on the road to Damascus, Paul was brought to realize the astonishing accomplishment of his former national hopes. Surprisingly, the exile has already ended! Israel has truly been delivered from her oppression and oppressors. There is no need to yearn for her redemption anymore. The Messiah has come. He has exhausted the curse of sin and death.[75] Besides, the gospel involves an extensive redefinition of Israel. She "is transformed from being an ethnic people into a worldwide family," including Gentiles.[76] Hence, what counts is grace, not race.[77] To put it simply, "The one true God had done for Jesus of Nazareth in the middle of time, what Saul had thought he was going to do for Israel at the end of time."[78]

---

[72] Wright, *People of God*, 271–72.

[73] Wright, "Paul of History," 65, 71.

[74] Wright, *People of God*, 268–79.

[75] Wright, *Climax*, 141–55.

[76] Wright, *Climax*, 240.

[77] Wright, *Climax*, 168, 194, 238.

[78] N. T. Wright, *What Saint Paul Really Said: Was Paul of Tarsus the Real Founder of Christianity?* (Grand Rapids, MI: Eerdmans, 1997), 36.

Obviously, a short summary cannot do full justice to the overall picture of Wright's analysis. He has much more to say on Jewish and Pauline theology. Even so, his specific theory of Israel in exile is to be examined more closely next.

Israel Still in Exile?

Old Testament

On the whole, Wright regards the so-called Deuteronomic view of history as "constitutive of the underlying narrative framework" in the Old Testament as well as in later writings.[79] He maintains that "a great many second-Temple Jews interpreted *that part of the continuing narrative in which they were living* in terms of the so-called Deuteronomic scheme of sin—exile—restoration, with themselves still somewhere in the middle stage, that of 'exile'" (especially Deuteronomy 27–30).[80] A similar sequence of events culminating in a continuing exile and an ultimate return emerges in Leviticus 26.[81] Both Ezra (Ezra 9:6–9) and Nehemiah (Neh. 9:32–37), in their great prayers, speak of a constant calamity, which amounts to a hapless exile.[82] Also, the prophet Daniel in Daniel 9 "poured out his heart and soul in prayer, insisting that it must be time for the exile to end" (because Jeremiah predicted that it would last for seventy years).[83] But he is informed by the angel that "the exile will not last for seventy years, but for *seventy times seven*." He ought not run ahead of reality. There will be an extension of the time schedule. Until then, the hoped-for restoration falls short.[84]

Despite some strong tendencies in the current academic debate, it has not been substantiated that Wright is correct in his analysis of

---

[79] N. T. Wright, *Paul and the Faithfulness of God* (London: SPCK, 2013), 162. See also 139–40, 142–43, 149–50.

[80] Wright, *Paul and the Faithfulness of God*, 140.

[81] Wright, *Paul and the Faithfulness of God*, 149–50.

[82] Wright, *Paul and the Faithfulness of God*, 151.

[83] Wright, *Paul and the Faithfulness of God*, 142.

[84] Wright, *Paul and the Faithfulness of God*, 142. See also 140, 143–46, 151, 160–62.

the biblical data.[85] Here, for obvious reasons, a full-scale evaluation of his arguments would go too far. Still, a number of germane aspects, not always taken at their face value, are needed.

The most common word for "exile" in the Old Testament is גלוֹה (גלוּת). It stems from the verb גלה, which literally means "to uncover" and is used in various contexts. The phrase "to uncover the ear"—with either man or God as its subject—means "to show" or "to reveal." Though not a technical term for "divine revelation," it conveys that meaning too. In Leviticus 18 and 20, the verb גלה occurs in the expression "to uncover the shame," which denotes sexual intercourse in proscribed circumstances, usually incest. It occurs also in the prophetic complaint that Israel has "uncovered her nakedness," a metaphor implying that she has thrown off her loyalty to the Lord. As a rough punishment, her land will be "uncovered" as the people go into exile (e.g., Ezek. 16:36; Hos. 2:10).[86] Here the idea of "uncovering" is associated with the conditions of a ruined land[87] and probably with the humiliation of the prisoners of war being led naked into captivity.[88] During the time of Israel's "scattering" among the nations, her whole holy terrain "will rest and enjoy its Sabbaths," a rest it did not have the entire time she lived in it (Lev. 26:33–34).

The Lord's judgment of leading all the Israelites out of the land into captivity functions as an appropriate contrast to his fulfilling the promises to lead them into the land at the beginning of their

---

[85] Cf. Wright's own evaluation in *Paul and the Faithfulness of God*, 139n263. He refers to James M. Scott, who suggests that the notion of the ongoing exile is now widely recognized and speaks of a growing consensus. That is—Wright reasonably fears—"over-optimistic."

[86] See especially Bruce K. Waltke, "גלה," in *Theological Wordbook of the Old Testament*, ed. R. Laird Harris, Gleason L. Archer, and Bruce K. Waltke (Chicago: Moody Press, 1980), 160–61. He regards it as "an open question whether we are dealing with one or two roots" and therefore discusses the verb גלה under two main meanings: "to uncover" and "to depart, to go into exile." However, the two main meanings are connected because "the land is uncovered when people are removed." See Allen P. Ross, "Exile," in *NIDOTTE*, 4:595.

[87] Ross, "Exile," 4:595.

[88] M. G. Klingbeil, "Exile," in *Dictionary of the Old Testament: Pentateuch*, ed. T. Desmond Alexander and David W. Baker (Downers Grove, IL: InterVarsity Press, 2003), 246.

history. Accordingly, his repeated warnings through the prophets to lead them out of the land correspond exactly to his recurring promises to the fathers to lead their descendants into the land.[89] Thus, as God remembers his covenant with Abraham, Isaac, and Jacob, he certainly remembers also the land at the same time (see Lev. 26:42). Both aspects are very closely intertwined. Indeed, the thought of an ongoing exile would be awkward in Old Testament theology. It does not make any more sense if the Lord would bring back his people into the Promised Land but then nevertheless leave them in a state of ongoing exile. He is a trustworthy God, not an arbitrary one.

Additionally, the notion of exile is both lexically and theologically linked with "nakedness." In other words, it is associated with heinous sins, such as idolatry (Israel uncovering her nakedness), forbidden sexual relationships (Israelites uncovering the shame of their relatives or neighbors), and constant violation of Sabbath rules. Those really loathsome connotations are included in the language of the Old Testament. Therefore, the theory of ongoing exile suggests that Israel is still involved in grievous transgressions in one way or another. I strongly suspect that it properly renders the common Jewish thinking after the rebuilding of the temple (see below).

To be precise, the Deuteronomic view of history does not amount to the scheme of sin—exile—restoration but rather to the scheme of sin—punishments—restoration (in which the exile is the climax of the punishments). In Deuteronomy 28, the exile arises recurrently during the whole chapter as the harshest chastisement (e.g., 28:21, 25, 32, 36–37, 41, 49–52, 63–68). The repetition aims to underline the seriousness and severity of the divine retribution. Transgressing the law ushers in a catastrophe. In Leviticus 26, the whole long story ends with the retribution of the exile (26:32–39). The line of thought is more linear, leading finally to the return and restoration of Israel (26:40–45).

The factual composition in Deuteronomy 28 and Leviticus 26 indicates, as Steven Bryan suggests, that the exile would take place "as the ultimate punishment invoked only when the other curses had at last failed to bring Israel out of its recurrent recalcitrance."[90]

---

[89] Waltke, "גלה," 161.

[90] Steven M. Bryan, *Jesus and Israel's Traditions of Judgement and Restoration*, SNTSMS 117 (Cambridge: Cambridge University Press, 2002), 17. Bryan

The long list of punishments reaches the culmination there, with the last one being the absolute worst. Cogently, if the exile is going on, at least most other chastisements (but not necessarily all and all the time) are likewise in force. In that case, Israel suffers as well from serious diseases, insanity, extreme drought and other environmental calamities, unceasing hunger and thirst, dire poverty, the burdens of huge debts, brutal robbery, constant oppression, the desire to be married to a woman but someone else ravishing her, building a house but not living in it, ploughing and sowing but not reaping the harvest, planting a vineyard but not enjoying its fruit, slaughtering an ox but not eating any beef, the curse of eating one's own children. To be sure, the Jews would not have been thinking about living in ongoing exile and on the whole suffering from this kind of chaos and anarchy after having returned from Babylonia back to the Promised Land. Without a doubt, life was hard in ancient times and circumstances, but it was scarcely *too* tough, especially if you were released from your captivity among foreign nations (see also below).

The books of Ezra and Nehemiah shed more light on the crucial aspects included in the concept of exile. The rest of Israel has returned from Babylon to the Promised Land. As a result, they have started to rebuild the temple and, soon after, the tumbled walls of Jerusalem. In the meantime, it is important to learn from the mistakes of the past, repenting of them and definitely not repeating them. Otherwise, the people run the risk of a new exile, in which they will be punished because of their inward stubbornness.

It is no coincidence that the books of Ezra and Nehemiah strictly forbid those sins that especially brought about the exile, in other words, offenses that are closely associated with "nakedness." Thus, Israel is not to "uncover her nakedness," showing disloyalty to God by failing to complete the rebuilding of the temple or the fallen walls of Jerusalem (Ezra 4:1–6:22; Neh. 3:17–6:19). Neither is Israel to "uncover the shame of others" by marrying foreigners (Ezra 9–10;

---

examines the book of Jubilees, and in contrast to seeing the exile as "the ultimate punishment," an "obvious way of reading the curses of Deuteronomy 32," in *Jubilees* 23 the significance of the exile has been reduced. . . . Captivity is simply one of a litany of curses." In the Old Testament the significance of the exile has not been downgraded but upgraded as the worst curse. See my arguments below.

Neh. 13:1–6, 23–31). Neither should Israel reject the Sabbath and cause the land to turn into "naked" (or desolate) conditions to enjoy its Sabbatical rest that it was not allowed to have under the Israeli regime (Neh. 13:15–22).

Further, it should also be borne in mind that the punishment for the sins associated with "nakedness" is nothing less than the exile. If Israel forsakes God, he, in turn, will forsake her as well as the land where she lives (as already shown in Deuteronomy 28). Likewise, prohibited sexual relationships result in captivity. In fact, there are, strictly speaking, no offerings that bring reconciliation in that case. If Israel defiles the land, it will simply vomit her out (see Lev. 18:24–28, cf. 20:22–24; 26:31). Similarly, if Israel does not keep the Sabbath laws, she will be driven out from her land, and the land will be laid waste. Then it will have the rest it needs (26:34–35).

The seriousness of the situation makes it more understandable why both Ezra and Nehemiah are ready to use or threaten violence in order to avoid intermarriage or prevent the recurring violation of Sabbath rules (Ezra 10:8; Neh. 13:15–22). Sins like those have resulted in exile, a fact that they both explicitly refer to (Ezra 9:10–15; Neh. 13:17–18). Thus, there is definitely no room for slackness and vagueness. Restricted violence is better than the whole hell of savagery and bloodshed, prompted by furious enemies who—if worse comes to worst—will take Israel into captivity once again.

Also, 4 Baruch (dated to the first half of the second century AD) shows much later the same line of thought. It announces the end of the exile. However, those who do not separate from their foreign wives have to return to Babylon. They go back but are not allowed to resettle there anymore. Therefore, they must come back and build a city (i.e., Samaria) for themselves (8:1–11). Here, a certain sin is closely connected with the punishment of the exile as in the Old Testament. This is to say nothing of the Gospels, where the Pharisees really do their utmost to especially keep the Sabbath rules and purity laws (not least those concerning sexuality). Without a doubt, their devout practice maintains to a large extent substantial continuity with the national revival of Ezra and Nehemiah.[91]

---

[91] For the Pharisees before AD 70, see particularly Jacob Neusner, *The Rabbinic Traditions about the Pharisees before 70*, 3 vols. (Leiden: Brill, 1971).

In addition, it is worth mentioning that the Deuteronomic scheme of sin—punishments—restoration (in which the exile is the ultimate punishment) is taken at face value in Haggai as well. Yet now the curses are made to function in reverse (or, so to speak, "backward"). They do not disappear all at once but rather in the long run. To be sure, the exile is over. The rebuilding of the temple has begun without being finished. Therefore, the prophet urges his kinsmen to complete it. If God's own house remains a ruin, there are no abundant blessings. So far, "the heavens have withheld their dew and the earth its crops" (Hag. 1:10). As soon as the work on the temple is making real progress and coming to an end, a fabulous change takes place. The Lord says, "From this day on I will bless you" (2:19). It denotes—as expected—the rich blessings of the heavens and the earth. To sum up, not long ago Israel has returned from Babylon to the Promised Land. In a little while she will live in abundance in the land flowing with milk and honey.

The future will be even much brighter. Notwithstanding the fact that the new temple seems "like nothing" in comparison with the old one (2:3), the Lord promises that he will fill it with glory (2:7). In the end, the glory of the new temple will be greater than the glory of the old one (2:9). The divine prophecy was fulfilled at least in two different ways: first, through the insane construction projects of Herod the Great as he enlarged the temple and made it one of the most astounding buildings in its own time; second, through the entering of the Messiah (Jesus) into that temple.[92]

All this shows that the full restoration of Israel does not occur at once. It takes time—much more time than originally thought. Yet it would be wrong to argue on that basis alone that the exile is still going on.

Daniel 9 infers nothing like the theory of the ongoing exile (whether at present or in the remote future). On the contrary, it "explicitly and positively recalls Jeremiah's prediction of seventy years, suggesting that the author regarded Jeremiah's prophecy not as incorrect."[93] By the

---

[92] Strictly speaking, the temple that Herod the Great enlarged was still the second one (not the third one), since the sacrificial cult was not interrupted during the long construction work. Thus, the prophecies in Haggai 2 were fulfilled in the long run.

[93] Bryan, *Jesus and Israel's Traditions*, 18.

same token, it assertively envisions the hope for the final atonement and everlasting righteousness (Dan. 9:24). In short, the exile will soon be over, but the full restoration will take time to be completed.

Largely, Wright's theory of Israel still in exile is backed up by no noteworthy biblical data. For sure, the next issue concerns whether it could be traced to other Jewish texts.

Other Jewish Texts

On the whole, Wright has to deal with the fact that Jewish writings "in which exile language occurs are rare." Therefore, much of the evidence for his case is drawn from a more wide-ranging perspective.[94] Accordingly, Wright expands the textual basis for his theory of ongoing exile. To support it, he quotes texts

1. reflecting on the Diaspora,
2. bemoaning the bondage of Israel (such as already seen in Ezra 9:8–9; Neh. 9:36–37), and
3. underlying the nonrestoration (or incomplete restoration) of Israel.[95]

Yet equating the Diaspora, the bondage of Israel, and the non-restoration of Israel with exile displays a serious methodological problem:

1. Accurately, the Diaspora and exile are not synonymous. In the latter case, prisoners of war are not allowed to return from the land(s) of their captivity. In the former case, they have become accustomed to living outside their home country and by their own choice reside where they are. They could go back where they (originally) are from, but at present—for one reason or another—they do not.
2. Similarly, living in bondage is not exactly tantamount to exile. In Old Testament times, Israel has been living in bondage in her own land every so often without living

---

[94] Bryan, *Jesus and Israel's Traditions*, 13, 19.
[95] Wright, *Paul and the Faithfulness of God*, 139–63.

in exile (which denotes the obligation to live in a foreign country).

3. To be precise, the nonrestoration of Israel does not absolutely suggest that exile still continues. For certain, there was plenty of room for future revelations and end-time perfection after the return of Israel from Babylonia as well. The end of Babylonian captivity was not the end of all eschatology in the proclamation of the prophets.

Despite the indisputable fact that Jewish writings "in which exile language occurs are rare," Wright remarkably assumes that "we can no doubt go on *fine-tuning the details of what kind of exile* people thought they were living in."[96] There are at least geographical, political, cultural, and theological adjustments to exile.[97] Yet "the sense of living within the middle term of the Deuteronomic scheme [of sin—exile—restoration]" is applied on all levels. This remains true, Wright argues,

1. whether, for those concerned, "exile" was still in fact a geographical reality, as it was for many in the Diaspora;
2. whether they were aware of the continuing theological and cultural oppression of foreign nations as indicating that Daniel 9 had not yet been fulfilled; or
3. whether they believed that in some sense they themselves were the advance guard of the "real return from exile," indicating that it had been going on right up to their time and still was for everyone except themselves (as in Qumran).[98]

Wright's efforts to fine-tune the details of what kind of exile we ultimately are talking about run into grievous methodological shortcomings. He equates here again exile with the Diaspora (point 1) and with the nonrestoration of Israel (point 2). To that extent, his conclusions are unwarranted—as already shown above. In addition,

---

[96] Wright, *Paul and the Faithfulness of God*, 140; italics added.

[97] Wright, *Paul and the Faithfulness of God*, 139–40.

[98] Wright, *Paul and the Faithfulness of God*, 140.

Wright argues from the sectarian viewpoint of Qumran that all other Israelites live in exile, as if the exclusive indoctrination of a religious minority correctly expressed the common Jewish desperation felt by the majority (point 3). Rather, one could understand the whole state of affairs very much to the contrary: while a rigorous sect like that in Qumran is not ashamed of asserting that all the others of their kinsmen still live in exile, this suggests that the Israelites themselves in general did *not* think along those lines (see below).

Overall, Wright fails to convince. His methodological fallacies call into question his conclusions. The "fine-tuning" of the details in the notion of exile remains a flop. A meticulous exegetical analysis of data is missing. Wright has not shown that his way of reading varied Jewish texts is possible—much less that it is even plausible. The proof of evidence lies on him.

Astonishingly, Wright himself admits that there are a number of remarkable exceptions to his theory of ongoing exile. As already stated, he considers the vast literature of the tiny sect in Qumran one of them. Additionally, he also mentions the books of Sirach and Judith.[99] All these examples draw attention to the fact that Israel has already returned from her exile to the Promised Land.

In the case of Tobit,[100] 1 Enoch,[101] and, as it seems, Jubilees,[102] Wright focuses on "a double return from exile." Certainly, the first return has already taken place. A number of Israelites have come back to the Promised Land. God has shown "mercy on them" (Tob. 14:5). Still, the second return will take place sometime in the future.

That said, Wright explains the double return from exile by downplaying the first one. He writes, "Yes, there had been a 'return from exile'—of sorts: but it had not been the real thing." Hence, Israelites have "experienced a kind of 'return,'" but are "still awaiting the *true* 'return.'"[103] On balance, the first return from exile does not

---

[99] Wright, *Paul and the Faithfulness of God*, 157–58.

[100] Wright, *Paul and the Faithfulness of God*, 154–55.

[101] Wright, *Paul and the Faithfulness of God*, 155.

[102] Wright, *Paul and the Faithfulness of God*, 156. After having acknowledged "a double return from exile" in Tobit and 1 Enoch, Wright continues: "So too with *Jubilees*."

[103] Wright, *Paul and the Faithfulness of God*, 155.

override the second one. In fact, the exile has not ended but at the present goes on as ever.

Frankly, Wright's devaluation of the first return seems unwarranted. The most natural interpretation of the double return from exile denotes the gathering of *all* Jews: at the outset merely the *southern* tribes of Judah from Babylon, then also and especially the *northern* tribes of Israel (including the rest of the other Jews as well) from different countries. Since the northern tribes never came back, their future gathering was an end-time dream. That vision will come true at long last—not before:

> God will again have mercy on them [i.e., the Israelites], and God will bring them back into the land of Israel; and they will rebuild the temple of God, but not like the first until the period when the times of fulfilment shall come. After this they *all* will return from their exile and will rebuild Jerusalem in splendour. (Tob. 14:5)[104]

As a result, the whole of Israel (all her tribes) will be saved.

The fulfillment of the traditional hope as to the redemption and restoration of all Israel in the end is the content of the double return from exile. It does not indicate that the first return is not essentially a "true" one. Neither does it suggest that the Jews at year zero in general regarded themselves as being in exile and estranged from God. Wright is not right. He does not even discuss other alternatives but only his own previously established and closed position, which assumes that no critical remark should be thought through.

On the contrary, Wright is correct that the view of an ongoing exile does occur in the book of Baruch. The alleged author is pseudonymous. He is portrayed as Jeremiah's secretary. Thus, the book has a fictive setting in the Babylonian exile, though it is usually dated to the second century BC.[105] In Baruch, there are indeed passages that state that Israel will return from her exile in the future. Jerusalem is admonished to rejoice since her children are coming from everywhere (4:37). She should take off her garments of

---

[104]The quotation according to Wright, *Paul and the Faithfulness of God*, 154.
[105]Wright, *Paul and the Faithfulness of God*, 151–52.

mourning and instead wear the marvelous clothes of divine glory at that moment (5:1).

Even so, the reader of Baruch is naturally supposed to understand that the "today of the exile" is simply a literary setting.[106] The long-promised foretelling as to the end of exile has already come true. Israel has returned from her captivity. What has been told to Baruch was verified long ago. Accordingly, he has been confirmed as a trustworthy man, sent from God. To be sure, the book of Baruch was not written to show that it for the most part has completely failed (conveying that Israel should return when in fact she did not)! In that case, it is not to be used as evidence for the theory of ongoing exile.[107]

Neither do the books of the Maccabees say what Wright thinks. Referring to "such exalted language about the results of Simon's rule,"[108] Wright, as expected, recognizes the difficulty "to imagine that in the heady days of Hasmonean success," the Jews generally "perceived themselves to be in exile."[109] However, he also now speaks of the "double return," asserting that God has already rescued Israel and will soon gather all Israelites everywhere.[110] On that basis, he then suggests that "the promised time of full blessing" has not arrived. Accordingly, he concludes that the curse of being in exile prevails.[111]

Once again, Wright rushes into his vague methodological point of departure and simply overemphasizes the eschatological language of Israel's complete restoration. As pointed out, his line of reasoning falls short on account of (1) the equating of incomplete restoration with exile and (2) the devaluing of the first return while recurring to the idea of the double return from the exile. Both methodological

---

[106]Seifrid, "Blind Alleys," 88.

[107]Pace J. M. Scott, "Restoration of Israel," in Dictionary of Paul and His Letters, ed. Gerald F. Hawthorne, Ralph P. Martin, and Daniel G. Reid (Leicester: InterVarsity Press, 1993), 796–99. Scott repetitively quotes the book of Baruch as evidence for an ongoing exile. A better understanding of the literary setting of the writing would have resulted in another conclusion.

[108]Wright, Paul and the Faithfulness of God, 159.

[109]Wright, Paul and the Faithfulness of God, 160, in reference to Bryan, Jesus and Israel's Traditions, 15.

[110]Wright, Paul and the Faithfulness of God, 159.

[111]Wright, Paul and the Faithfulness of God, 159–60.

fallacies cause Wright to misinterpret the obvious meaning and sense of the books of the Maccabees.

In the case of Josephus, Wright asserts that "the period of life under Rome was a time of *douleia*, 'slavery,' and it was all Israel's own fault."[112] Therefore, he concludes that because of that enslavement, Israel still lives in exile. But this is simply a blatant *non sequitur*. The equating of bondage (or slavery) with exile is another methodological fault that leads astray (as shown above).

What is more, Wright must know well that Josephus "regards the beginning of Jewish slavery as having occurred because of the Jewish civil strife leading to Pompey's entrance."[113] Thus, as Steven Bryan observes, "Inasmuch as Josephus regards the enslavement that began under Pompey as the end of a preceding period of liberty, it is difficult to see how or why he would have connected this new situation of bondage with exile."[114] Astonishingly, the more detailed facts like these are hidden in a footnote and hastily forgotten.[115] Why? It is obvious that as a consequence the view of an ongoing exile completely collapses. To put it bluntly, Wright distorts the plain meaning of the original text by his tendentious interpretation. He forces his sources to say what he likes.[116]

All in all, the theory of an ongoing exile lacks evidence. It does not do justice to the Jewish texts and their apparent message. On the contrary, a more comprehensive inquiry into the data shows that a number of Israelites have indeed returned to the Promised Land. The end of exile was generally perceived and recognized. Not even the notion of a double return entails that the first return is not a "true" one.[117]

---

[112]Wright, *Paul and the Faithfulness of God*, 159.

[113]Bryan, *Jesus and Israel's Traditions*, 15.

[114]Bryan, *Jesus and Israel's Traditions*, 15. Wright is acquainted with the arguments here; see *Paul and the Faithfulness of God*, 160–62.

[115]Wright, *Paul and the Faithfulness of God*, 159n332.

[116]Texts like 4 Ezra (see Wright, *Paul and the Faithfulness of God*, 156) are not discussed here since they are written after the devastation of the temple in AD 70. As a result, a new age of exile was launched.

[117]Cf. Seifrid, "Blind Alleys," 87. He writes with more caution: "More precisely stated: the early Jewish tradition of an extended period of exile for Israel is more complicated than recent advocates of this perspective often have taken

Paul and His Pharisaic Past

All things considered, the theory of an ongoing exile is not to be assumed as Jewish background for the interpretation of the New Testament. As it happens, the Gospel of Matthew begins with the genealogy of Jesus, where the author makes a clear distinction between the age before and after the exile to Babylon (1:11–12, 17), a kind of prelude that acts as a fitting introduction to the other canonical books. That is an important lesson to be learned from it!

Once, Paul, as a devout Pharisee, did not think of himself as living in exile because of his own fault or as a result of the guilt of all Israel. He returned from the Diaspora to Jerusalem in his youth. In addition, he regarded his former practice of the law as "blameless" (Phil. 3:6). There is no hint that he felt culpable. Paul was one of the best and advanced in self-righteousness, beyond many others (Gal. 1:14). Further, his declaration of "the earthly Jerusalem being enslaved with her children" does not derive from the ongoing Roman occupation but rather is a consequence of Israel's failure to believe the gospel (Gal. 4:25). In Romans 9–11, it rather seems that a new exile has begun (or shortly will begin) in Israel's unbelief![118] It is well known that this prediction was fulfilled in concrete history through the fall of Jerusalem in AD 66–70 (cf. also the later revolt in AD 132–135).

There is no reason to dwell further on details in the Pauline letters. To state the obvious: the idea of Israel still living in exile fails to carry conviction. Accordingly, it is not to be taken for granted in the reading of the New Testament on the whole. A more comprehensive exegesis of certain features, particularly in Galatians and Romans, confirms that such is the case.

---

into account. Dissatisfaction with the condition of Jerusalem and the Temple is not precisely the same as the theme of a continuing exile. And to view the exile as in some sense continuing is not the same as regarding 'all' of Israel as being in exile or estranged from God."

[118]Mark A. Seifrid, *Christ, Our Righteousness: Paul's Theology of Justification*, NSBT 9 (Downers Grove, IL: InterVarsity Press, 2000), 21–25.

Concluding Remarks on Wright

As usual among the proponents of the New Perspective, Wright rejects
the notion of the "introspective conscience" in Pauline thinking. Paul
did not struggle with an anguished mind and spirit before his conversion. Rather, he and all Israel have lamented their corporate failures.
This is what the theory of the ongoing exile implies. Conversely, the
proclaiming of the gospel is the difference; it insists that the end of
the exile has already arrived in Jesus's cross and resurrection.[119]

In truth, to shift from speaking of the burden of personal guilt
to that of the nation is a mere variation on an older theme. It represents no real movement away from psychologism. "The Paul of the
introspective conscience is ushered out the door," whereas "the Paul
of the social conscience is welcomed in." Oddly, "an early twentieth-century existentialist Paul is replaced by a late twentieth-century
Paul disturbed by the malaise of the world."[120]

Even worse, the compulsive need to explain the majority of the
Jewish texts through the category of the ongoing exile characterizes the
kind of interpretation that is to a great extent artificial, as if practically
the whole Jewish religion simply was an abject fiasco and in dire need
of the reparation kit of the arising Christianity. Wright pushes through
his theory whenever he thinks it feasible. When not, then he speaks
of *exceptions*. Alternatively, he speaks of a double return from exile,
underlining that the first one is not a *true* one. In addition, he confuses
the idea of exile with that of the Diaspora, the bondage of Israel, and the
nonrestoration of Israel. Finally, he asserts that he has confirmed his
main thesis as much as possible: since Israel lives in exile, she has failed.

Surprisingly, Wright's new perspective is increasingly coming
to resemble the outdated old perspective. The common denominator is the exaggerated proclivity to represent the Jewish religion as
a failure that paves the way for the definite triumph of Christianity.
Previously, the focus was laid on works righteousness (with basically
no sense for God's grace). This time, the emphasis is placed on the

---

[119]Wright, *People of God*, 268–79. See the well-known article by Krister
Stendahl, "The Apostle Paul and the Introspective Conscience of the West,"
HTR 56, no. 3 (1963): 199–215.

[120]Seifrid, "Blind Alleys," 90–91. See also Seifrid, *Christ, Our Righteousness*, 22.

life in exile (with principally no sense for any relief). In both cases, a flagrant distortion of the facts follows.[121]

It is no longer possible to discuss Wright's interpretation of the Pauline doctrine of justification. In part, it seems to be determined by his theory of Israel still being in exile. At least some anomalies in his overall thinking are easier to overcome on that basis. For instance, he affirms that justification first and foremost is a declaration of status ("you are already in") but not ultimately a declaration of entrance ("welcome in"), as if the question concerns living in the Promised Land or outside it.[122] Likewise, Wright asserts that justification is twofold and presupposes "the work of the Spirit," as if he is thinking of the new life in the Promised Land, including the readiness to accomplish basic obligations in various conditions and circumstances therein. Moreover, Wright speaks of future justification and maintains that it is on account of the entire life, as if he is imagining a continued existence in the Promised Land.[123]

---

[121]Wright refers frequently to Odil Hannes Steck, *Israel und das gewaltsame Geschick der Propheten: Untersuchungen zur Überlieferung des deuteronomistischen Geschichtsbildes im Alten Testament, Spätjudentum und Urchristentum*, WMANT 23 (Neukirchen-Vluyn: Neukirchener Verlag 1967). Wright notes, "The fundamental study for this remains that of O. H. Steck, and I suspect from some of the reactions to further presentations of the theme that his work has remained unread." *Paul and the Faithfulness of God*, 139. But does Steck's notion of an ongoing exile in the end represent the *old* perspective on Judaism, something that Wright uncritically has adopted? Steck writes in his book, "Die Gegenwart ist bestimmt von der Andauer des Gerichts, von der Andauer der Schuld des Volkes und von Umkehr und Gesetzesgehorsam als dem einzig möglichen Weg zu Jahwe"; (203) and, "Muss es darum auch immer Verkündigung gegeben haben, die sich auf das vorfindliche Israel im ganzen richtete, es zur Umkehr aufrief, zum Gehorsam mahnte und darüber belehrte, was der Gebotswille Gottes ist. Entsprechend sind wir [. . .] immer wieder auf den Vorgang solcher Umkehrpredigt und Gesetzesbelehrung im Volk gestossen." *Israel und das gewaltsame Geschick der Propheten*, 203, 215–16. Similar passages are to be found also elsewhere. They outline the central thesis of the whole book (cf. 64–80). See also Odil Hannes Steck, "Das Problem theologischer Strömungen in nachexilischer Zeit," *EvT* 28, no. 9 (1968): 445–58.

[122]Wright, *What Saint Paul Really Said*, 139, 157.

[123]Wright, *What Saint Paul Really Said*, 128–30, 159–79. See also Wright, *Justification: God's Plan and God's Vision* (London: SPCK, 2009), 122–24, 158–68.

In any case, the cornerstone of Wright's theological position is his well-known theory of the ongoing exile. The floundering of his main thesis together with the critical re-marks against his interpretation of "works of the law" as "badges of identity" and his neglect of synergistic propensities in Judaism—all this calls into question the credibility of his overall view.

John M. G. Barclay
Diverse Graces—Different Meanings

Recently, John M. G. Barclay has made an important contribution to the present-day debate. He has studied the occurrence and meaning of the different words for *gift* in the sociopolitical context of the Greco-Roman and Jewish frames of reference. Within that wider perspective, he then situates the Pauline teaching on grace. His thorough exegetical analyses provide the basis for a taxonomy of theologies of God's mercy.[124]

Barclay suggests that *gift* can be "perfected" (or drawn out into some essential or ultimate form) in a number of ways. He enumerates six perfections:

1. superabundance: the extravagance and overwhelming scale of the gift
2. singularity: the attitude of the giver as marked solely and purely by benevolence and including no punishment for evil
3. priority: the timing of the gift always before the recipient's initiative
4. incongruity: the bestowal of the gift without any regard to the worth of the recipient
5. efficacy: the impact of the gift on the nature or agency of the recipient

---

It is in this light that I understand what Seifrid wrote to me in an email dated April 24, 2017: "I do think that there is a subtle connection between 'return from exile' and Wright's conception of justification—and his eschatology: it pictures redemption in terms of the transformation of the present world and opens the door to the minimizing of the final judgment that appears in Wright's thought."

[124]See Barclay, *Paul and the Gift*.

6. noncircularity: no expected return for the gift, no cycle of reciprocity[125]

As a result, *gift* is a polyvalent symbol. One does not necessarily have all six definitions in mind when using the word.[126] Definitely, there may be more perfections of gift. Still, no single one of them should be regarded as *conditio sine qua non*. Each has its own worth. Hence, it need not be completed by other meanings.[127] Nor is it the case that the more perfections various ancient texts have, the better off they are.[128]

Further, Barclay claims that scholars often talk past each other by sharpening and perfecting gift or grace in one way but not making any allowance for another way of sharpening and perfecting gift or grace. He does his best to avoid that kind of dichotomy, which derails academic debate from the outset. Thus, he provides a stable foundation for moving forward to an in-depth analysis of the ancient texts.[129]

In view of his methodology, Barclay's treatment has strengths and weaknesses. As a specialist in New Testament theology and a professional scholar in the academic world, he is certainly a competent judge for his case. Yet he follows a procedure that has turned out to be problematic at least since the publication of Gerhard Kittel's standard dictionary, *Theologisches Wörterbuch zum Neuen Testament*. First, the entries appeal to the secular Greek literature, then the Old Testament as well as other Jewish sources, and finally relevant New Testament writings. This kind of reading runs the obvious risk of imposing an external model on the analysis of target texts (the canonical books), which should instead be interpreted in relation to their own defining characteristics.[130]

---

[125] Barclay, *Paul and the Gift*, 70–75, 185–86; for the concept of "perfection," see 67–68.

[126] Barclay, *Paul and the Gift*, 75–76.

[127] Barclay, *Paul and the Gift*, 68–70, 76–77.

[128] Barclay, *Paul and the Gift*, 69–70.

[129] Barclay, *Paul and the Gift*, 67–70.

[130] See *Theologisches Wörterbuch zum Neuen Testament I–X/2*, ed. Gerhard Kittel (Stuttgart: Kohlhammer, 1933–1979).

In the case of Barclay, he starts with some insights into cultural anthropology. Then he proceeds to the ancient Greco-Roman literature and analyzes most of it with discernment. Next, he surveys selected Jewish writings. In his inquiries, he principally concentrates on the concept of *gift* while examining the Pauline teaching on grace. Barclay works as if he is making a long entry in Kittel's *Theologisches Wörterbuch*. He paints with a broad brush and creates a canvas moving from the distant past to New Testament times, and even explores the contours of church history.[131] Yet it is questionable whether the content is rendered as accurately as possible.

The Pauline Teaching on Grace

As to the Pauline teaching on grace, Barclay particularly emphasizes the concept of incongruity but also the subjects of superabundance, priority, and efficacy.[132] His argument appears predominantly sound, so there is no need to go into the details. However, it seems that none of his six perfections of *gift*, in truth, depicts the Pauline notion of *grace*. Barclay himself properly delineates the exceptional understanding of God's mercy primarily in Romans and Galatians. His exegetical analysis is helpful in its basic outline. He affirms that "grace effects a new reality." It is "no ordinary existence, but the product of an impossibility, the resurrection of Christ." Hence, it is "a life whose source lies outside of themselves [Christians], the life of the risen Christ." In other words, it "is not some reformation of the self, or some newly discovered technique in self-mastery." On the contrary, it is rather an "eccentric" phenomenon or an "extrinsic" incident.[133] Further, it "is permanently at odds with the natural (post-Adamic) condition of the human being," no matter how much some Christians "may (and should) grow in holiness." Their inner "capacity depends on a transformation of the self or, better, a *new* self, derived from the risen Christ."[134] They do not achieve "a series of 'graces' won by increases in sanctification."

---

[131]Cf. Barclay's definition of his task in *Paul and the Gift*, 77–78.

[132]Barclay, *Paul and the Gift*, 569.

[133]Barclay, *Paul and the Gift*, 500–501.

[134]Barclay, *Paul and the Gift*, 503.

Neither do they acquire a set of "competencies added to their previous capacities, nor an enhancement of their previous selves." What is given to them "is a death and the emergence from that death of a new self."[135]

In view of the Pauline definition and interpretation of God's amazing grace, all other perfections of gifts outside the new reality, present in the risen Christ alone, fall short since they actually do not alter the human conditions and circumstances radically and completely but only improve them more or less. In such cases, nothing has been changed ultimately, even though there are improvements of different kinds. No real transformation has taken place. The old life and the old being are still the same in the midst of religious reformation agendas and programs. Thus, a general divine benevolence, discovered in the many-faceted forms of gifts, does not make any difference. It does not amount precisely to the special divine grace as substantiated in Pauline theology. This general divine benevolence and special divine grace are not strictly on a par with each other. The soteriological focus moves from the reparation of the old self in the former case to the rebirth of the new self in the latter case. For that reason, the gift in Greco-Roman culture can never replace God's grace in Pauline theology, which alone brings forth a totally new existence in contrast to the conventional old way of being and living.

The transformation of reality is centered on the "Christ event" (his death and resurrection), not elsewhere, irrespective of how much talk there is about a general divine benevolence. Once again in line with Barclay, it is apparently neither about "a narrative progression in human history" nor "an additional chapter in a developing human story." It is "no process of maturation," nor any series of "preceding epochs of human history," but more accurately "the *reversal* of previous human conditions." It "represents not continuity, but interruption," even "miracle," indeed, "a new creation in the midst of the present evil age."[136] In brief, it is an "impossibility"[137] that surprisingly turns into a possibility and reality. Hence, it is "not a goal yet to be

---

[135] Barclay, *Paul and the Gift*, 518.
[136] Barclay, *Paul and the Gift*, 412–13.
[137] Barclay, *Paul and the Gift*, 421.

attained or a favor yet to be gained from God."[138] It already exists in the risen Lord.

On the whole, after having dusted down the fundamentals and distinctive understanding of grace in Pauline theology, Barclay astonishingly concludes as follows:

> It would be a mistake to regard the incongruity of grace as ubiquitous in Judaism, but equally wrong to consider this notion uniquely Pauline. Paul's is one Jewish voice in a chorus of divergent opinions, distinctive in certain respects, but not qualitatively or quantitatively *more distinct* than the voices of other Jews. Paul stands *among* fellow Jews in his discussion of divine grace, not *apart from* them in a unique or antithetical position.[139]

This quotation shows a blatant non sequitur compared with what Barclay in his exegetical analysis has brought forward. Here the nonbiblical taxonomy of *gift* is imposed on the understanding of *grace* in Pauline theology, and the meaning of grace is reduced to one sense of gift, namely, that of incongruity. The conclusion is neither justified nor substantiated in any way. The evidence points in another direction: none of the six perfections of gift encompasses the Pauline definition of grace. This absolutely ruins the entire taxonomy used by Barclay in his investigation. But he still remains stuck in his own categories, without perceiving that they do not work in the soteriological matrix of Romans and Galatians. The methodological flaw like that in Kittel's *Theologisches Wörterbuch* has caught up with him. To repeat, not even the incongruous perfection of the gift as recognized in the sociopolitical context of the Greco-Roman and Jewish frames of reference does justice to the Pauline concept of grace, which assumes a totally new reality extrinsic to special human efforts and general divine benevolences.

By and large, the necessity of a totally new reality in the risen Christ makes all the definitions or perfections of gifts to depend on human cooperation, notwithstanding many-faceted divine benevolences. Therefore, the Pauline understanding of grace really makes

---

[138]Barclay, *Paul and the Gift*, 446.
[139]Barclay, *Paul and the Gift*, 565.

the difference. It does not fit into a straitjacket of modern exegetical taxonomy taken from the sociopolitical context of the Greco-Roman and Jewish culture. Barclay admits that the idea of "pure gift" is a late interpretation. He does not find any traces of it in his ancient texts.[140] That may be right. (I have to leave it to the experts to resolve.) But at least the notion of "pure *grace*" does occur as an essential element in Pauline theology. It takes the form of a new creation, an extrinsic existence in the risen Christ. As such, it is absolutely independent of any human efforts, even though a response certainly is expected or intended in return.

Oddly, it seems that Barclay's taxonomy of perfections of gifts does not have any sense for synergism in a soteriological setting. At the very least, he intentionally circumvents that kind of speech.[141] Instead, everything is labeled as a perfection of God's grace. The obvious methodological tendency of Barclay sticks out especially in the question of the Pelagian controversy. He asserts that both Augustine and Pelagius (and those in favor of his position) agree "in their emphasis on the priority of grace."[142] The latter "clearly believed in the *priority* and *superabundance* of grace."[143] However, the former insisted on the *priority, incongruity*, and *efficacy* of grace.[144] Thus, the controversy between them was in fact about different perfections of grace. The traditional question of synergism is conspicuous by its absence. Moreover, there is no clear-cut explanation for the shift of the focus.[145] To be sure, old theological disputes are open to modern and fresh interpretations. That in itself is a good thing. But how can it be that Pelagius and his spiritual followers, who were declared heretics (by the First Council of Ephesus in 431) on account of their synergism, are unexpectedly the ones who have "perfected" God's grace in their own way? Why condemn them at all, then? It seems,

---

[140] Barclay, *Paul and the Gift*, 59–63, 66.

[141] Quite strangely, it seems that Barclay only addresses the issue of synergism by criticizing me and others for making use of "the terminology of the Reformation tradition." Barclay, *Paul and the Gift*, 168–69.

[142] Barclay, *Paul and the Gift*, 92.

[143] Barclay, *Paul and the Gift*, 93.

[144] Barclay, *Paul and the Gift*, 97.

[145] Barclay, *Paul and the Gift*, 92–97.

at the least, that Barclay owes a clarification to his readers. He does not pursue his investigation through to the end.

Even so, Barclay's clear statement of the impossibility of the "pure gift" is evidence for the synergistic thinking that permeates Greco-Roman and Jewish theology, something that he repeatedly shows in his analysis. In this respect, he fully agrees with the other main proponents of the New Perspective, particularly with Sanders, Dunn, and Wright. Despite all the differences in their overall positions, they share at least one common denominator: they take for granted that the Jewish soteriology without a doubt indicates a strong synergistic feature. On the other hand, the Pauline understanding of divine grace radically differs from that kind of tendency. It is not based on human efforts or cooperation (as already recurrently recognized above). Salvation is found in the risen Lord, in a reality called into being through the gospel, in an existence extrinsic to oneself. In brief, it is an impossible possibility, an exceptional life, where truly "I no longer live, but Christ lives in me" (Gal. 2:20). As a result, it necessarily ushers in a breakdown of the Jewish soteriology.[146]

Beyond the New Perspective?

In his conclusions, Barclay regards his special contribution as going beyond the New Perspective, in other words, as "a reconfiguration of 'the new perspective,' placing its best historical and exegetical insights within the frame of Paul's theology of grace."[147] His

---

[146]To be sure, "Paul does not have to play the agency of the believer off against the agency of Christ / the Spirit," and "God's grace does not exclude, deny, or displace believing agents; they are not reduced to passivity or pure receptivity." Barclay, *Paul and the Gift*, 518, 519; cf. 503n17. Nevertheless, it is true that Paul lives only because Christ lives in him (Gal. 2:20) or that he lives together with Christ only after having been put to death together with him (Rom. 6:4). In this sense, the real agent is indeed Christ (*pace* Barclay). See Laato, *Paulus und das Judentum*, 199–204; Laato, *Paul and Judaism*, 158–62.

[147]Barclay, *Paul and the Gift*, 573. On the other hand, Barclay regards his special input "as a re-contextualization of the Augustinian-Lutheran tradition, returning the dynamic of the incongruity of grace to its original environment where it accompanied the formation of new communities." *Paul and the Gift*, 573.

analysis of "works of the law," a central issue in Pauline theology and absolutely decisive for the overall view of Dunn and Wright, as already shown above, serves particularly well as a test case for his self-evaluation.

Right from the outset, Barclay emphasizes that works of the law refer to the practice of the Jewish law. The expression is, for certain, Pauline shorthand. It echoes the scriptural commands to "do" the Torah.[148] But even so, "what is significant is not the bare fact of practices (and thus not 'works' as such) but that they derive from, and are oriented to, the Torah." Palpably, the Gentile mission threw some works into special relief (e.g., circumcision and dietary regulations). Yet "there is no reason to restrict the referent of ἔργα νόμου" principally to "those rules that created boundaries between Jews and Gentiles (*pace* Dunn)." Rather, "the issue is the validity of the Torah" in defining and establishing righteousness. Then, "it becomes clear" that the real question is about "the practice of the Torah as though it were the authoritative cultural frame of the good news."[149]

Despite his stout criticism of works as mere "identity markers," Barclay still shares Dunn's conviction that the major shift in the ἔργα νόμου "may be interpretation of traced in the deutero-Pauline letters, where works are refocused as moral achievements" (Eph. 2:8–10; 2 Tim. 1:9; Titus 3:5).[150] Neither does boasting indicate "the cultural confidence of the Jew in the Torah (or of the Greek in wisdom), but pride in achievement" (Eph. 2:9).[151] Concisely, the previous apostolic missionary theology is now "turned inwards."[152]

Principally, Barclay's critique of the practice of the Torah as "the authoritative cultural frame of the good news" derives from his downplaying of synergism in the Jewish soteriology. *Therefore*, he

---

[148]Barclay, *Paul and the Gift*, 373–74.

[149]Barclay, *Paul and the Gift*, 374; see also 444, 567–68.

[150]Barclay, *Paul and the Gift*, 571. Earlier, Barclay makes the following clarification: "What changes is not that a specific Pauline rule ('works of the Law') becomes generalized as 'works,' but that Paul's critique of the *criteria* of worth being applied in the formation of the community becomes a critique of the *achievement* of worth whose criteria, in an established Christian tradition, are themselves unproblematic." *Paul and the Gift*, 546n57.

[151]Barclay, *Paul and the Gift*, 571.

[152]Barclay, *Paul and the Gift*, 571.

has to find out some other reasons for the apostolic disapproval of works of the law. Despite the fact that he explains his reading of the Pauline texts at length, the exact meaning of his interpretation remains vague. It leaves the impression of unnecessary hairsplitting. In the end, how precisely does Barclay come to his conclusion that works of the law express "the authoritative cultural frame of the good news" and should be discarded for that very reason? Elsewhere, I have argued that Paul in Galatians raises the requirement of not only a quantitatively but even a qualitatively impeccable law observance.[153] Thus, he "maintains that those who rely on works of the law fail to do the works of the law!"[154] The question is simply about works as such. Accordingly, the severe denunciation is leveled against synergism in so-called covenantal nomism.[155]

Evidently, there is no alteration of the interpretation in the allegedly deutero-Pauline letters. The line of thought is similar everywhere in *corpus Paulinum*. For instance, Ephesians 2:8–10 summarizes the theological substance in Romans and Galatians. It remains unmistakable that works of the law stand for every kind of human striving and yearning in a soteriological context. It follows that Barclay's analysis here fails to carry conviction.

Summary

All in all, considering soteriological issues, the most popular advocates of the New Perspective to a large extent ignore the principal importance of anthropology in that context. To be sure, they do agree and admit that Judaism is synergistic. Yet they try to downplay that observation one way or another. This is true in the cases of E. P. Sanders, James D. G. Dunn, N. T. Wright, and John M. G. Barclay.

It seems that strong synergistic facets in Judaism are regarded as problematic because they easily explain why Paul disregarded his former Pharisaic past. As a result, many alternative ways of expounding his conversion, advocated by the representatives of the

---

[153] Laato, "Paul's Anthropological Considerations," 353–59.

[154] Laato, "Paul's Anthropological Considerations," 357.

[155] Laato, "Paul's Anthropological Considerations," 359.

New Perspective, fail to carry conviction or else fall short as an overall account of it. Dunn especially raises the question of synergistic
inclinations in Pauline theology but wisely rejects them in the end.
Those outdated and old-fashioned (in the deepest sense, heretical)
accusations hardly fit the image of the *New* Perspective.

It follows that an anthropological approach is surpassed neither by a Christocentric nor by an ethnocentric reading of Pauline
theology—important as these are in themselves. Works of the law are
not eradicated simply for the reason that they are not based on Christ
(*pace* Sanders) or that they are based on ethnic privileges (*pace*, in the
first place, Dunn and Wright). On the contrary, they are abandoned
because they are human efforts (for certain, not to the exclusion of
divine grace) to guarantee one's own salvation. Therefore, different anthropological presuppositions lead to different soteriological
conclusions. A correlation exists between them both. Paul emphasizes
the necessity of becoming an entirely new creature. He promotes a life
outside oneself, attained in the risen Christ alone. In view of that, all
various definitions of gifts in the sociopolitical context of the Greco-
Roman and Jewish culture and all divine benevolences perfected in
them do not prevail. They do not actually do justice to the meaning
of pure grace in Pauline theology, which stands out as a unique masterpiece in the midst of the ancient religious world (*pace* Barclay).
Besides, the theory of Israel's ongoing exile as the black background
of the New Testament proclamation of salvation in the risen Lord is
to be rejected (*pace* Wright).

Thus, this chapter as a whole ushers in a conclusion that is
stressed elsewhere but that I inevitably want to make my own:

> That Luther, to this extent at least, gets Paul "right" is part of what I
> intended when I once suggested, somewhat epigrammatically, that
> Pauline scholars can learn from the Reformer. . . . Still, one has only
> to read a few passages of his writings (most any will do) to realize
> that, in crucial respects, he inhabits the same world, and breathes
> the same air, as the apostle. . . . Such kindredness of spirit gives
> Luther an inestimable advantage over many readers of Paul in "cap-
> turing" the essence of the apostle's writings. On numerous points
> of detail, Luther may be the last to illumine. For those, however,
> who would see forest as well as trees, I am still inclined to propose

a trip to the dustbins of recent Pauline scholarship—to retrieve and try out, on a reading of the epistles, the disregarded spectacles of the Reformer.[156]

Long ago, Ernst Käsemann published an article that initiated a new quest for Jesus. The old by itself was not bad in his eyes. Actually, he went forward by going backward. Hence, he found the historical Jesus all over again. In the Reformation Jubilee year 2017, the New Perspective on Paul was forty years on (after Sanders published his book *Paul and Palestinian Judaism* in 1977). During all those years, many scholars have pointed out faults and flaws in its basic structure. What is left now? When all is said and done, the fact remains that the Jewish soteriology was synergistic despite divine benevolences and compassion in the covenantal context. To be sure, the most acknowledged advocates of the New Perspective admit it, although not showing a lot of enthusiasm for the result. Nevertheless, the breakthrough draws closer: obviously, the strong synergism of Jewish soteriology launched the morbid reproach especially in Romans and Galatians (the denunciation of works of the law). If so much is agreed on, then, the longed-for new quest for Paul is about to begin.

Recommended Resources

Barclay, John M. G. *Paul and the Gift*. Grand Rapids, MI: Eerdmans, 2015.

Dunn, James D. G. "The New Perspective: Whence, What, Whither?" In *The New Perspective on Paul: Collected Essays*, 1–88. Tübingen: Mohr Siebeck, 2005.

Laato, Timo. "'God's Righteousness'—Once Again." In *The Nordic Paul: Finnish Approaches to Pauline Theology*, edited by Lars Aejmelaeus and Antti Mustakallio, 40–73. Library of New Testament Studies 374. London: T&T Clark, 2008.

———. *Paul and Judaism: An Anthropological Approach*. Translated by T. McElwain. South Florida Studies in the History of Judaism 115. Atlanta: Scholars Press, 1995.

---

[156]Westerholm, "'New Perspective' at Twenty-Five," 37–38.

———. "Paul's Anthropological Considerations: Two Problems." In *Justification and Variegated Nomism*. Vol. 2, *The Paradoxes of Paul*, edited by D. A. Carson, Peter T. O'Brien, and Mark A. Seifrid, 343–59. Wissenschaftliche Untersuchungen zum Neuen Testament, 2nd ser., vol. 181. Grand Rapids, MI: Baker Academic, 2004.

Sanders, E. P. *Paul and Palestinian Judaism: A Comparison of Patterns of Religion*. Minneapolis: Fortress, 1977.

———. *Paul, the Law, and the Jewish People*. Philadelphia: Fortress, 1983.

Seifrid, Mark A. "Blind Alleys in the Controversy over the Paul of History." *Tyndale Bulletin* 45, no. 1 (1994): 73–95.

———. *Christ, Our Righteousness: Paul's Theology of Justification*. New Studies in Biblical Theology 9. Downers Grove, IL: InterVarsity Press, 2000.

Westerholm, Stephen. "Finnish Contributions to the Debate on Paul and the Law." In *The Nordic Paul: Finnish Approaches to Pauline Theology*, edited by Lars Aejmelaeus and Antti Mustakallio, 3–15. Library of New Testament Studies 374. London: T&T Clark, 2008.

———. "Paul's Anthropological 'Pessimism' in Its Jewish Context." In *Divine and Human Agency in Paul and His Cultural Environment*, edited by John M. G. Barclay and Simon J. Gathercole, 71–98. London: T&T Clark, 2008.

Wright, N. T. *Paul and the Faithfulness of God*. London: SPCK, 2013.

General Index

Scripture Index